IMAGES
of America

SHEBOYGAN COUNTY

PIONEERS OF COMMERCE

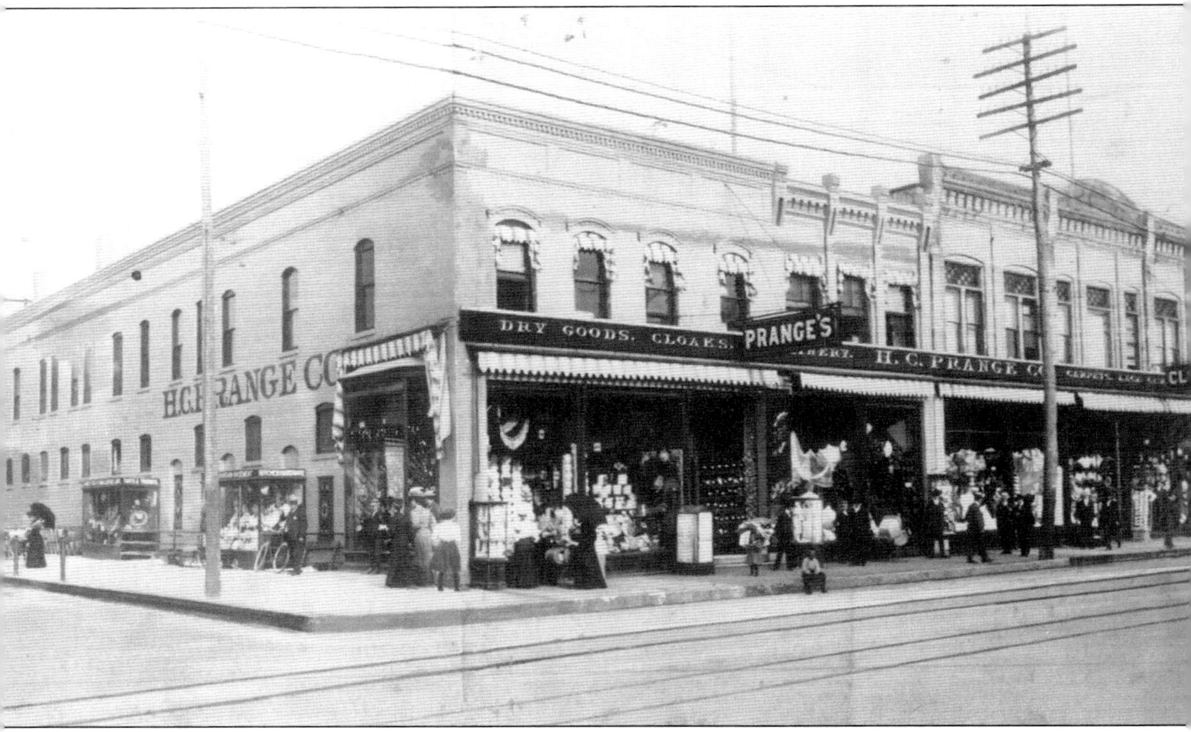

H.C. PRANGE STORE. Located at the corner of 8th Street and Wisconsin Avenue, Prange's was for years the focal point of business life in downtown Sheboygan. "Down by Prange's" was a favorite term of all Sheboygan old-timers.

IMAGES
of America

SHEBOYGAN COUNTY

PIONEERS OF COMMERCE

Sheboygan County
Historical Research Center

Text by Janice Hildebrand, Elmer Koppelmann, James Rindt and Beth Dippel

ARCADIA
PUBLISHING

ISBN 978-0-7385-2012-4

Published by Arcadia Publishing
Charleston, South Carolina

Printed in the United States of America

Library of Congress Catalog Card Number: 2002108574

For all general information contact Arcadia Publishing at:
Telephone 843-853-2070
Fax 843-853-0044
E-mail sales@arcadiapublishing.com
For customer service and orders:
Toll-Free 1-888-313-2665

Visit us on the Internet at www.arcadiapublishing.com

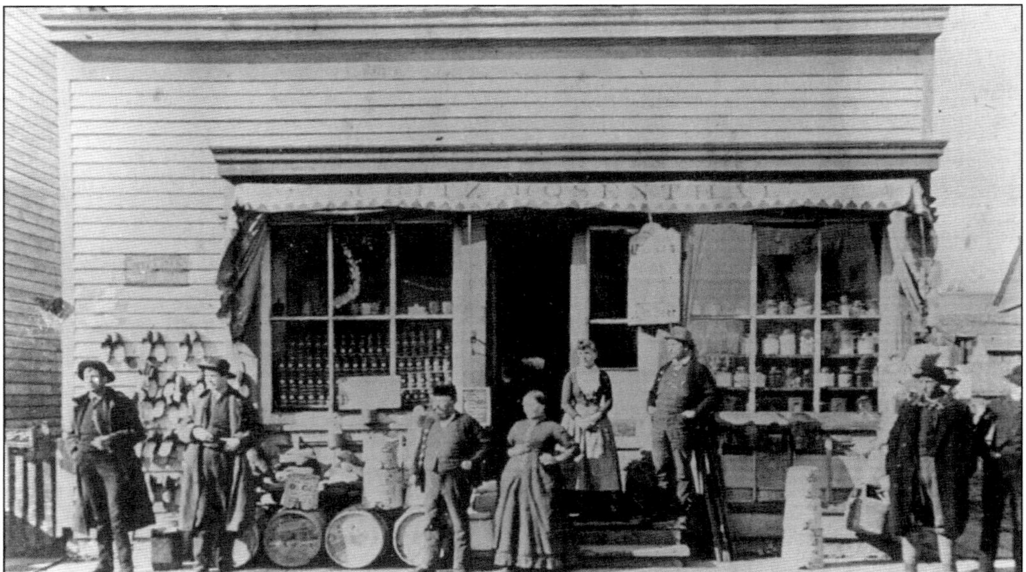

FRITZ ROSENTHAL GENERAL STORE. This store, built about 1850, was located at 816 North 8th Street in Sheboygan.

Contents

Acknowledgments		6
Introduction		7
1.	Mercantile and Trade	9
2.	Hotels and Hospitality	37
3.	Gambling and Vice	59
4.	Specialty Manufacturing	63
5.	Early Transportation	91
6.	Odds and Ends	109

ACKNOWLEDGMENTS

This book, and the preservation of hundreds of business images and files of information, has been made possible through the generosity of the Clicquennoi Foundation. Since Jacob and Nellie Ver Hage Clicquennoi came to the United States from Cadzand, Zeeland, the Netherlands, in 1880, their family has been business and civic minded. The Clicquennois were carpenters, painters and butchers. We especially want to remember Jacob Clicquennoi, owner of Clicquennoi Auto Body in Sheboygan, for his keen interest in business. He was the "Keeper of Sheboygan Business Trivia." We remember his daughter, Joanne Clicquennoi, for her generosity to the community of Sheboygan. The Clicquennois and their family-run businesses represent the pioneer spirit that makes America strong. That spirit will be shared through this pictorial remembrance of the changes in Sheboygan County commerce. The information available in Sheboygan County is too diverse and voluminous to be contained in one volume. This book will be a beginning. Thousands of other files and photos are stored at the Sheboygan County Historical Research Center and are ready to be utilized by the public. Please visit SCHRC and take a trip through time.

We also wish to thank the Sheboygan Rotary Club Foundation, Inc. The Sheboygan County Historical Research Center received a generous grant from the Sheboygan Rotary Club Foundation for the purchase of a new computer system. This new system enables SCHRC staff to preserve and share the vast collection of photos, slides and negatives (some 200,000+) with residents and students of Sheboygan County.

The Clicquennoi Foundation and Sheboygan Rotary Club Foundation, Inc. are important supporters of Sheboygan County's local historical community. This book is dedicated to them.

INTRODUCTION

The citizens of Sheboygan County excel in the preservation of history like no others. Thousands of people are involved each year in the collection and documentation of all things historic. They are active participants in their heritage. They realize its value, and the urgency of the preservation process.

In 1944, a man named Gustave Buchen researched and wrote the finest history of early Sheboygan County available. For this introduction to Sheboygan County, we borrow some of his own words. A few phrases have been updated, but for the most part, his thoughts are not to be improved upon. Buchen said, in essence:

Sheboygan County has a past as colorful and romantic as can be found anywhere. For over 150 years the steady stream of men and events that make up its history has proceeded onward: Native Americans lived and hunted in the thick forests and swamps; Wandering hunters and traders thoroughly at home in the wilderness and ever in quest of the coveted furs and peltries with which the region abounded; Black-robed missionaries counting their beads as they plodded the weary miles, their one thought the salvation of souls; Adventurous government surveyors running their survey lines across hitherto unexplored and unknown country; Greedy speculators searching out the most desirable tracts of land ahead of settlers; Hardy pioneers forsaking their old home-places and pushing westward by vessel and covered-wagon to seek their fortunes in a new land of opportunity; Courageous home-seekers carving homes and farms out of the unyielding forest, and laboring unremittingly to wrest a livelihood from the virgin soil; The building of highways, ships and railroads to reach the outside world; The founding of farms, towns, schools, churches and factories to provide the comforts of life and the amenities of civilization where only raw and untamed nature had since the dawn of time held sway.

All this and more is the story of Sheboygan County.

This book contains representative images that tell the story of Sheboygan County from about 1870 until 1950. The photos cover many facets of the entrepreneurial spirit in the bustling region of east central Wisconsin. There are photographs of buildings and occupations, many of which no longer exist. Special emphasis is given to the city of Sheboygan because of the availability of quality images, and because it was the centerpiece of immigrant life in the county. More immigrants passed through the port of Sheboygan than through Wisconsin's largest port, Milwaukee.

In early images we see horse-drawn wagons, sawmills, harness makers, bicycle liveries, hitching posts, wooden sidewalks, and cobblestone streets. Later we see Model Ts and Hupmobiles, mechanized knitting machines, pianos, dry goods stores, city hotels, and lumberyards. Finally, we see things like Spic 'N Span Dry Cleaners, tire recapping, and McDonald's.

As generation after generation of people in the 20th century developed and made use of new technology, the county changed in practically every respect. Businesses, jobs, and new products were created, markets were expanded, buildings erected, others were demolished, and living conditions improved for the average citizen. Life got easier. Leisure time increased.

Sheboygan County's strong manufacturing base of the 1900s remains intact, although the makeup of the industries has changed a great deal. From the furniture factories and ship building companies of the late 1800s to the plastics and generator companies of today, progress continues.

The businesses featured in this book reflect, for the most part, the "mom and pop" companies that made up the majority of the enterprises in the county. We have chosen not to spotlight the largest for a couple of reasons. They tend to write their own histories, and do a wonderful job of it. Most have published books commemorating their 100 or 150th anniversaries in business. We salute these mainstays of Sheboygan County. Also, the small businesses are truly the "Forgotten Store Fronts." In our need to preserve the history of all Sheboygan County residents, we focus on these smaller commercial ventures.

Andrew Clicquennoi

Automobile and Carriage Painting

Painting and Repairing Promptly Attended to

Refinishing of Automobiles

First-Class Work—Best Materials used—Valentine's Vanadium Varnish, Murphy's, Beckwith-Chandler's, and other high-grade varnishes.

During the winter months your car could be getting a fine new finish instead of standing idle. Call or telephone and I'll arrange to handle your job. Do it now, so you can be sure of delivery at the right time.

I Also Refinish Wagons, Carriages, etc.

SHOP	RESIDENCE
1520 North Thirteenth Street	1832 North Eighth Street
Telephone 720 White	Telephone 509 White

SHEBOYGAN, WISCONSIN

One

MERCANTILE AND TRADE

Every city and county has hundreds of "Forgotten Store Fronts;" those businesses that existed for a few years, then disappeared and are now forgotten. This very fate can also happen to a business that spanned decades, especially when the landscape is changed by progress. Documentation like this book is important in the effort to preserve this fragile history. Included in this chapter are grocery stores, hardware stores, banks, and many other store fronts which were a part of our ancestors' daily lives.

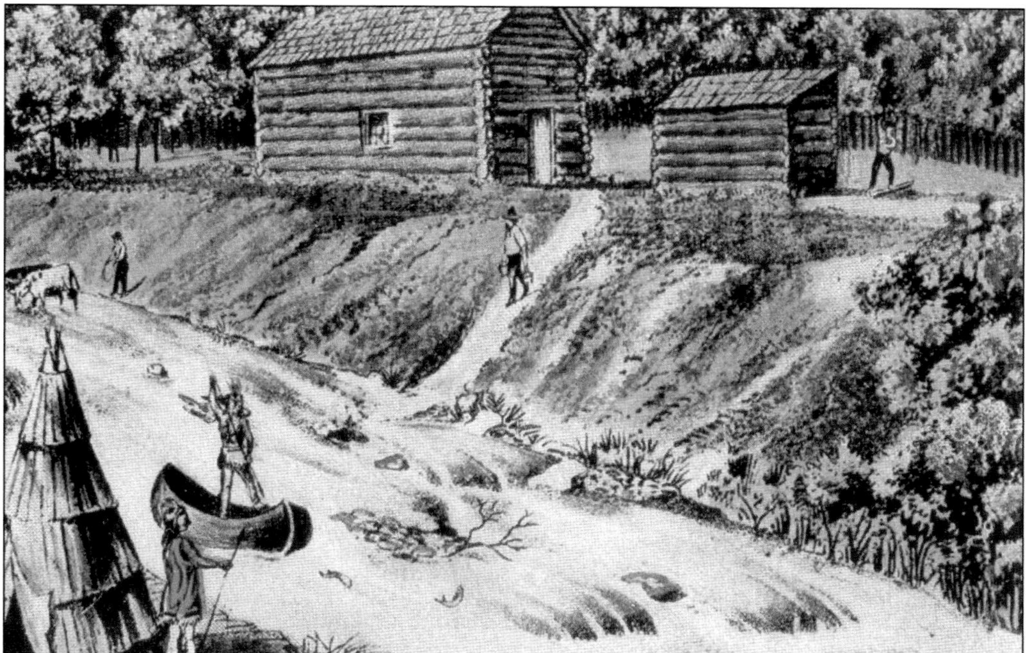

CROCKER AND PAINE. This picture from an unknown artist's rendering shows a log cabin built at the site of the first sawmill on the Sheboygan River. William Paine and Colonel Oliver Crocker constructed the mill in 1834. The mill was built at the site of the first rapids on the river. The mill and property were later sold to William Farnsworth, founder of Sheboygan. Paine and Crocker never owned the land. The U.S. government was the land owner.

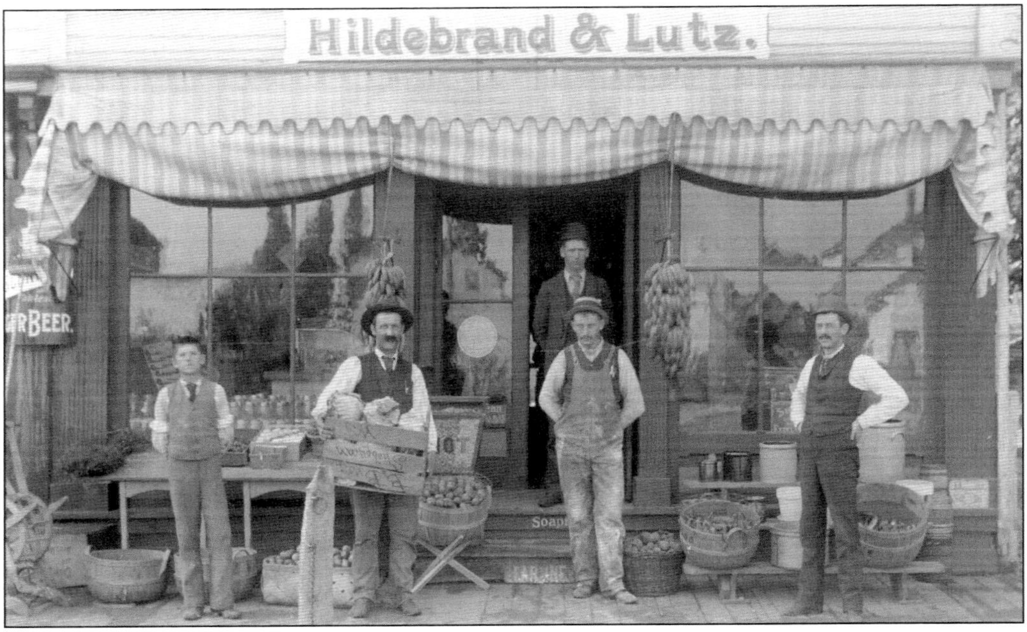

HILDEBRAND AND LUTZ GROCERY. This grocery was located at 1015 Michigan Avenue, Sheboygan. It was in business from about 1888-1902. The fresh bananas hanging outside the shop were a luxury of the time. Note the B. Bros., Sheboygan, Wis on the box of cabbage, the crocks for sauerkraut near the windows and the fresh, hot roasted peanut machine.

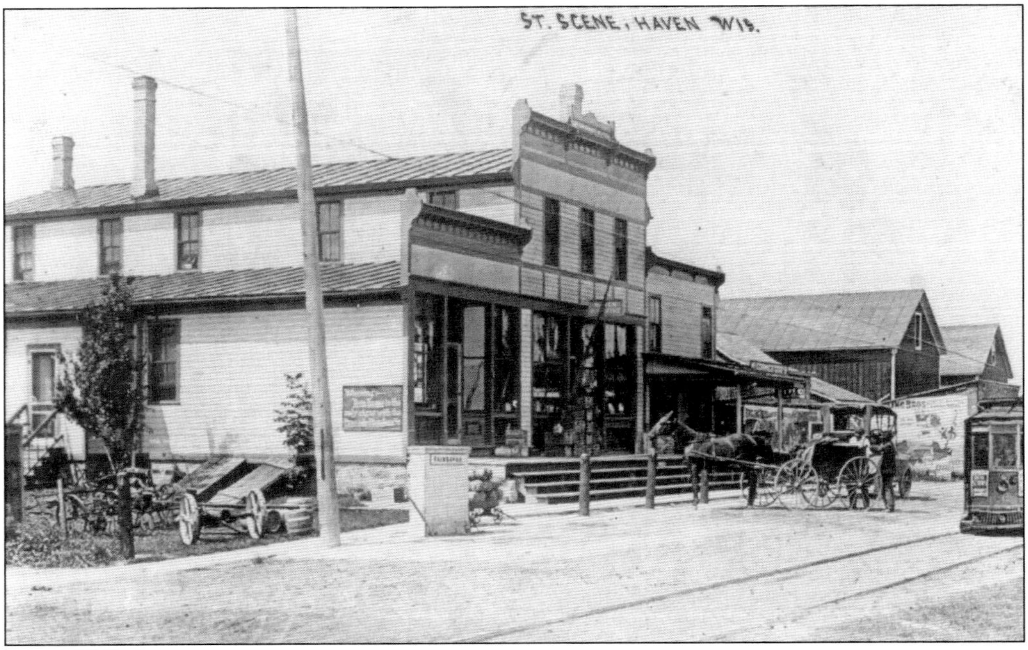

HAVEN GENERAL STORE. This image of Haven's main thoroughfare is interesting for a number of reasons. Note the three modes of transportation shown: horse and buggy, early motorcar, and Interurban. In reality, the Interurban never passed through Haven. This promotional piece may have been made to encourage the Interurban lines being built in the county.

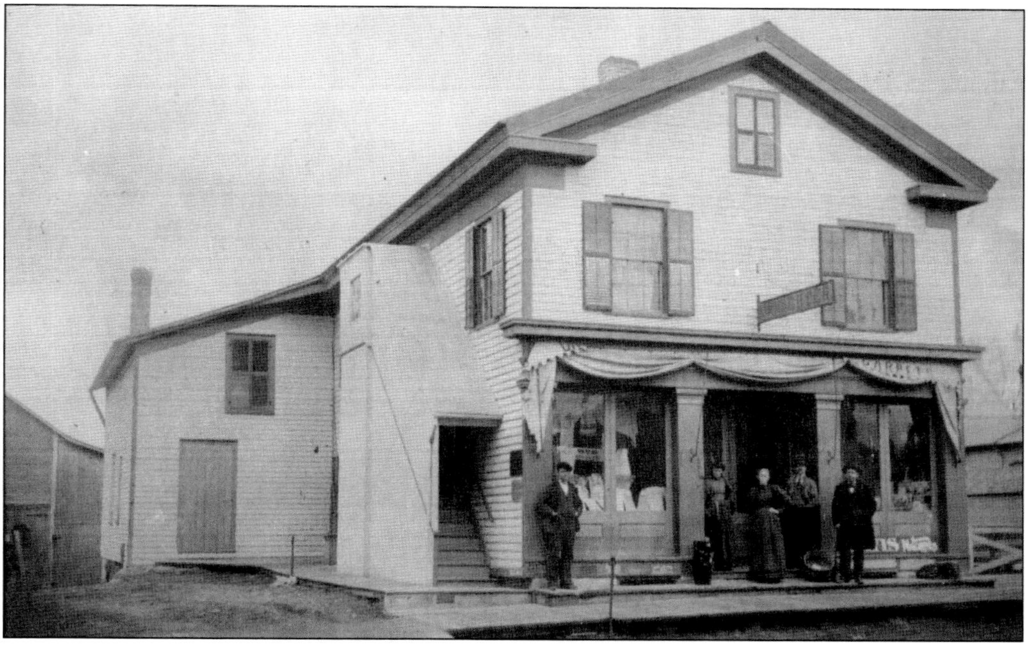

WACHTER'S STORE. Located at 215 Pine Street, Sheboygan Falls, this exterior shot features from left to right, August Wachter, Lena Wachter, Josephine Mallman, Charles A. Wachter, and Adolph Wachter, Sr.

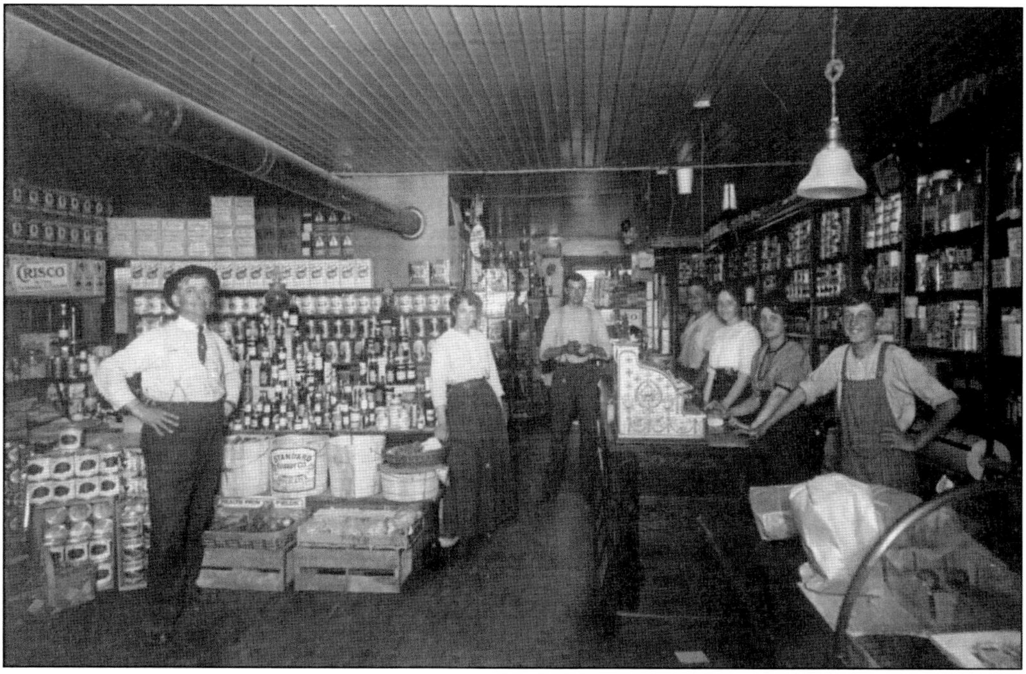

WACHTER'S STORE INTERIOR. From left to right are Charles A. Wachter, Lena Wachter, Oscar Fiedler, Raymond Wachter, Alma Mallman, Odana Henke, Mrs. Emil Heining, and Milford Wachter.

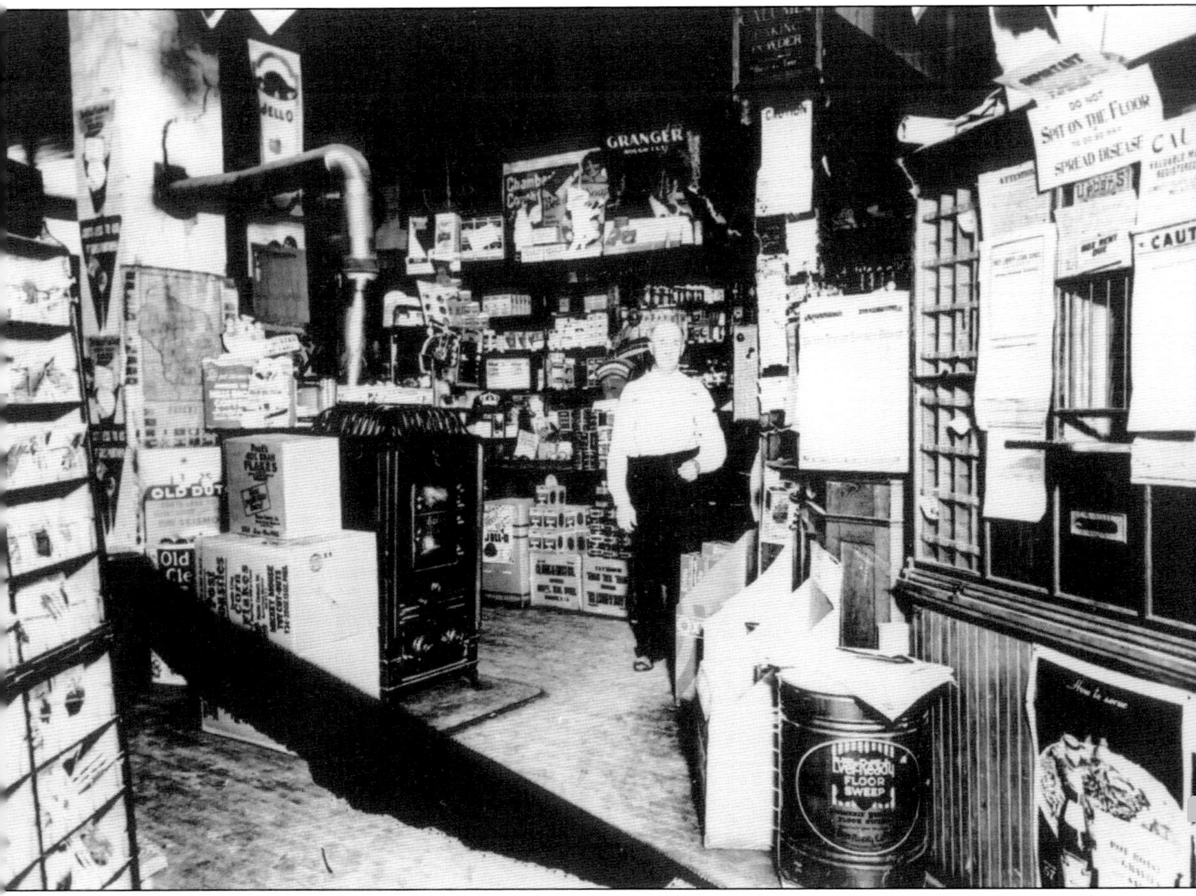

POOLE'S GENERAL STORE. Mr. George Poole ran the Hingham general store and post office from 1913 to 1940. The postal window at right can be seen with its many advertisements and announcements including a reminder atop the window that patrons "Do not spit on the floor, to do so may spread disease," a very common problem in days gone by. Among the notable brand names still around today are Hill Bros. Coffee, Calumet Baking Powder, Kellogg's Corn Flakes, and a relatively new product introduced to radio audiences everywhere when Jack Benny began his program with "Jello Folks." Currently a water filtration business owned by Mr. Larry Shaver occupies the site.

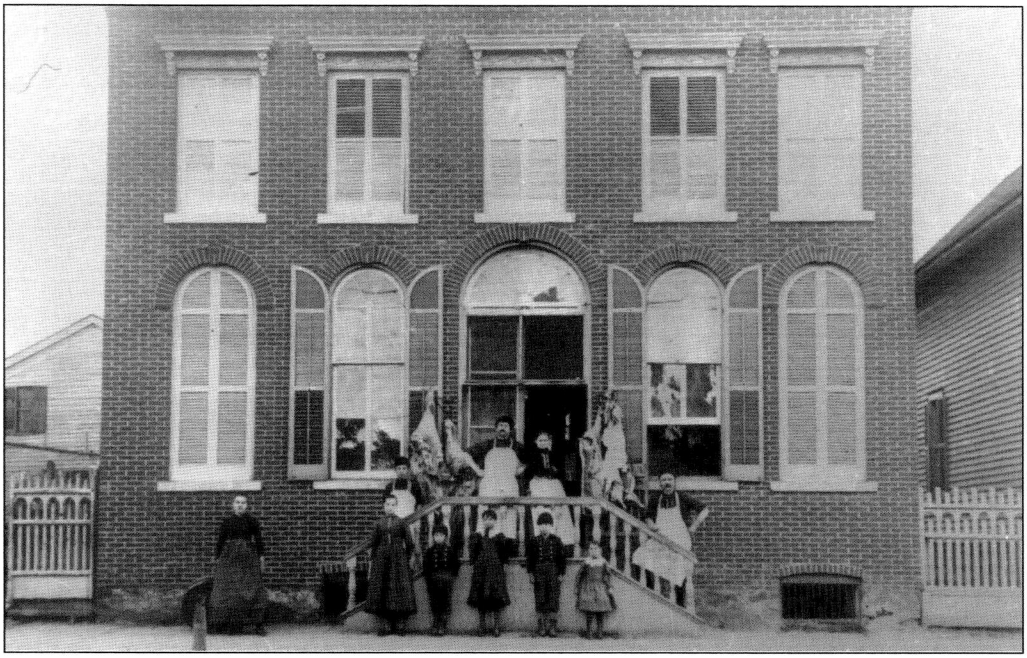

CHARLIE KOLL BUTCHER SHOP. Located on New York Avenue in Sheboygan, the Koll family stands proudly in front of its new facility displaying a number of items available to the public. From left to right are Martha Koll Wendland, Elizabeth, Charles, Jr., Minnie, Gustave, Clara Koll Muhs, Emil, Charles, Sr., and Mrs. Koll.

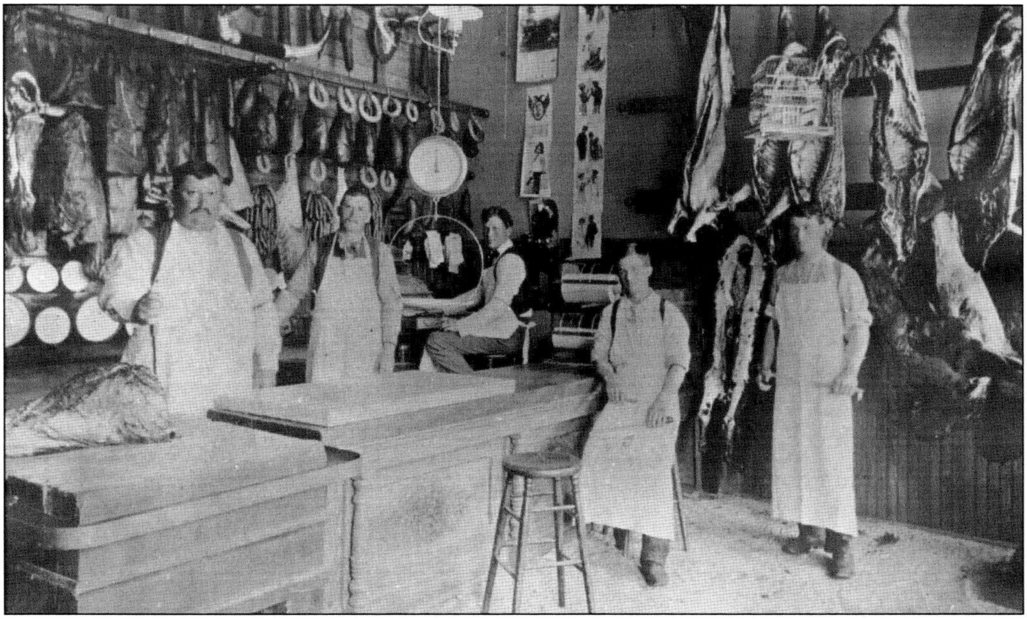

HEERMAN BROTHERS BUTCHER SHOP. Located at 1126 Michigan Avenue, Sheboygan, in 1899, the store was founded by Henry Heerman (left) about 1885. An unskinned calf carcass can be seen in the background. In 1899, he formed a partnership with his brother William. The business was dissolved in 1952 and the building was sold. From left to right are Henry Heerman, William Heerman, Gust Heerman, Otto Schultz, and William Schultz.

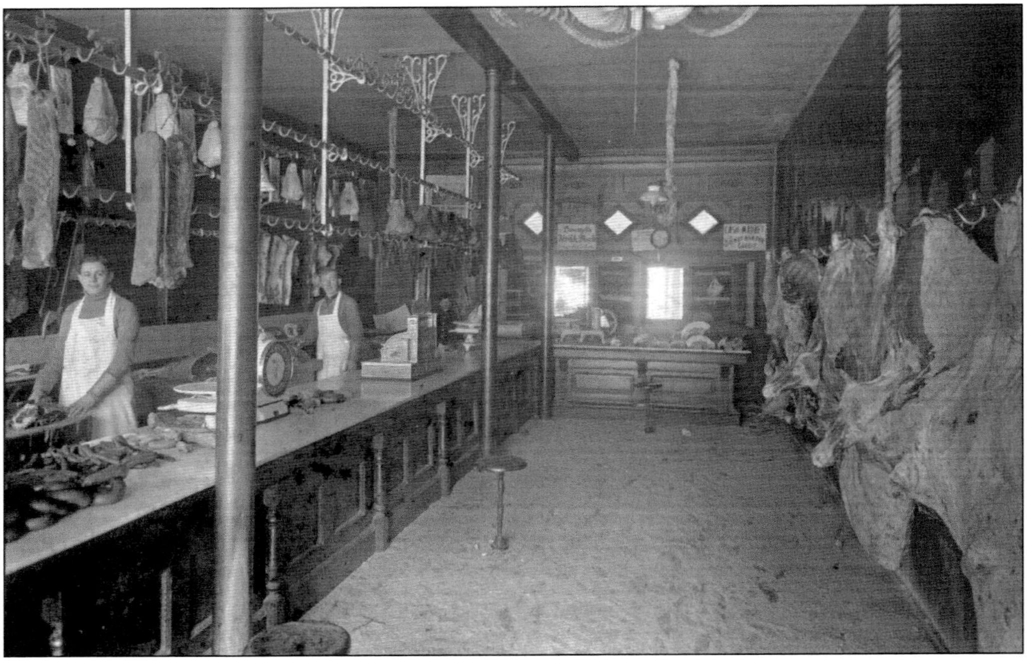

ROMAN STEPHANIE AND JOHN HETTINGER BUTCHER SHOP. Notice the sawdust on the floor, sausage on the counter, and the No Credit sign at the rear of the store. Elaborate light fixtures, stools for customers, and decorative meat hanging apparatus made the store a pleasant place to shop.

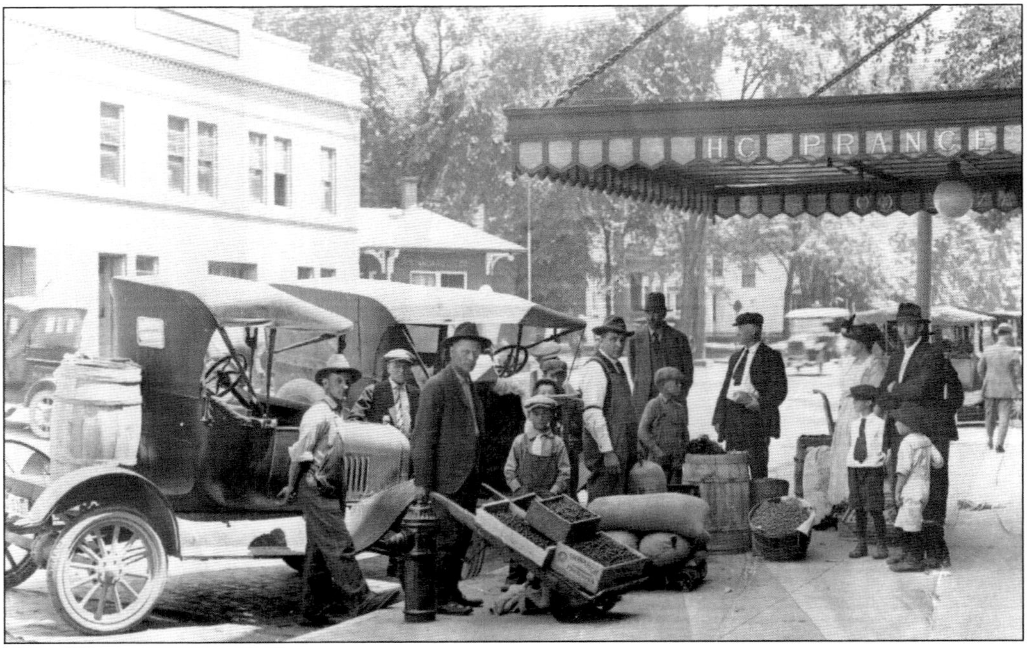

H.C PRANGE. Farmers brought produce to sell to the H.C. Prange Company in Sheboygan. In exchange for their produce they were issued "Due Bills" that the farmer could then spend on whatever he needed or wanted from the store. This picture is taken looking east to Seventh Street.

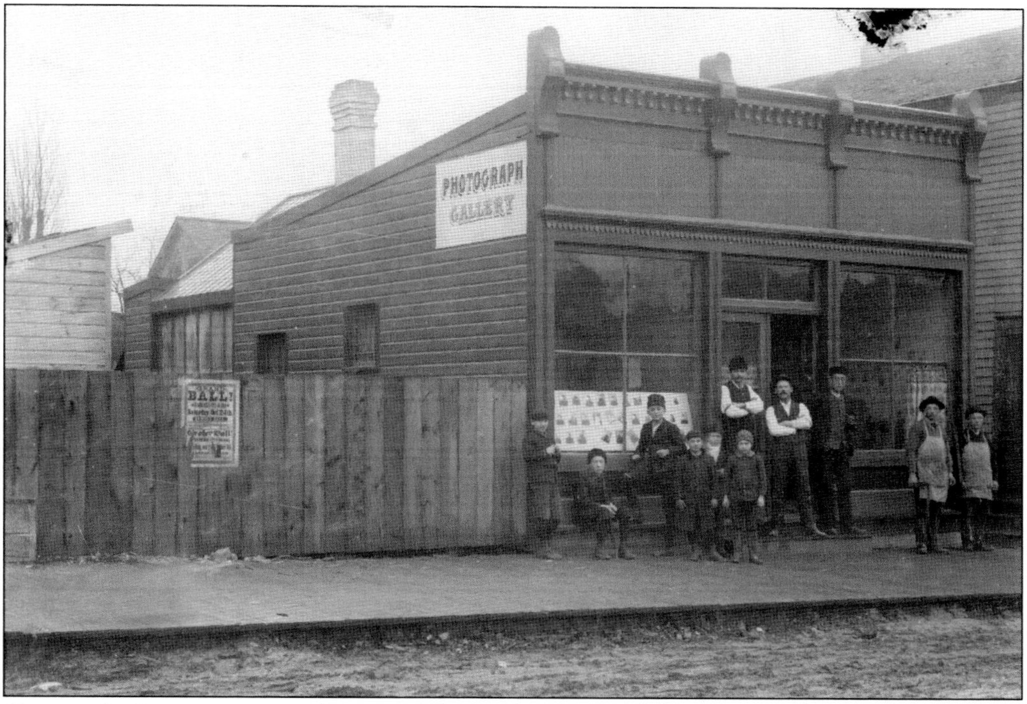

Glaeser's Photographic Studio. This early photo of the Glaeser Photographic Studio, dated 1891, shows the business that was located at Eighth and Jefferson Streets in Sheboygan. Note the slanted panes of glass on the side of the building. This was designed to give the photographer the maximum use of natural light. Also, notice the poster painted on the board fence. This was a most common way of promoting upcoming events.

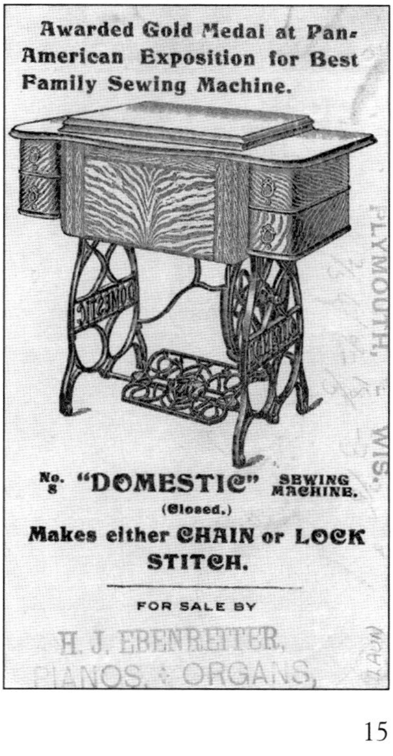

Ebenreiter Sewing Machine Ad. H.G. Ebenreiter of Plymouth sold everything from sewing machines to pianos and organs. This ad for an elaborate treadle sewing machine speaks of the model's award winning moments at a Pan-American Expo.

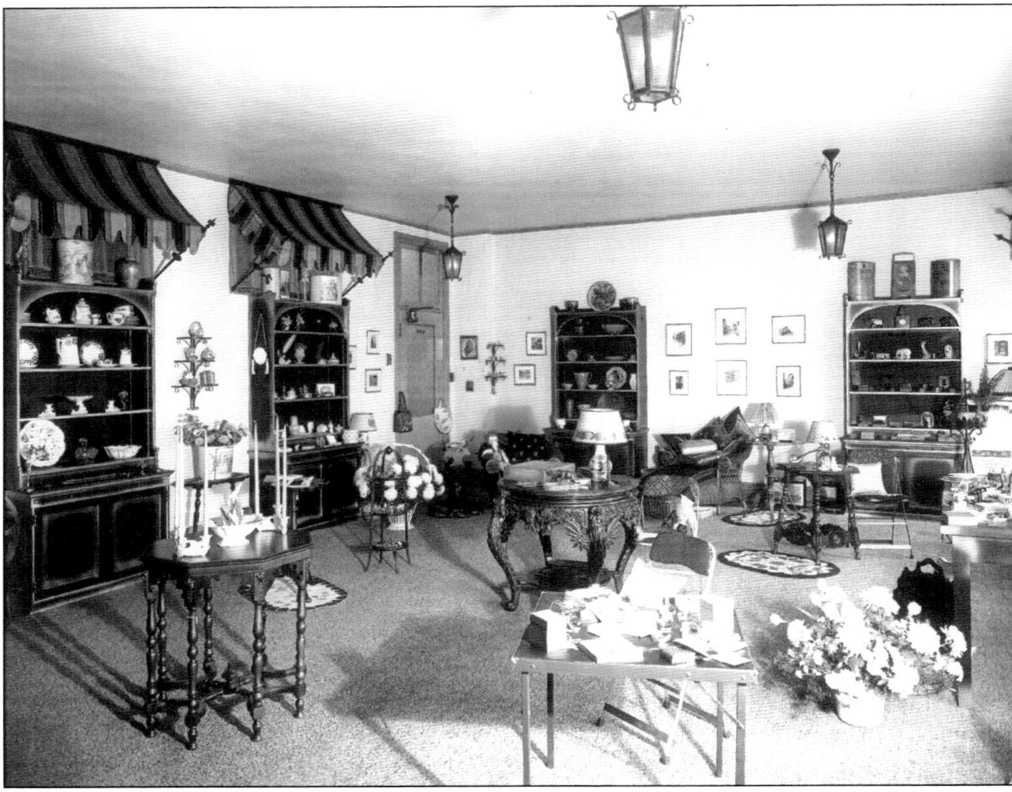

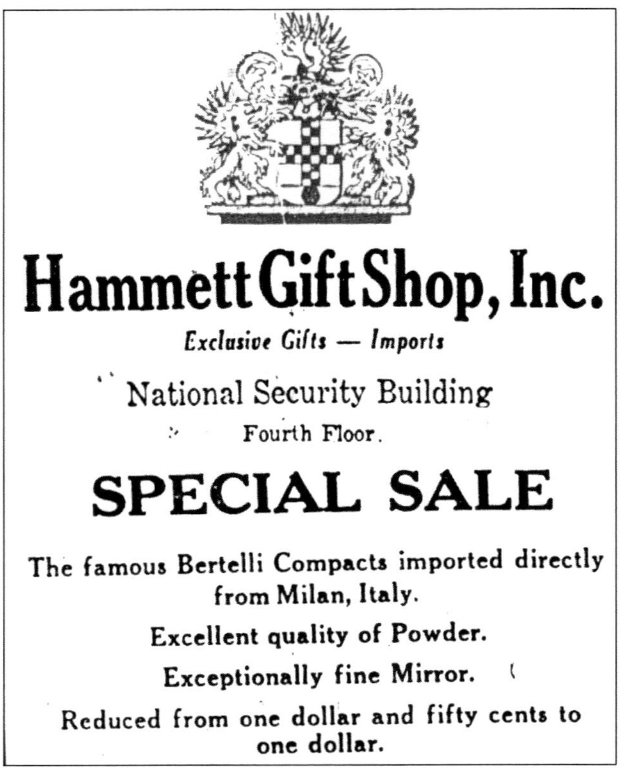

HAMMETT GIFT SHOP. Operated by Edward Hammet, this early gift shop was located on the 4th floor in the Security National Building in Sheboygan. The *Sheboygan Press* states in a 1927 issue that "Sheboygan will soon have a new shop where it will be possible to buy exclusive novelties, imported directly from Italy." Officers of the company included Edward Hammett, Sr., president, Edw. Hammett, Jr., vice president, and Mrs. Edward Hammett, secretary and treasurer.

HAMMETT GIFT SHOP. This sale advertisement from the Sheboygan Press urges shoppers to see the imported items available for sale. Another ad listed the company as importers, wholesalers, and retailers.

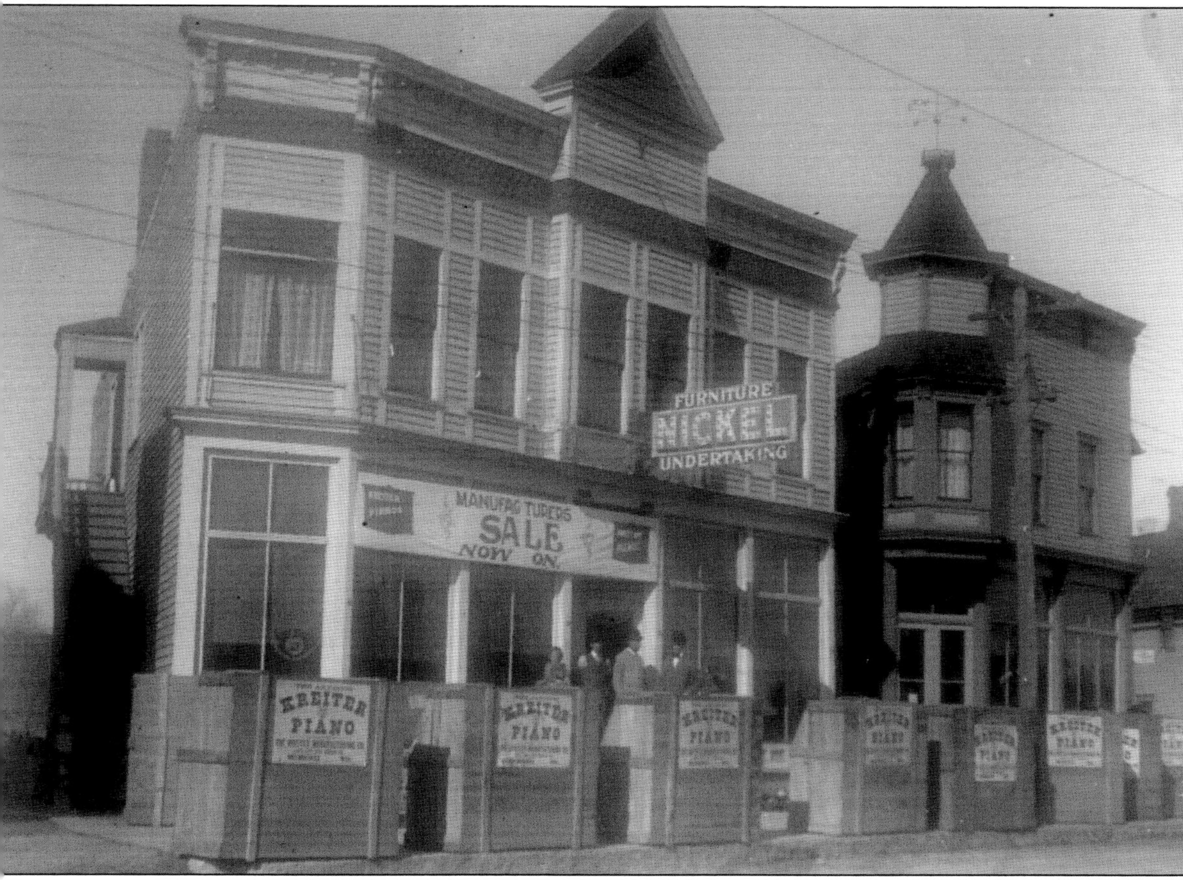

NICKEL AND DIEHL FURNITURE. This photo is a great advertisement for the Kreiter Manufacturer's piano sale. Nine boxed pianos await eager customers at the curb. The furniture store, located in the 1500 block of Calumet Drive in Sheboygan, stayed in operation until the 1960s. The business was started in 1892.

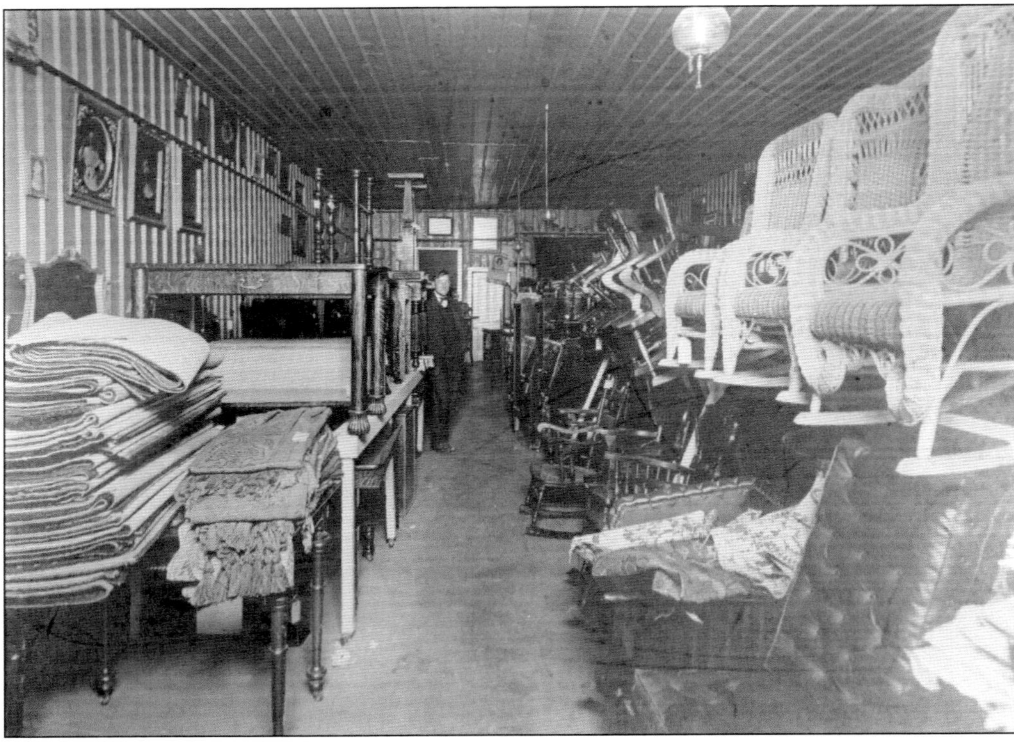

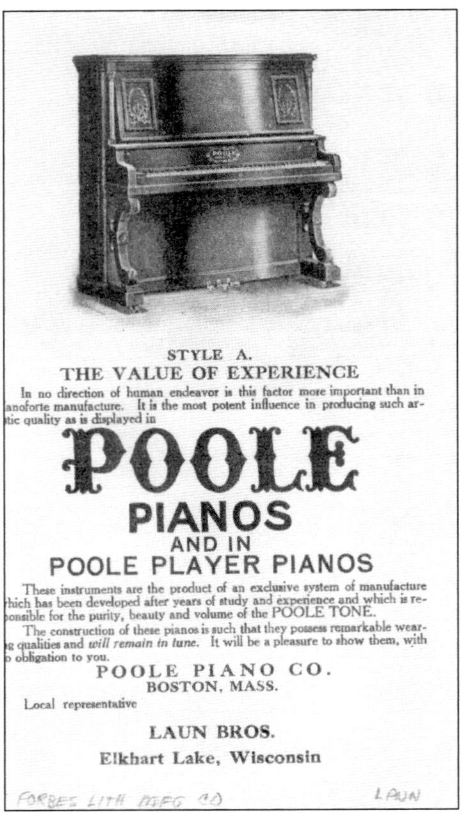

LAUN FURNITURE COMPANY. Shown here is the interior of the Laun Furniture Company. The Laun brothers, Jacob, Louis, Henry, and Alfred, of Elkhart Lake were the first conglomerate in this part of Sheboygan County. They pooled their resources to form a number of furniture and lumber companies. In Elkhart Lake, they built the feed mill and furniture company. They also dealt in coal, grains, accessories and mortuary services.

POOLE PIANO ADVERTISEMENT. Sold by Laun Furniture of Elkhart Lake, this ad for Poole Pianos extols the virtues of the new player piano.

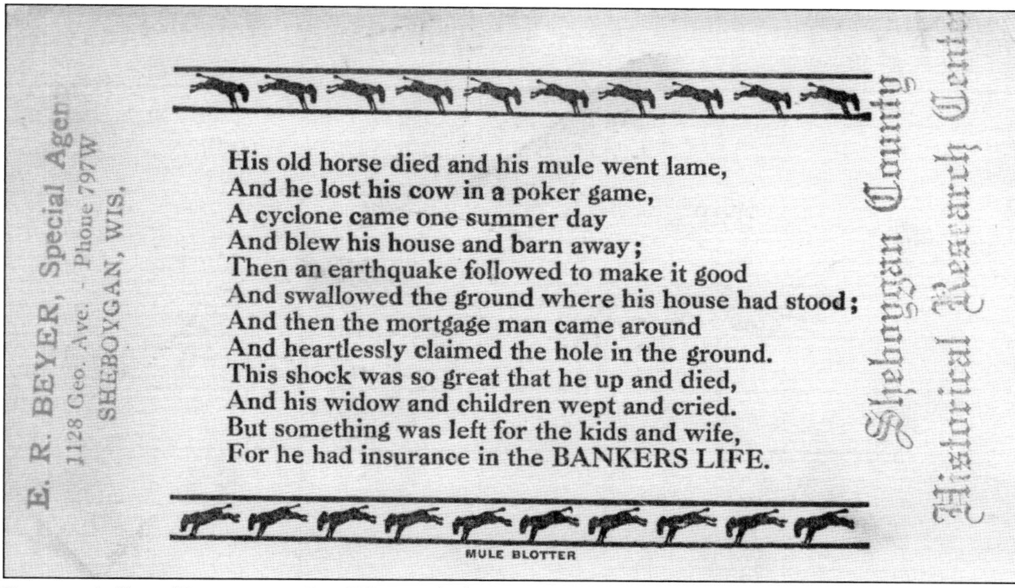
E. R. BEYER, Special Agen
1128 Geo. Ave. - Phone 797W
SHEBOYGAN, WIS.

His old horse died and his mule went lame,
And he lost his cow in a poker game,
A cyclone came one summer day
And blew his house and barn away;
Then an earthquake followed to make it good
And swallowed the ground where his house had stood;
And then the mortgage man came around
And heartlessly claimed the hole in the ground.
This shock was so great that he up and died,
And his widow and children wept and cried.
But something was left for the kids and wife,
For he had insurance in the BANKERS LIFE.

MULE BLOTTER

BANKER'S LIFE POEM AND AD. This early business card, presented to customers by E. R. Beyer of Center Avenue in Sheboygan, notes the benefit of carrying Banker's Life insurance, while at the same time making the customer chuckle.

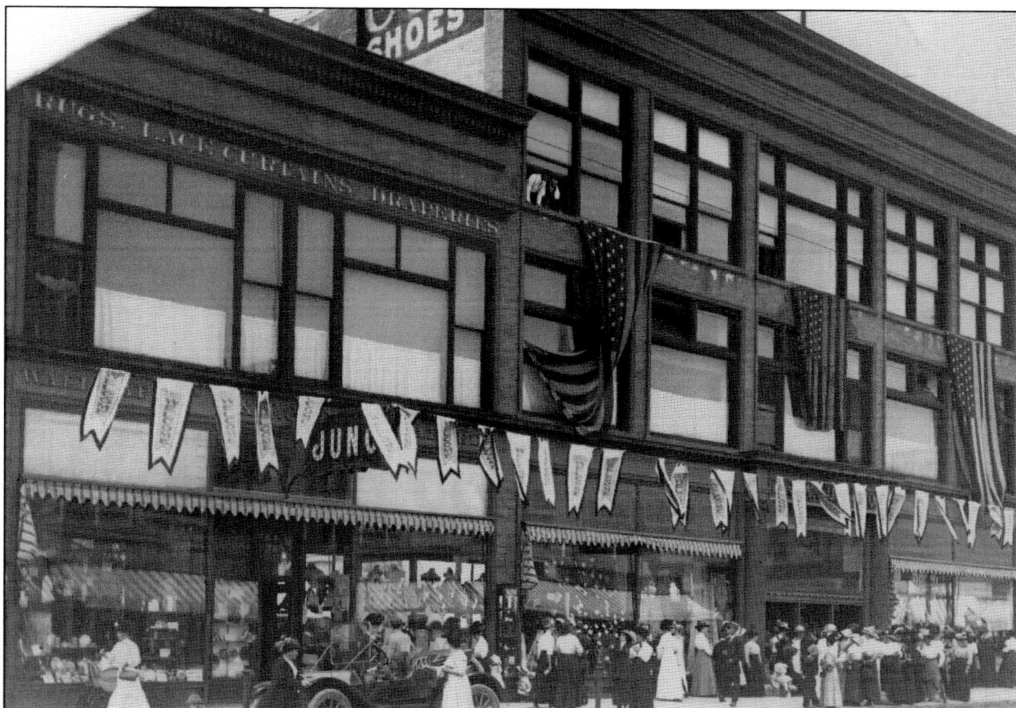

JUNG'S DRY GOODS. On February 17, 1909, the J. & W. Jung Company opened their new grocery and dry goods store on Wisconsin Avenue in Sheboygan. They carried shoes, cloaks, suits, millinery, carpets, curtains, wallpaper, paints, crockery, glassware, woodenware, hardware, and so much more. The store bore the Jung name until 1927, when it was changed to Sheboygan Dry Goods and finally to Hill's Department store in 1950. It was demolished in April of 1973.

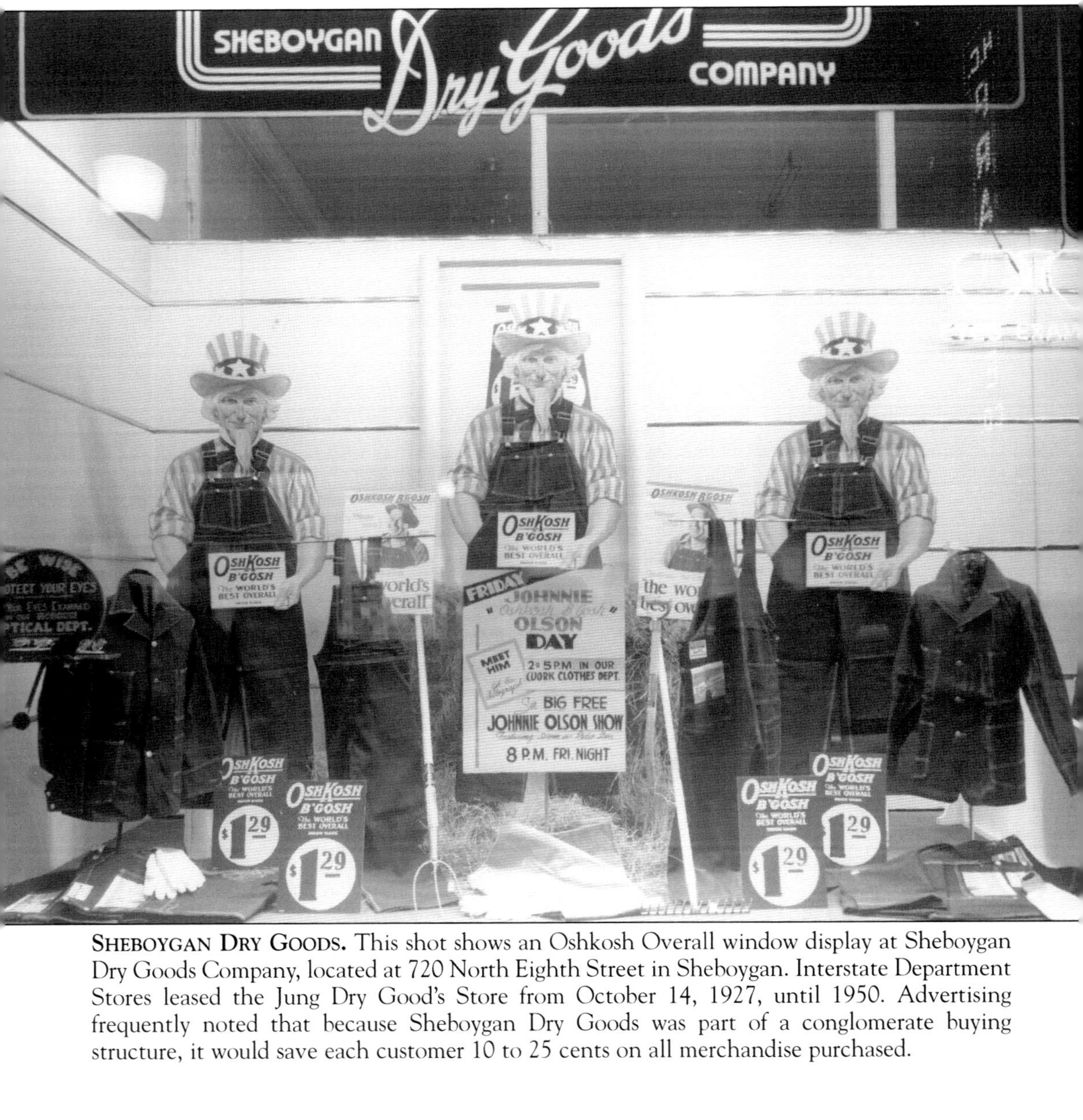

SHEBOYGAN DRY GOODS. This shot shows an Oshkosh Overall window display at Sheboygan Dry Goods Company, located at 720 North Eighth Street in Sheboygan. Interstate Department Stores leased the Jung Dry Good's Store from October 14, 1927, until 1950. Advertising frequently noted that because Sheboygan Dry Goods was part of a conglomerate buying structure, it would save each customer 10 to 25 cents on all merchandise purchased.

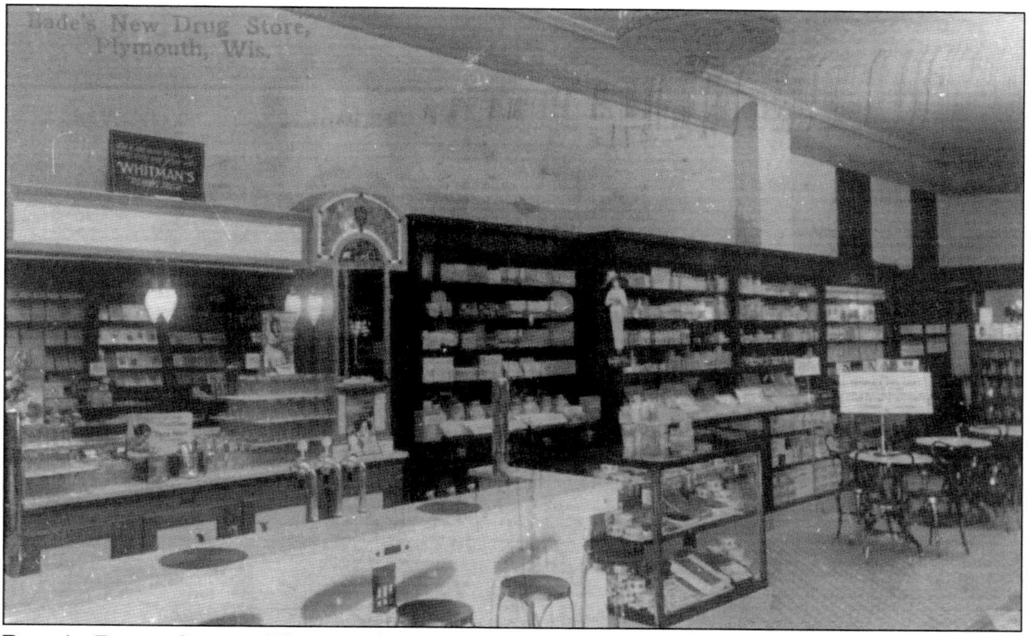

Bade's Drug Store. The grand opening of Bade's Drug Store in Plymouth was held in September of 1914. This interior shot, taken in 1926, shows the Sanitaire Soda Fountain made of marble, opal glass, and German silver. It was ten feet long and equipped with the latest improvements for serving of sodas, sundaes, and ices. Customers would sit at the counter stools or at the tables in the background while enjoying an ice crème soda or sundae. The prescription area was located at the rear of the store.

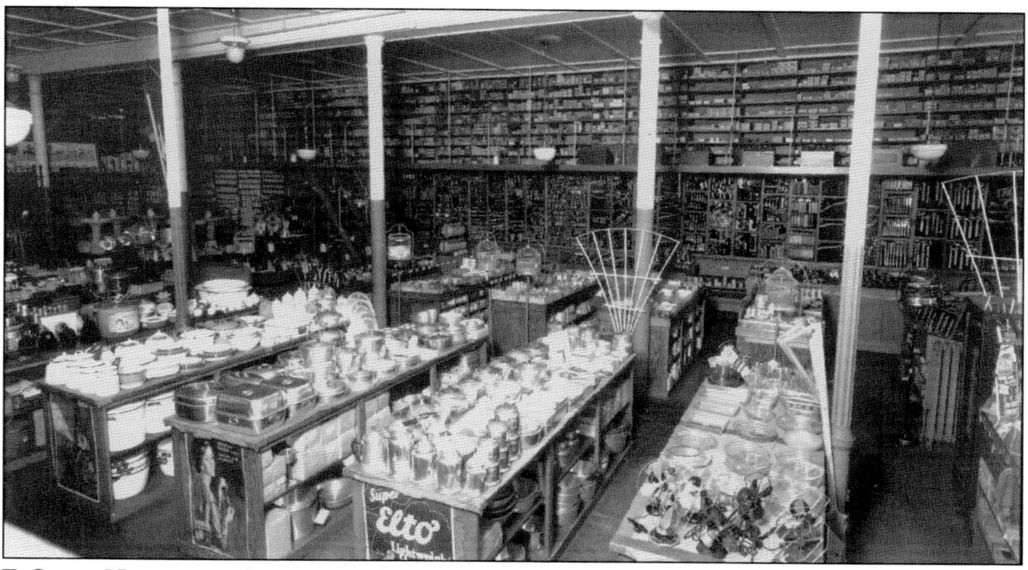

F. Geele Hardware Company. The Frank Geele Hardware Store opened in 1850, three years before the start of the city of Sheboygan. The business, located at the Corner of Eighth and Center in Sheboygan, carried everything a homeowner could want. The *Sheboygan Press* stated that "the large warehouse-type structure was filled with heavy hardware, sash doors, blinds, paints, oils, glass, tools, and the finest instruments." This interior shot was taken in 1932. The building was razed in 1961.

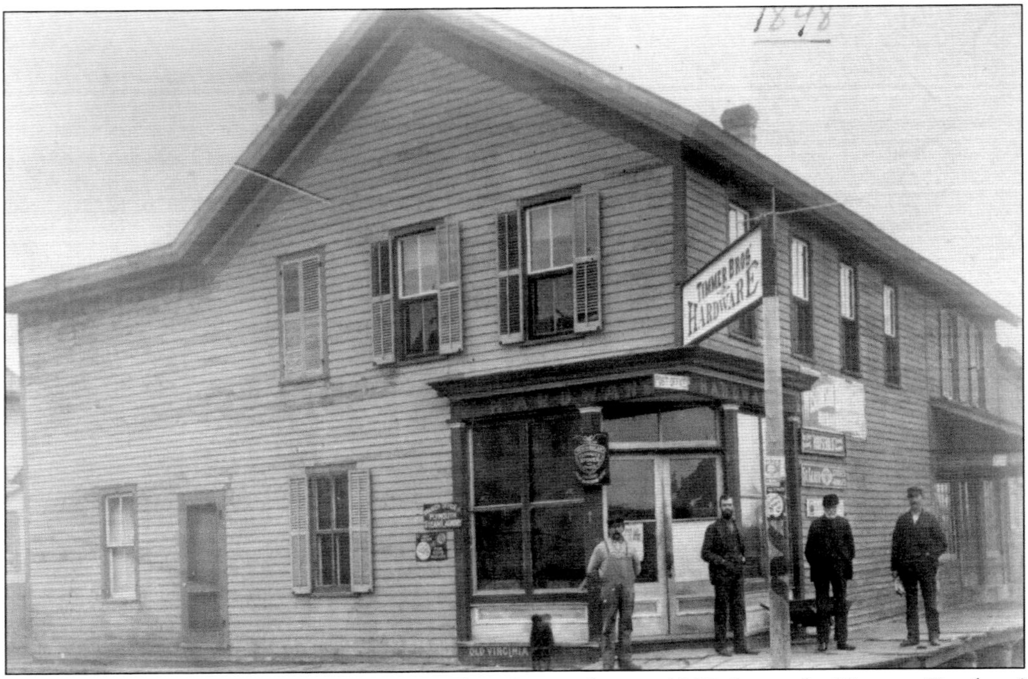

TIMMER BROTHERS HARDWARE STORE. This photo taken in 1898 shows the Timmer Brothers' hardware store in Waldo. The building now houses the United States Post Office.

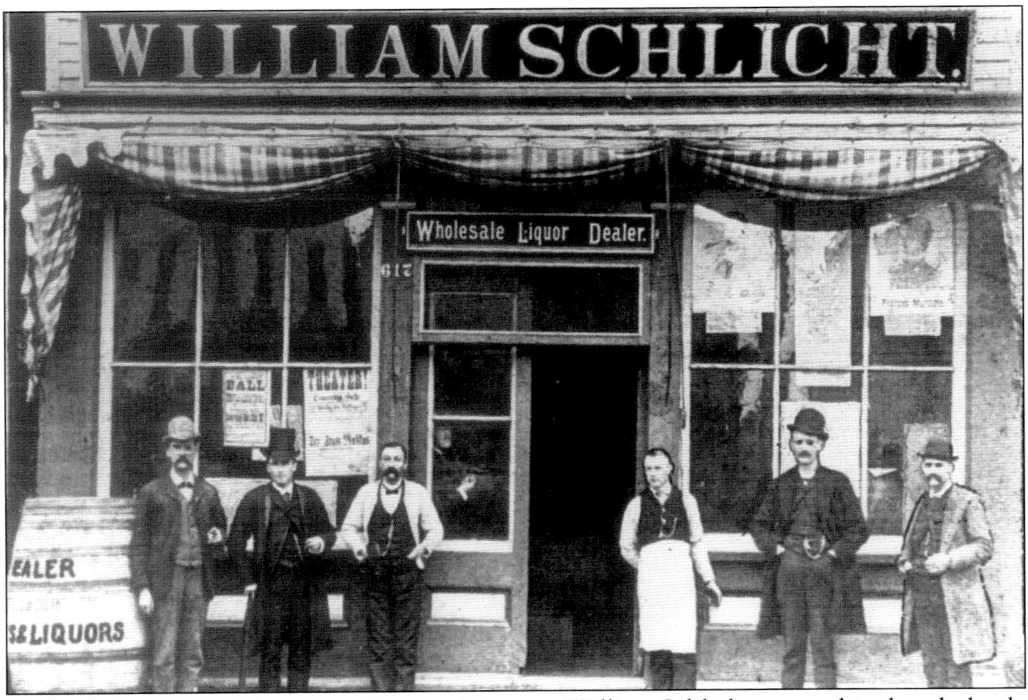

WILLIAM SCHLICHT WHOLESALE LIQUOR DEALER. William Schlicht engaged in the wholesale liquor business beginning in 1873. He was later joined by his brother Jacob, and the two men ran the business until William retired in 1896. Jacob continued the business. The store was located at 615 N. Eighth Street, Sheboygan.

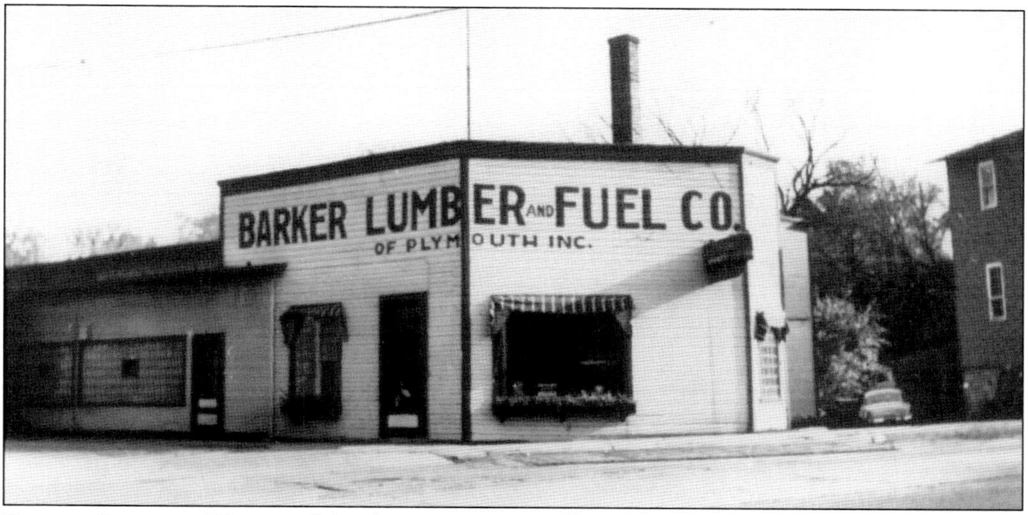

BARKER LUMBER. This small lumber company was located in Plymouth on the south side of Stafford Street, where Stayer Park is now situated.

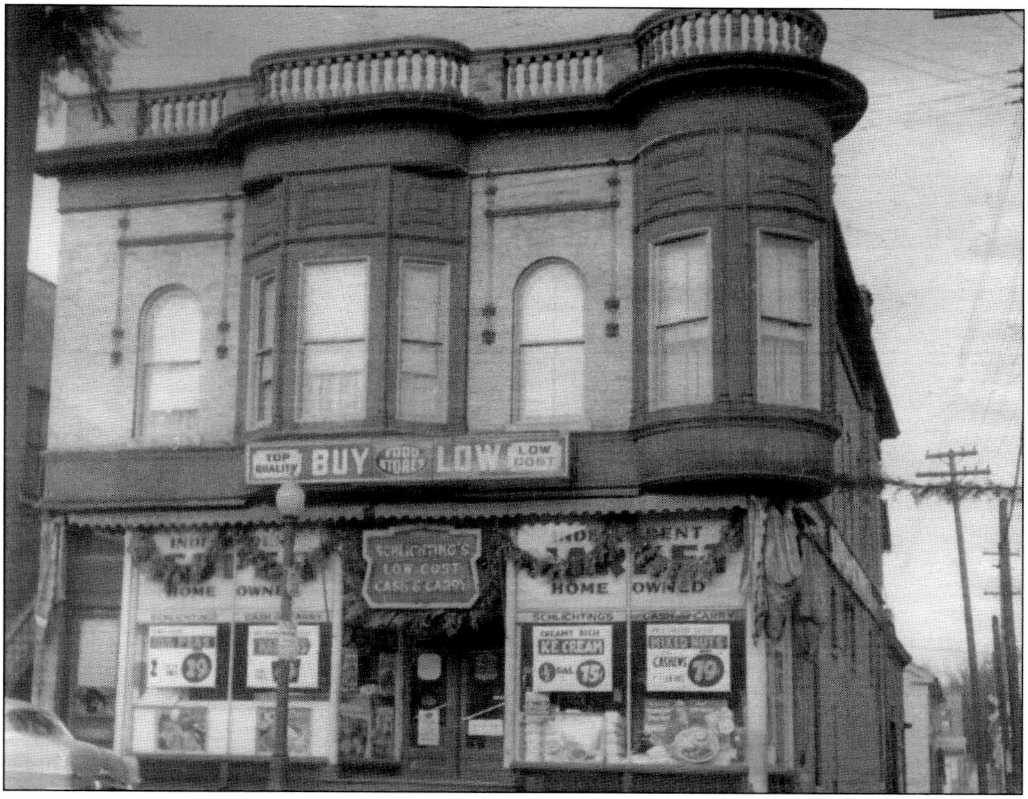

SCHLICHTING BUILDING. Henry Schlichting came to this country from Mecklenburg, Germany, on July 5, 1835. He was initially a blacksmith. In 1894, he finished the building shown in this 1895 print of the exterior of the Schlichting block. It was located at the corner of Buffalo and Pine in Sheboygan Falls. The Schlichting family discontinued its grocery business in 1976, at which time the Richardson family purchased the site. Richardson Furniture Emporium now occupies the site. Note the Ariel and bay windows.

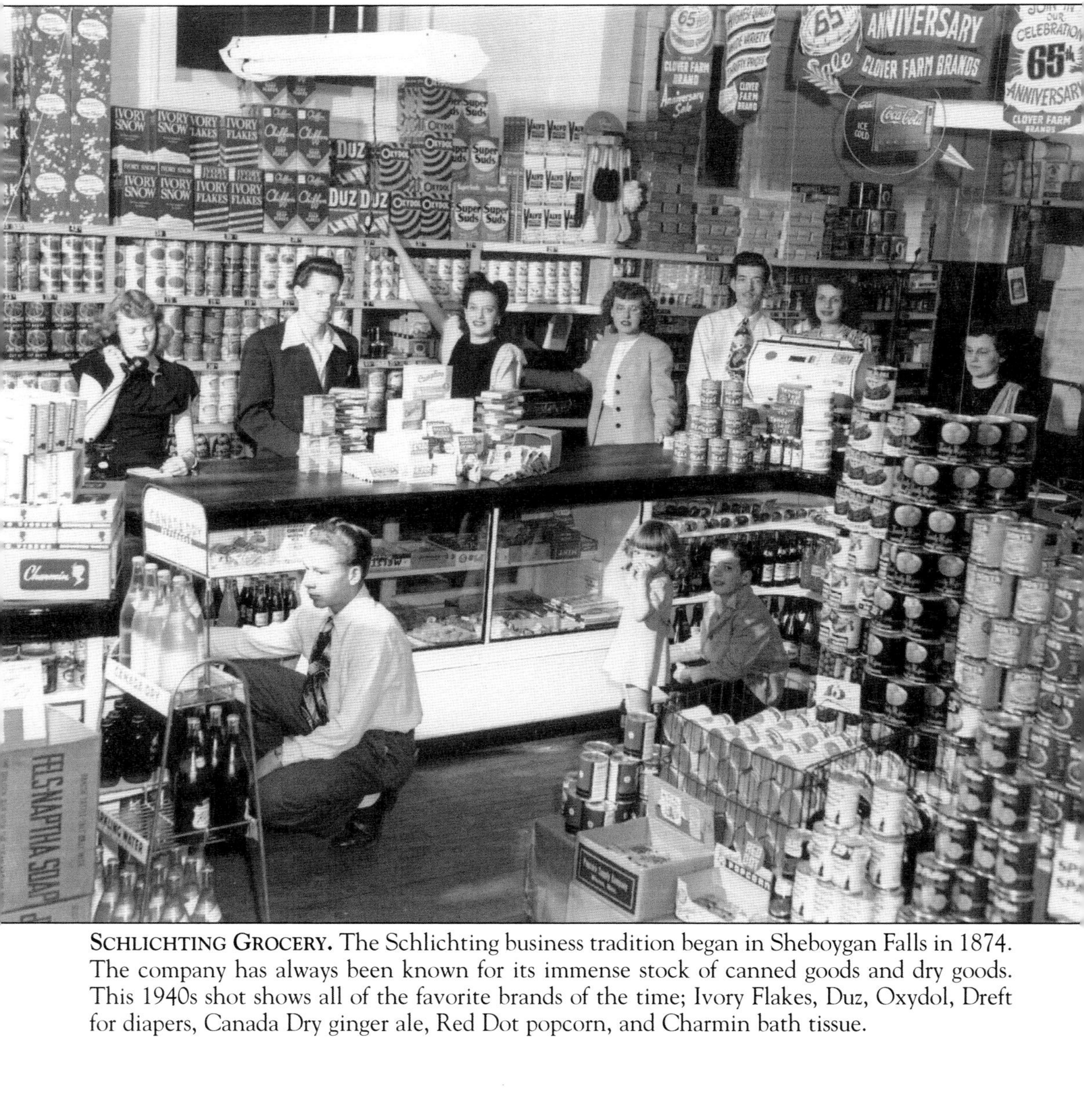

SCHLICHTING GROCERY. The Schlichting business tradition began in Sheboygan Falls in 1874. The company has always been known for its immense stock of canned goods and dry goods. This 1940s shot shows all of the favorite brands of the time; Ivory Flakes, Duz, Oxydol, Dreft for diapers, Canada Dry ginger ale, Red Dot popcorn, and Charmin bath tissue.

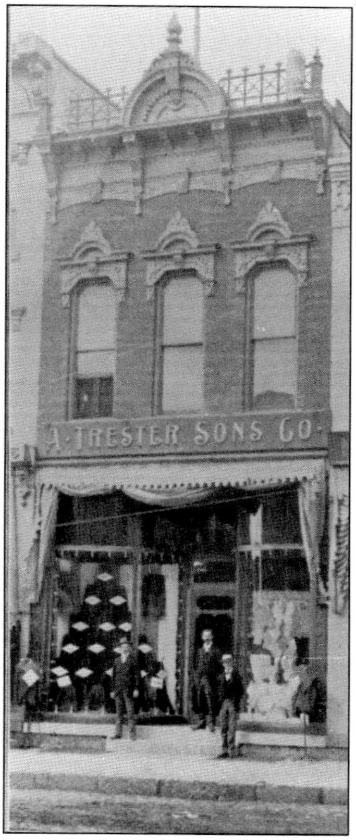

TRESTER CLOTHING STORE. Adam Trester, a native of Coblenz, Germany, learned the tailor's trade in his native land. In 1858 he came to Sheboygan where he established a small tailor shop. His store was one of the first to be established in Sheboygan, and was one of the largest stores of its kind. This building, erected c. 1860, still stands at 514 N. Eighth Street, Sheboygan.

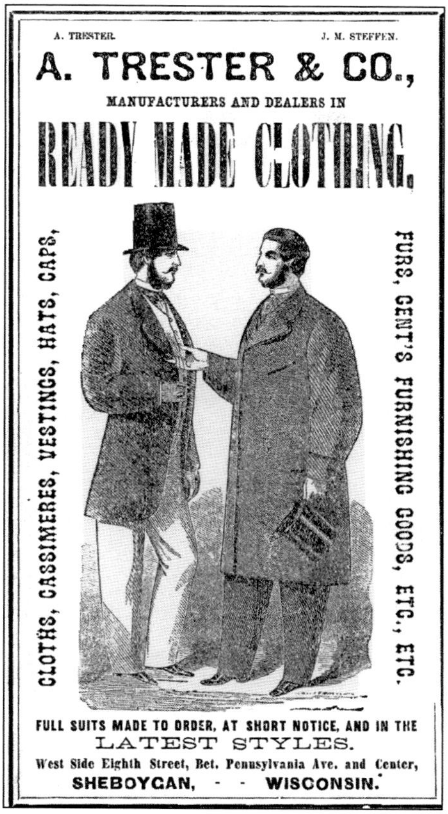

TRESTER ADVERTISEMENT. Shown here is an advertisement for men's ready-made clothing. The day of the tailor was beginning to pass.

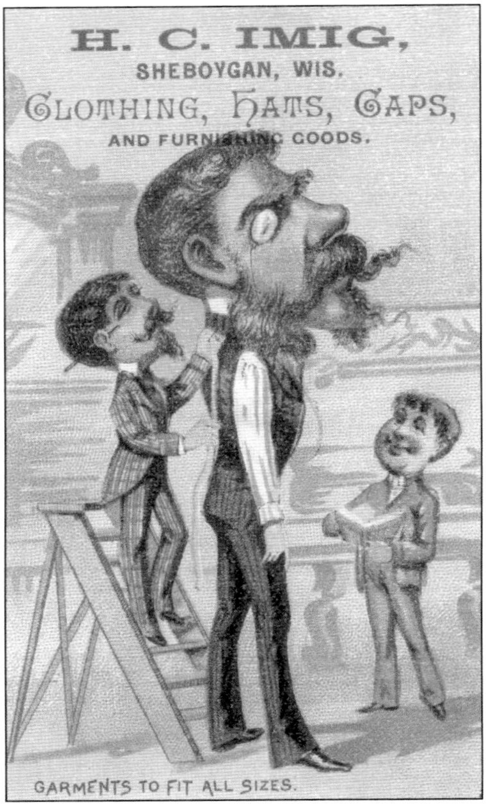

H.C. IMIG CLOTHING ADVERTISEMENT. The name Imig has been a part of Sheboygan's clothing vocabulary since 1852. Michael Imig opened a tailor's shop on Pennsylvania Avenue when it was still "Sheboygan's main street" and plank roads were in vogue. But, his sons continued this tradition of commerce. The advertisement shown is one of a series of color display cards touting the benefits of shopping at a quality clothier like Imig's.

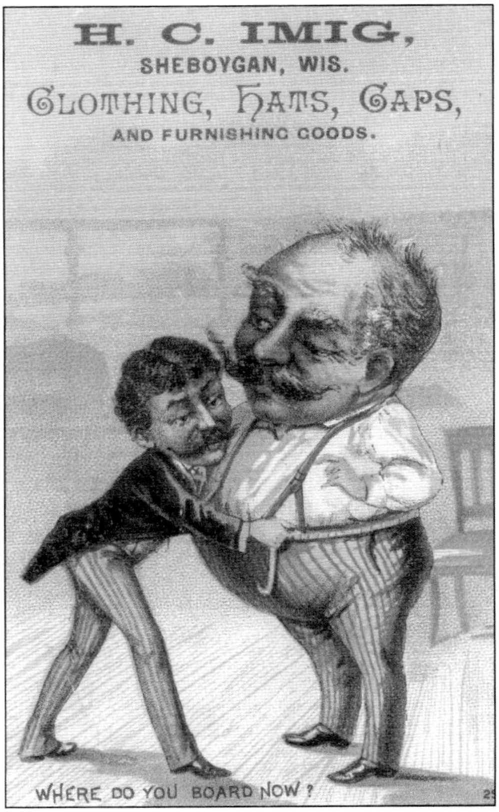

H.C. IMIG CLOTHING ADVERTISEMENT. Another of Imig's clever advertising items and souvenirs.

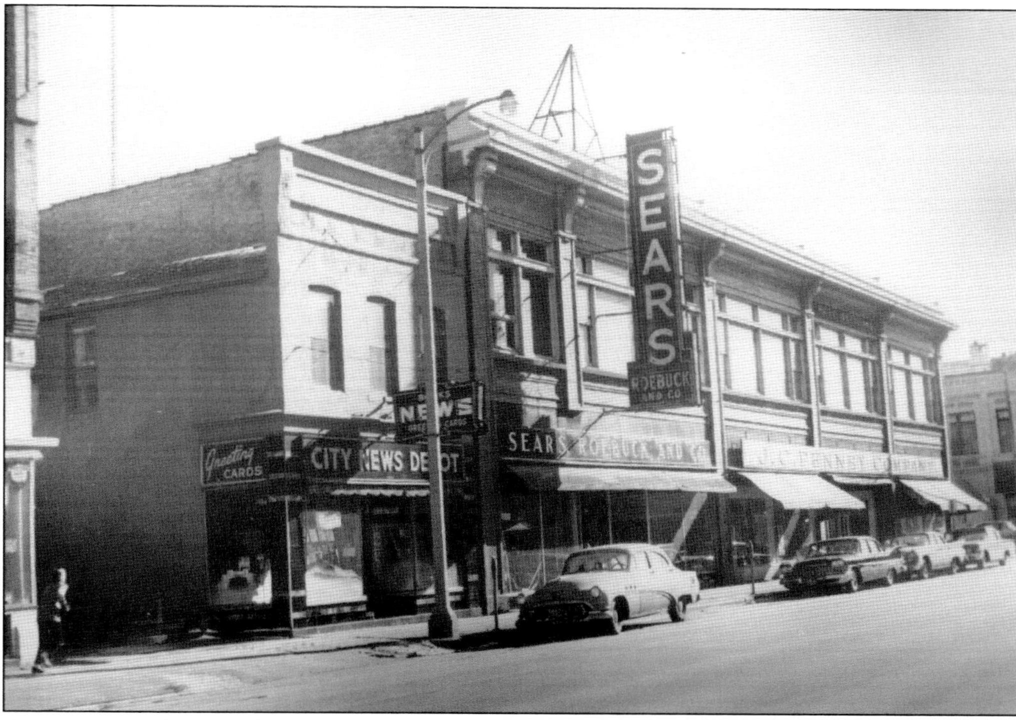

Sheboygan's Main Street. Located on one of the busiest stretches of Eighth Street in Sheboygan were J.C. Penney, Sears Roebuck and Company, and City News Depot.

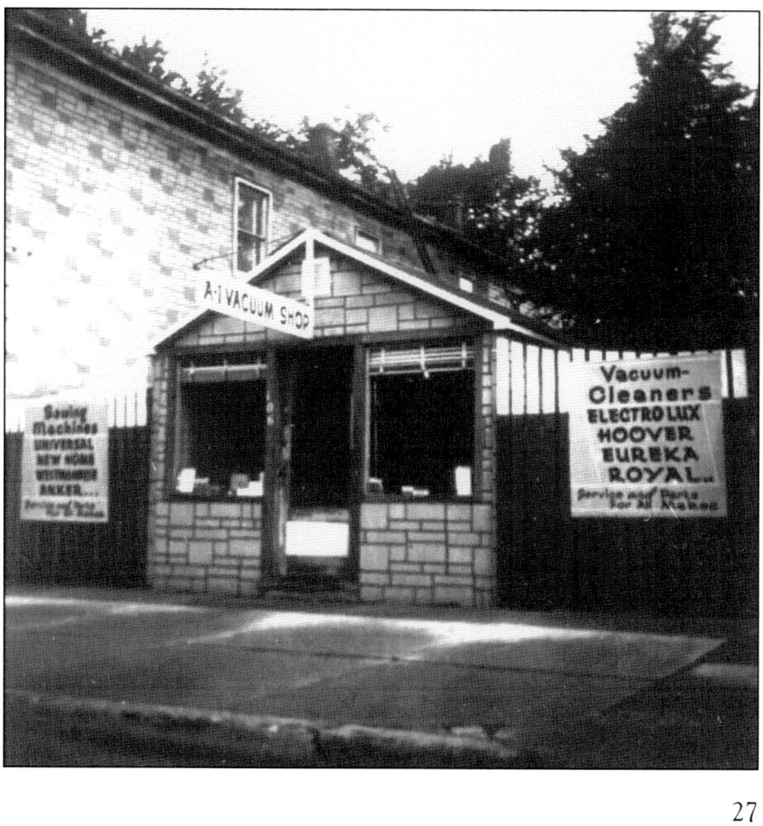

A-1 Vacuum Shop. An early view of a tiny business once located at 106 E. Mill, Plymouth. This photo was taken c. 1959. All the popular models were sold; Electrolux, Hoover, Eureka, and Royal.

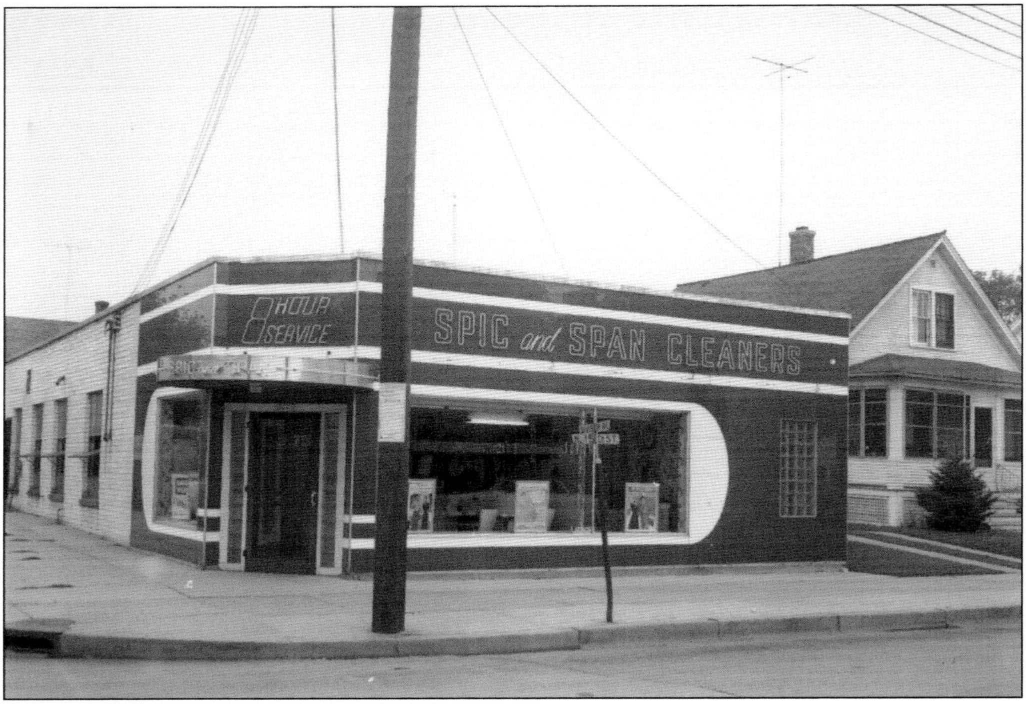

SPIC 'N SPAN CLEANERS, INC. Located at 2602 North Fifteenth Street in Sheboygan in 1953, the front of this building had a unique Art Deco design. The colors of the façade were cobalt blue and white. It later became the home of Bytehead Computers.

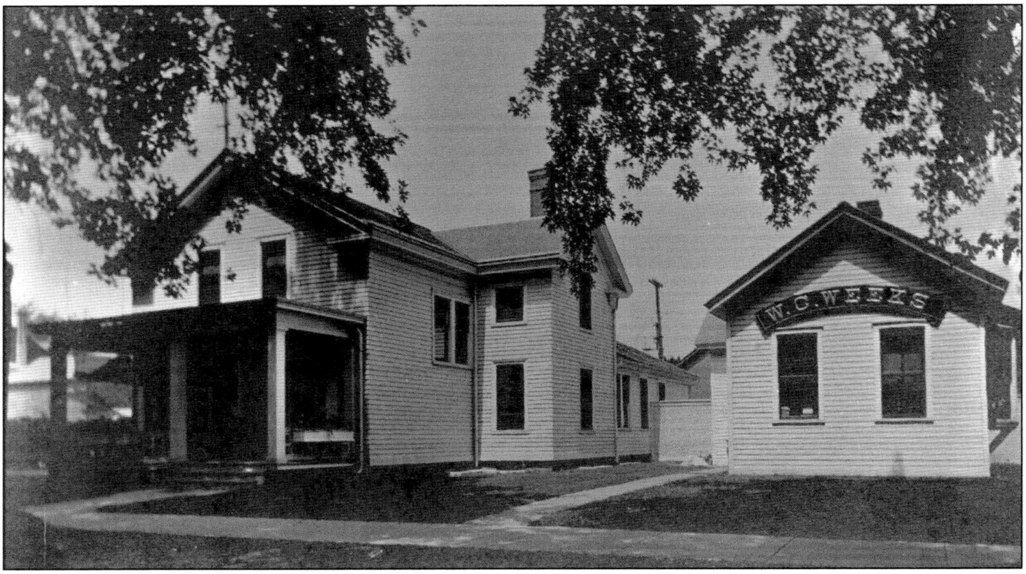

OFFICE OF W.C. WEEKS, ARCHITECT. The Weeks family was a family of architects. Four members of the family were actively involved in the design and construction of public buildings, churches, and residences in Sheboygan. Buildings designed by members of the Weeks family include Corporate Headquarters of Plastics Engineering at 3518 North Fifteenth Street, W. B. Hawkins house at 434 Erie Avenue, and the Otto Jung home at 318 St. Clair Avenue. The office shown here was located at 720 Ontario in Sheboygan.

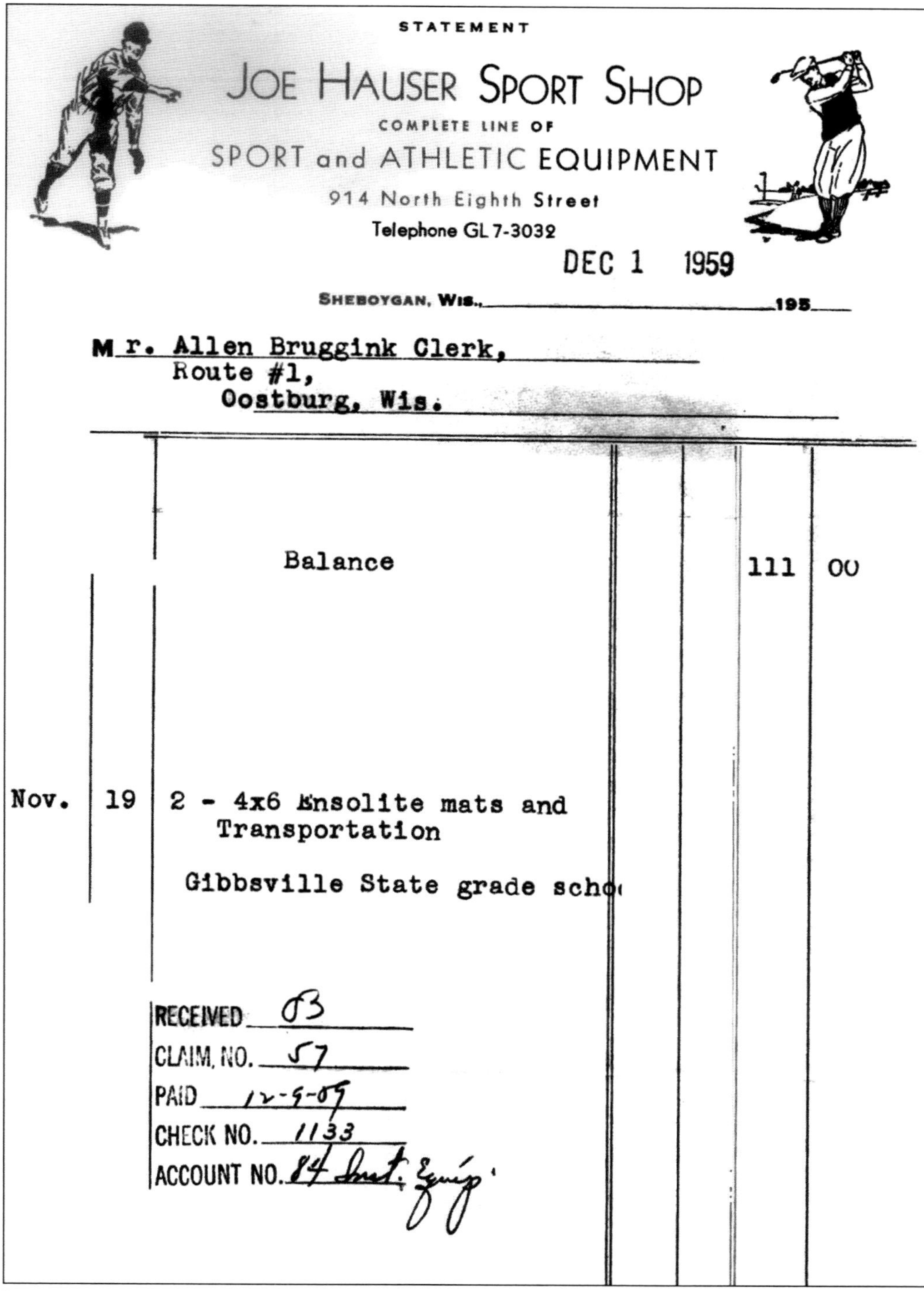

STATEMENT

JOE HAUSER SPORT SHOP

COMPLETE LINE OF

SPORT and ATHLETIC EQUIPMENT

914 North Eighth Street

Telephone GL 7-3032

DEC 1 1959

SHEBOYGAN, WIS., 195

Mr. Allen Bruggink Clerk,
Route #1,
Oostburg, Wis.

		Balance	111 00
Nov.	19	2 - 4x6 Ensolite mats and Transportation	
		Gibbsville State grade scho	

RECEIVED 83
CLAIM. NO. 57
PAID 12-9-59
CHECK NO. 1133
ACCOUNT NO. 84 Inst. Equip.

UNSER CHOE'S SHOP. This invoice from Joe Hauser's Sport Shop, located at 914 North Eighth Street, is dated December 1, 1959. Joe was a native of Milwaukee. He began his baseball career as a 19-year old pitcher for the Philadelphia Athletics in 1918. The next year he was sent to the Brewers in Milwaukee. He came to Sheboygan in 1937 as manager of the Chairmakers. He died in 1997 at the age of 98.

—Jake Clicquenoi, employed by Blust Bros, struck a gold mine last Thursday when he wasn't even prospecting and what's more he found the yellow metal already coined. While examining the stomach of a heifer he had just butchered he was greatly surprised to find therein a bright five dollar gold piece. Nails and various other articles are frequently found in the stomachs of cattle but gold pieces seldom and we would suggest to the Sheboygan county farmers who feed their cattle such rich food that they do their own butchering. 5-27-03

BUTCHER SHOP SURPRISE. In 1903, butcher Jake Clicquennoi found a five dollar gold piece in the stomach of a cow he had just butchered. This newspaper article mentions that nails and other items are frequently found, but rarely a five-dollar piece. Who kept the money? The farmer, the butcher shop, or Mr. Clicquennoi?

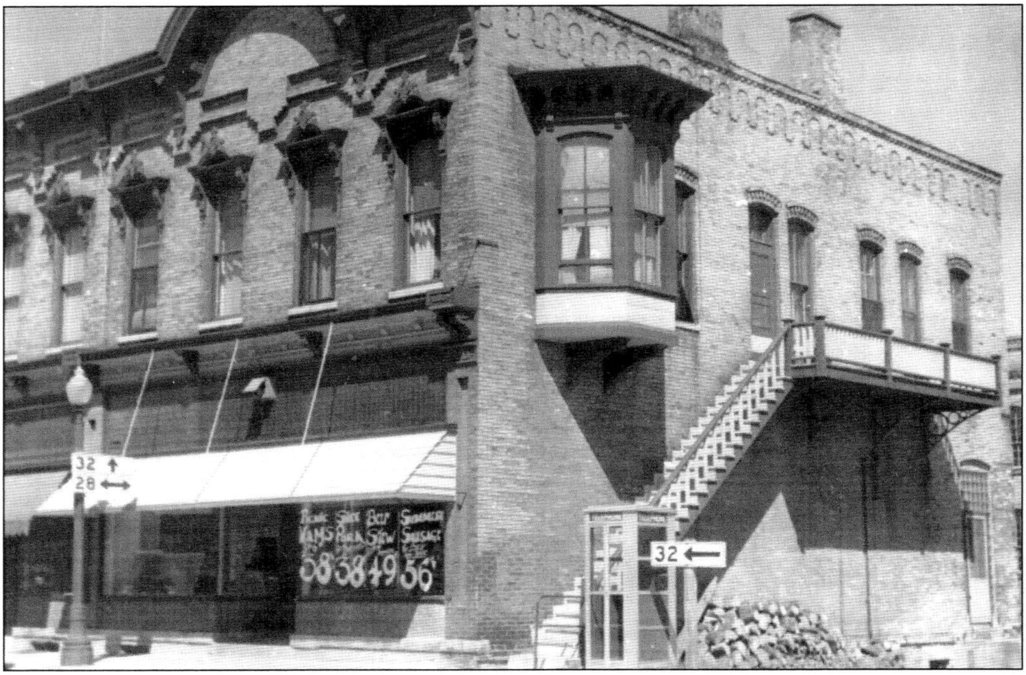

BROADWAY MEAT MARKET. This 1955 photo of the Broadway Meat Market in Sheboygan Falls advertises picnic hams and side pork for \$0.38 per pound, summer sausage for \$0.56 per pound, and beef stew meat for \$0.49 per pound. Jacob Clicquennoi owned this business from 1925 until the fall of 1947. Mr. Clicquennoi was born in the Netherlands on January 29, 1875, coming to this country at the age of nine. At 11, he began to work in a neighborhood butcher shop. In 1899, he came to Sheboygan Falls and worked for Frank and John Blust for nine years. Those were the days, according to Jake, "that meat prices were really reasonable." Beef roast was eight cents and chicken was 10 cents per pound. The butcher would also give a piece of bologna to children as a treat.

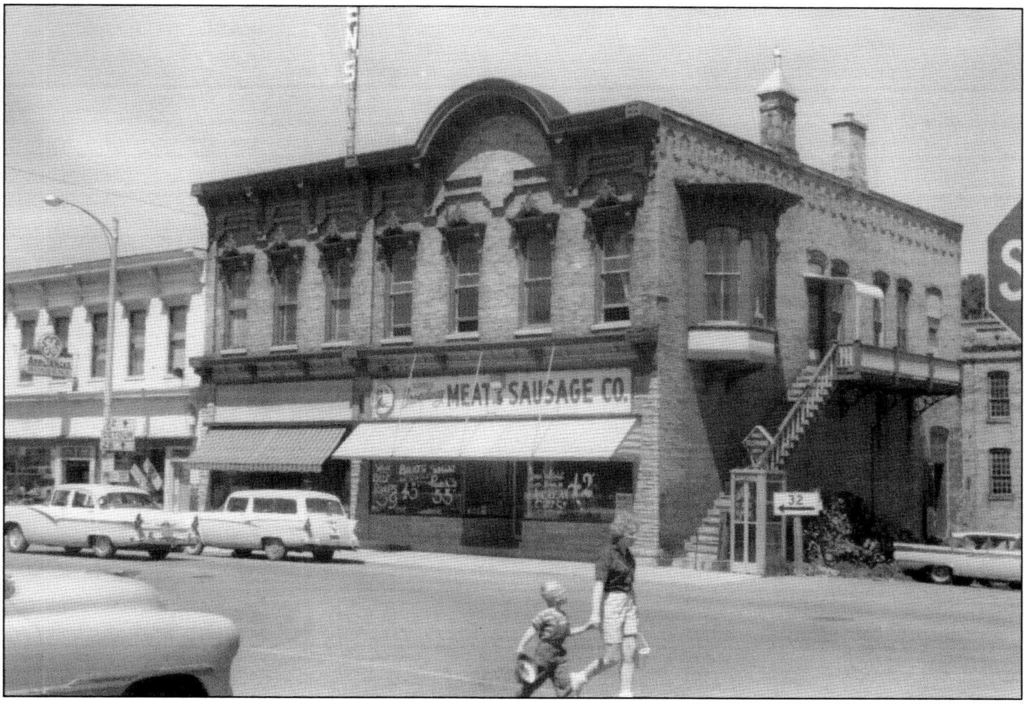

MORE BROADWAY. The Broadway Meat Market is shown here in 1961. It is located on Broadway Street in Sheboygan Falls, just north of Pine Street. The building houses the Bemis Company Outlet Store today.

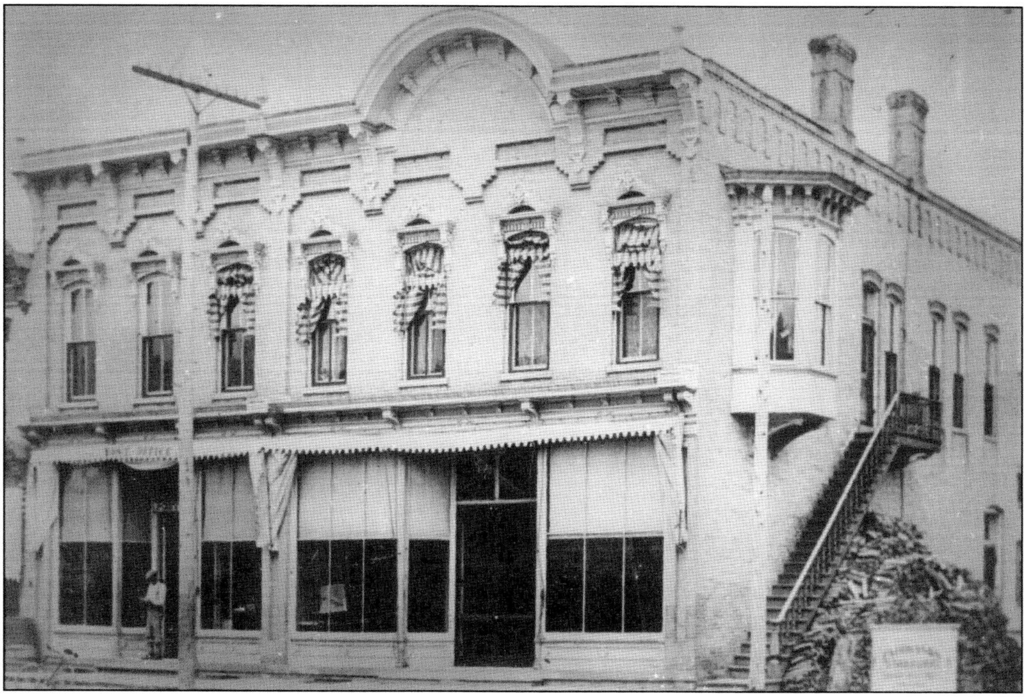

CLICQUENNOI MEAT MARKET. Old Post Office and Blust Meat Market. This is the oldest view of the Clicquennoi Meat Market.

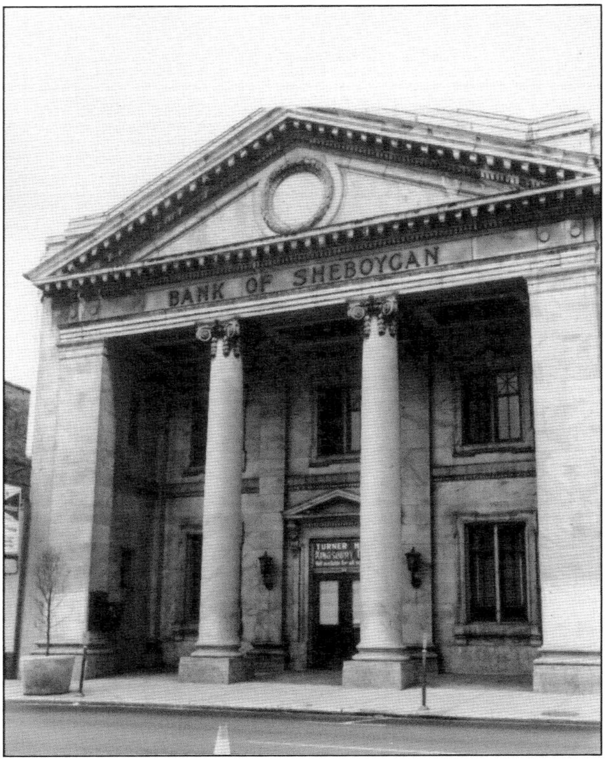

BANK OF SHEBOYGAN. This beautiful marble-columned, Greek Revival style bank was built in 1910 at a cost of $80,192. It was located on the west side of Eighth Street in Sheboygan, one block south of Mead Library. When it was demolished in the 1970s, the columns were unceremoniously dumped into Lake Michigan near the Reiss Coal property.

PLYMOUTH EXCHANGE BANK. This bank was established in 1896, opening its doors for business on May 5 in the Wolf Building on Division Street in Plymouth. The building pictured here at Division and Stafford was erected in 1907. The bank became a victim of the Great Depression of the 1930s. Today, the upper floors contain apartments and small businesses occupy the lower level.

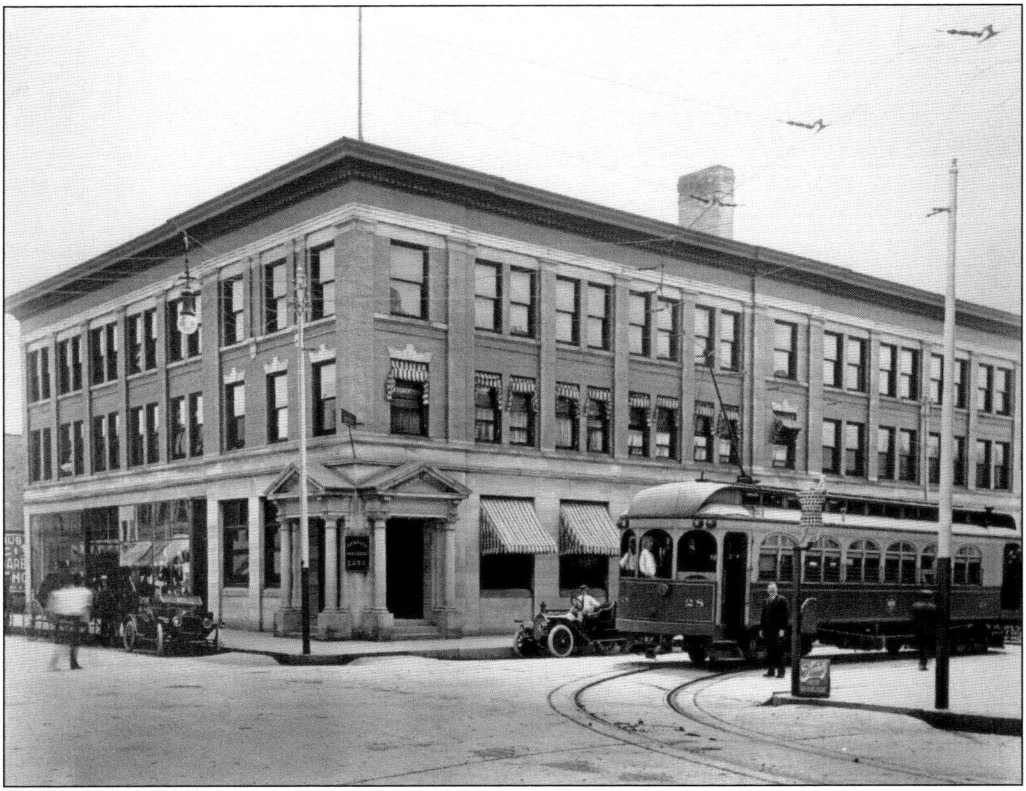

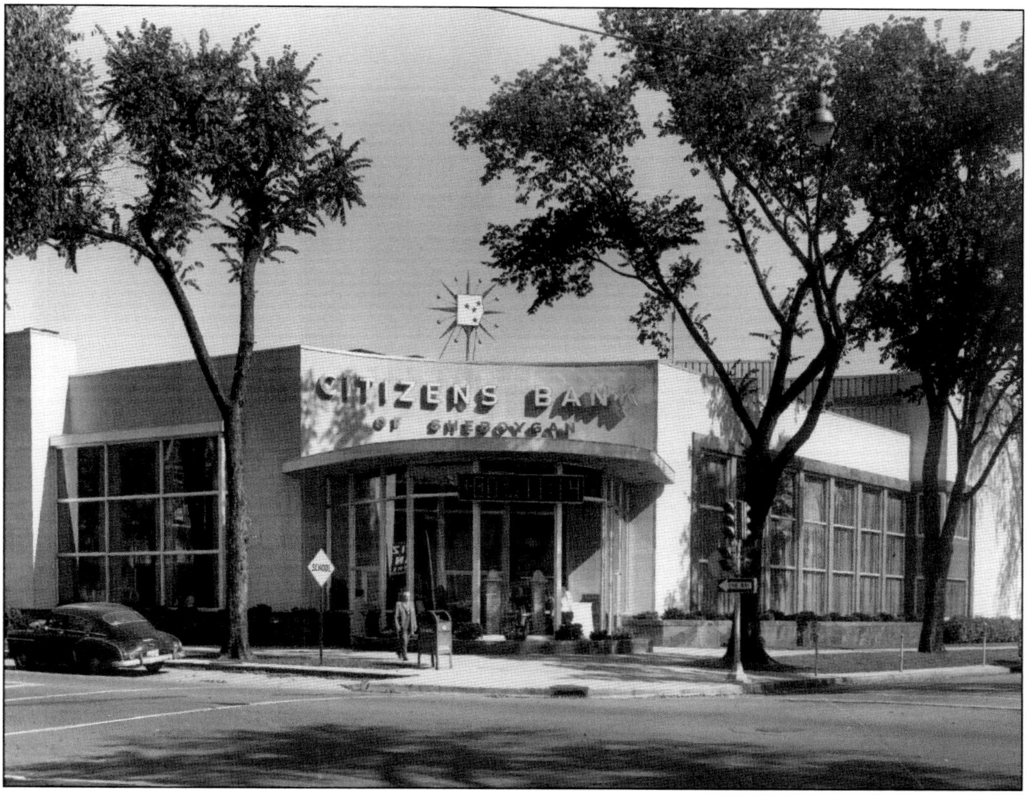

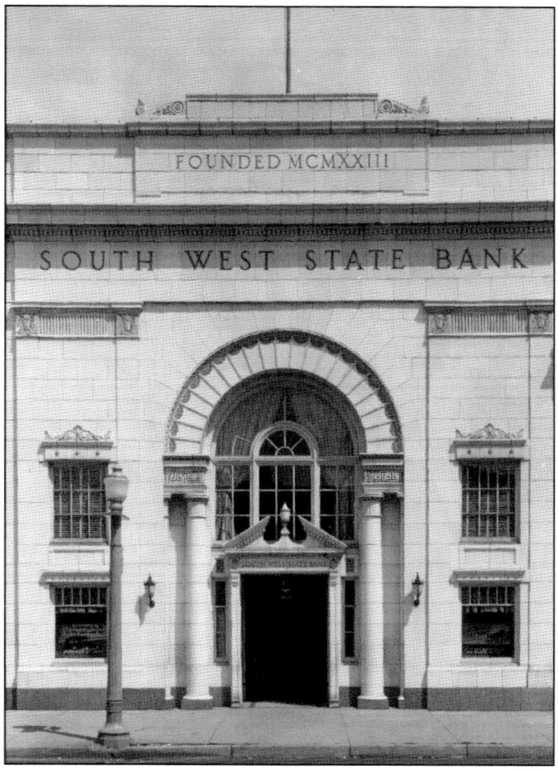

CITIZENS BANK, SHEBOYGAN. This building was completed in November of 1957. Atop the building, the bank's "sunburst" emblem symbolizes Citizens Bank of Sheboygan's county-wide service. It is located on the northeast corner of Seventh Street and Wisconsin Avenue in Sheboygan. Citizens Bank was heavily involved in outreach activities with its customers. It was the home of "Breezy the Clown" and the annual "Dress A Doll" contest, which raised money for needy Sheboygan County children at Christmas.

SOUTHWEST STATE BANK. Founded in 1923, this bank was located at 1510 South Twelfth Street in Sheboygan. A 1942 newspaper article says, "The bank was equipped with the latest security vault for bank funds and safety deposit boxes, and the walls are protected by a burglar alarm system." It is pictured here on August 4, 1948. The building still stands in the Heritage Square area of Sheboygan.

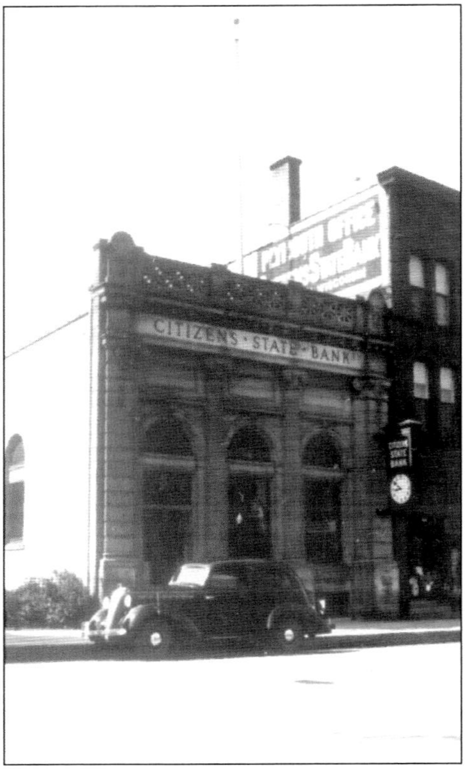

CITIZENS BANK OF PLYMOUTH. Located at 433 East Mill Street in Plymouth, this bank was built in 1904. It is shown here in 1938. The bank later became First Interstate Bank and then in 1990, Norwest, and finally, Wells Fargo.

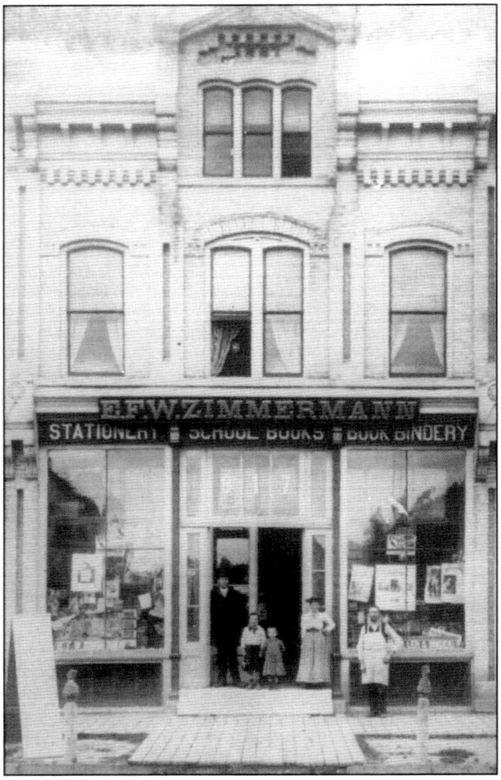

ZIMMERMANN BOOK STORE. In 1887, this building, located at 817 New York Avenue in Sheboygan, was constructed to house Edward F.W. Zimmermann's book and stationery store on the main floor and the Zimmermann family upstairs. In 1937, 63 years after it was started, the business was terminated. Gottsacker Realty bought the building in 1975, and restored it to its former beauty.

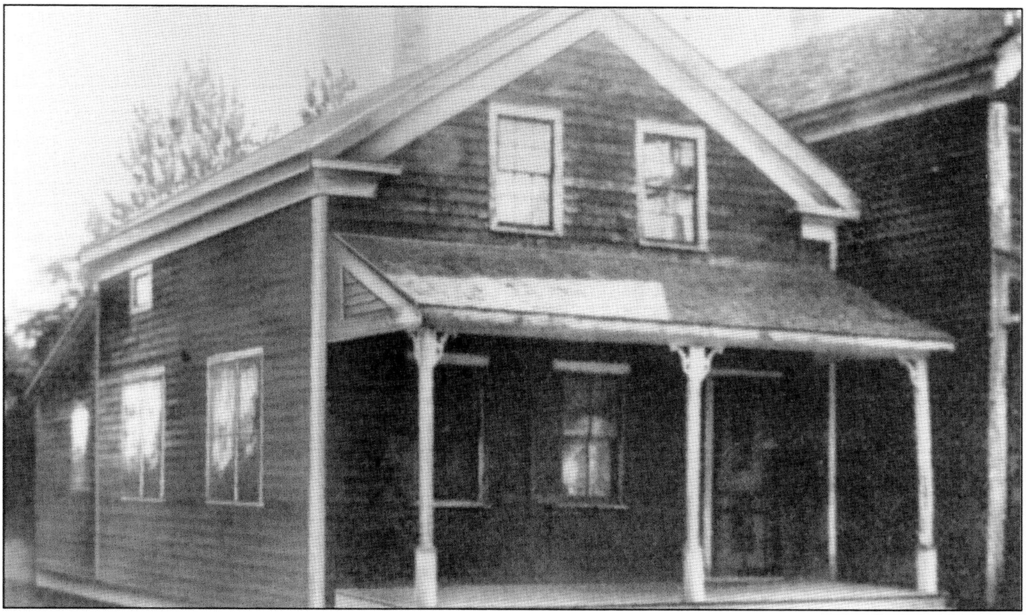

Heritage Insurance Home Office. On July 20, 1925, 45 men met at Schieb's Hall in Franklin to form a local insurance company. It was named Mutual Automobile Insurance Company of Wisconsin. The company moved to Sheboygan in 1960 as Heritage Mutual Insurance Company. This photo shows the original office space in the Henry Griebe Store, Franklin, *c.* 1925-30.

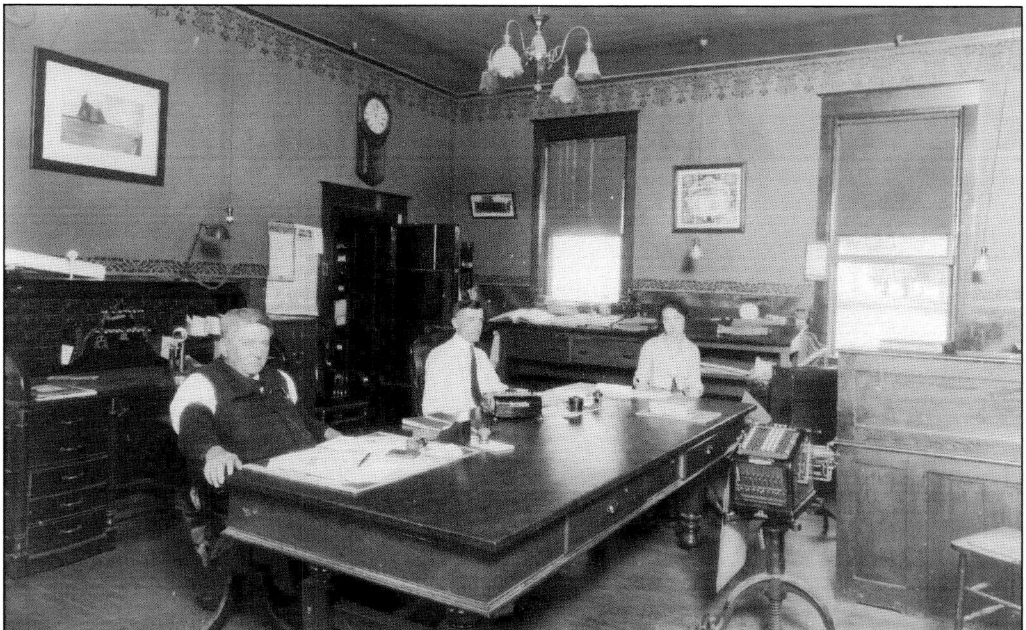

Sheboygan Falls Mutual Insurance Company. Organized on May 3, 1899, the company was originally known as Sheboygan Falls Mutual Fire Insurance Company. The present name was adopted in 1934. This interior shot was taken inside the offices at 323 Buffalo in Sheboygan Falls. It also housed the Sheboygan Falls Savings and Loan.

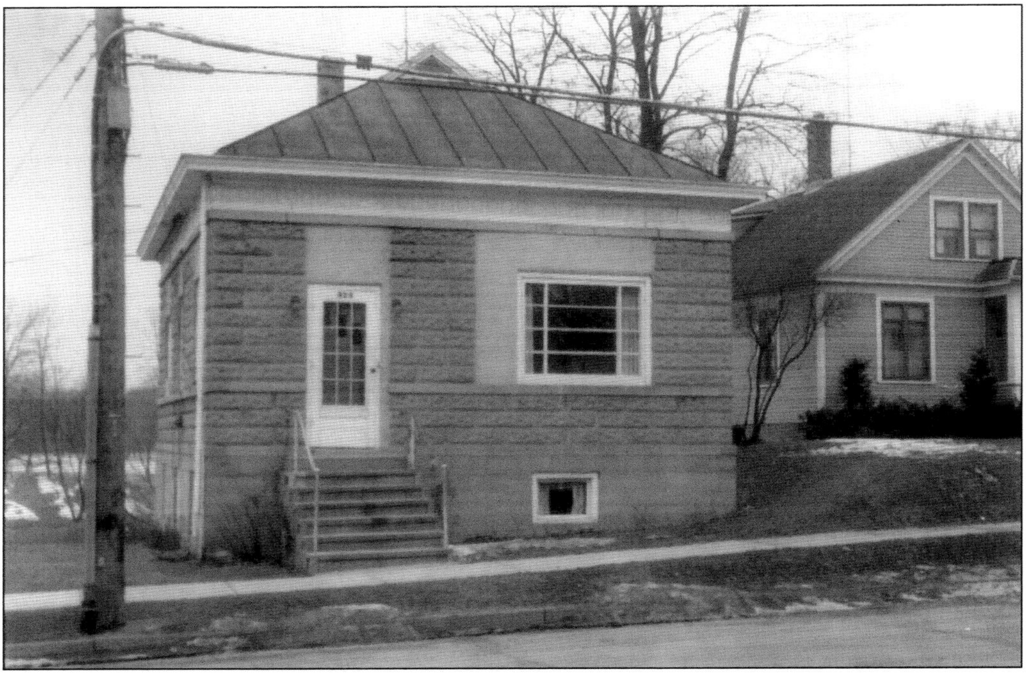

SHEBOYGAN FALLS MUTUAL. This exterior shot shows the building located on Buffalo Street in Sheboygan Falls. This building was built in 1909 at 323 Buffalo Street. The company remained there until 1937, when spatial requirements necessitated its moving to 504 Broadway. In 1971, the company moved to "Rock Ledge" at 511 Water Street.

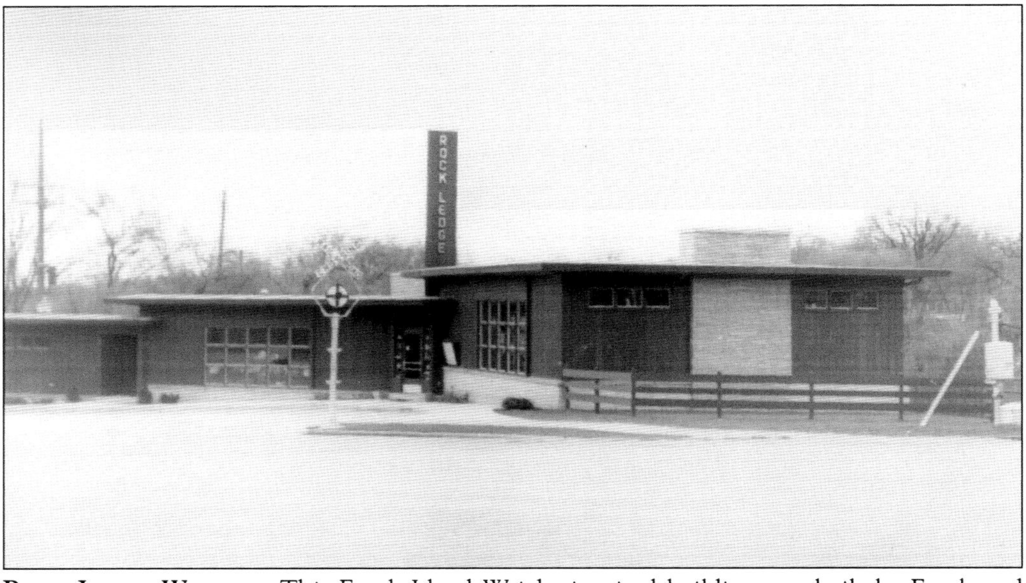

ROCK LEDGE WONDER. This Frank Lloyd Wright inspired building was built by Frank and Helen Stroub in 1952. "Rock Ledge" stands on the site of the Stedman Mill, the first industry in Sheboygan Falls. The mill was built in 1836 and disappeared in a later flood. The Brickner Woolen Mills warehouse also stood there for many years. The site had become overgrown and weedy, when the Stroubs decided to get involved in the early 1950s. The wonderful site is now the home of Sheboygan Falls Mutual Insurance Company.

Two

HOTELS AND HOSPITALITY

The old time saloon has all but vanished, at least in name, but it exists in even greater numbers under such names as bar, bar and grille, tavern, and cocktail lounge. Some of the elements of the saloon have vanished as well. The darkened windows, sawdust on the floor, separate ladies entrances and side rooms, the nude painting over the bar, and spittoons have all gone. Today the saloon keeper is known as the tavern keeper or bartender. Another item that has disappeared is the free lunch. It used to be, prior to Prohibition, that a very sumptuous repast could be had at almost any saloon. Today the "free lunch" consists of a dish of peanuts or bowl of popcorn and that only in some establishments. The free drink "on the house" is yet another tradition that has dropped by the wayside. Hotels are now part of a chain. A bed and breakfast is the closest thing we have to the old rooming house or hotel. Restaurants, too, are chains. The following group of businesses had a character unique to themselves.

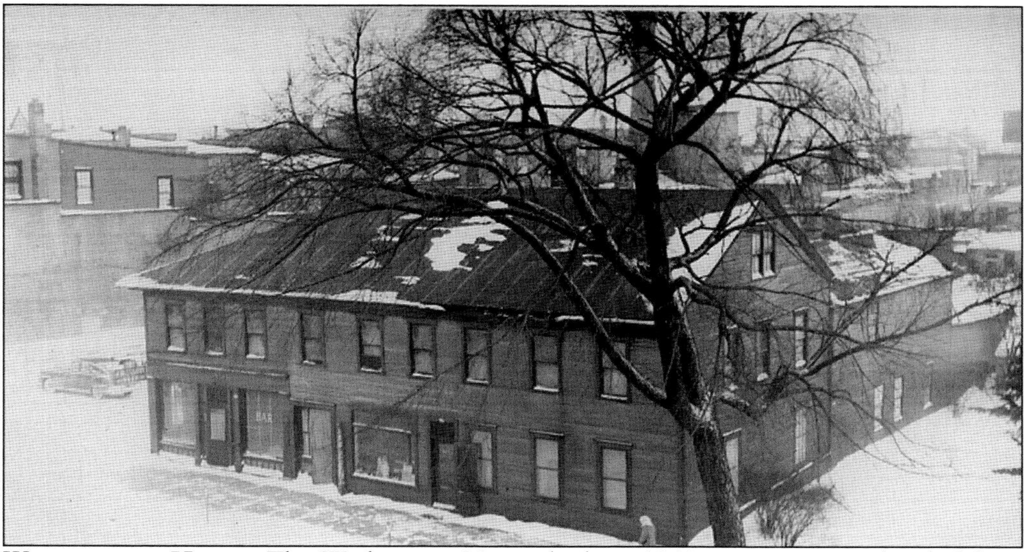

WASHINGTON HOUSE. The Washington House, built in 1860, was a center of early life in Sheboygan. The building was located at 823 Center Avenue. It was known throughout the state for its hospitality. Farmers congregated there every Monday to sell cheese. It had little German bands, scissor and organ grinders, and patent medicine troops as patrons. The building was razed in 1953.

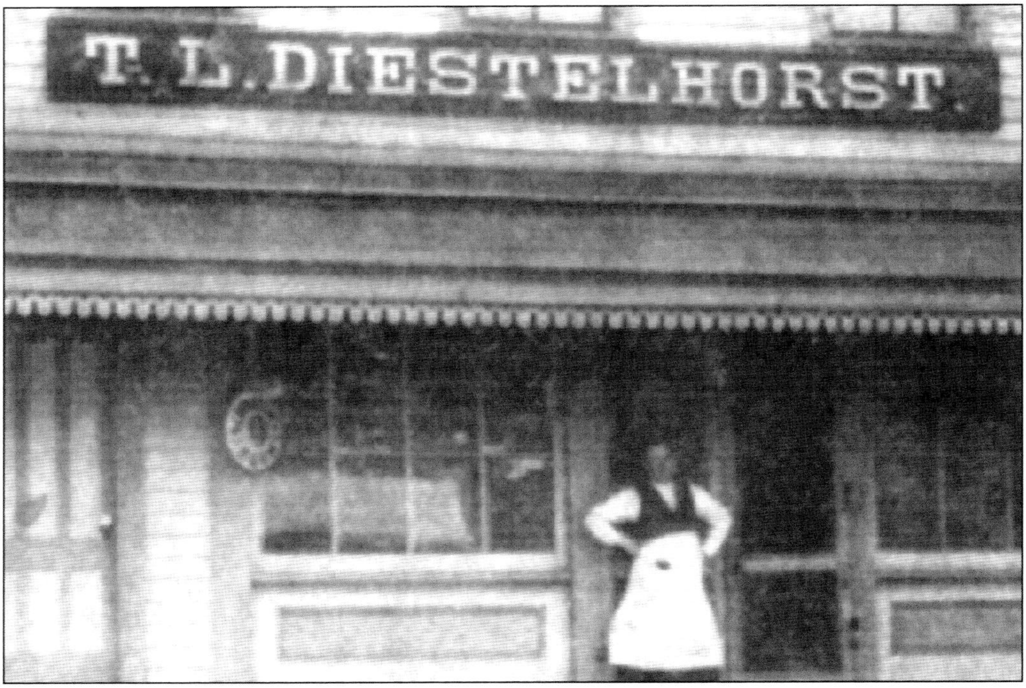

DIESTELHORST TAVERN AND BOWLING ALLEY. Owned and operated by Theodore Diestelhorst, this saloon was located at 815 North Eighth Street in Sheboygan. The establishment also boasted an early bowling alley.

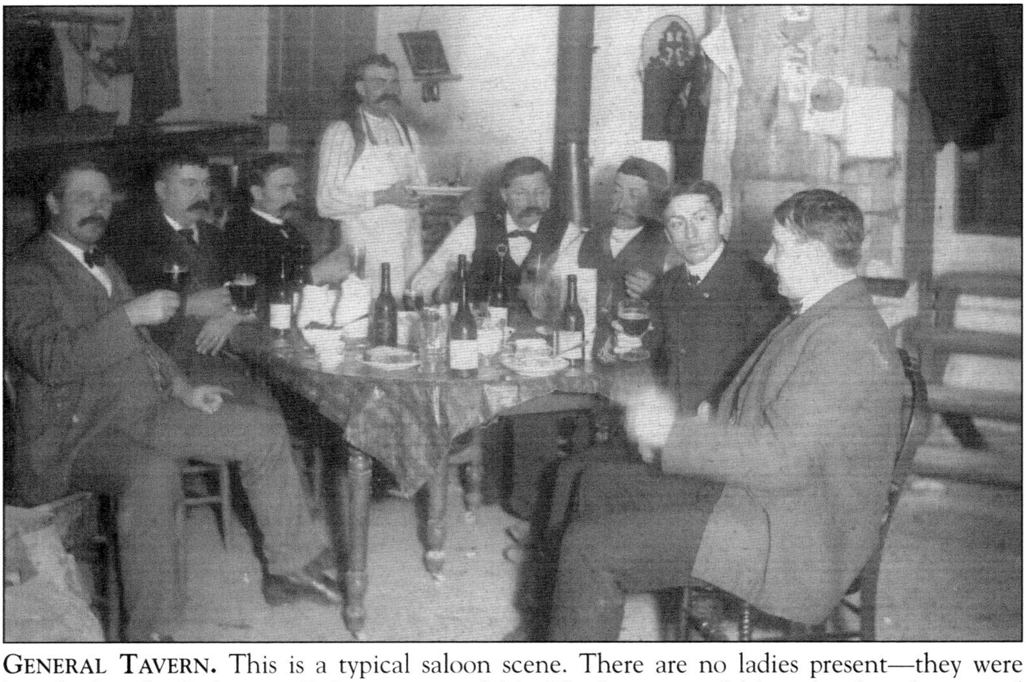

GENERAL TAVERN. This is a typical saloon scene. There are no ladies present—they were banished to the "side room," if one was available. The beer is available in bottles, glasses, and mugs, rather than cans and plastic cups. The potbellied stove sits directly behind this group of men. This table would be considered the best seat in the house during the winter.

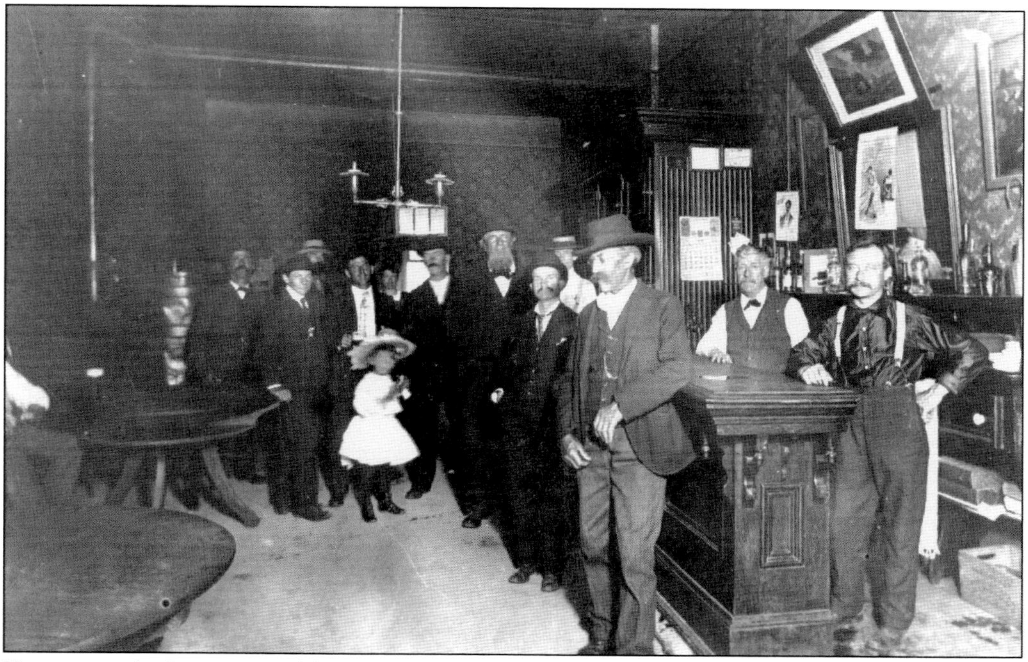

KAMPMANN'S SALOON. Although it was not considered appropriate for women to enter a saloon, it was entirely appropriate for men to bring their children along. Many times, while farmers and their children waited for their feed to be ground at the neighborhood mill they spent time in a nearby tavern. Kampmann's was located at 609 N. Eighth, Sheboygan.

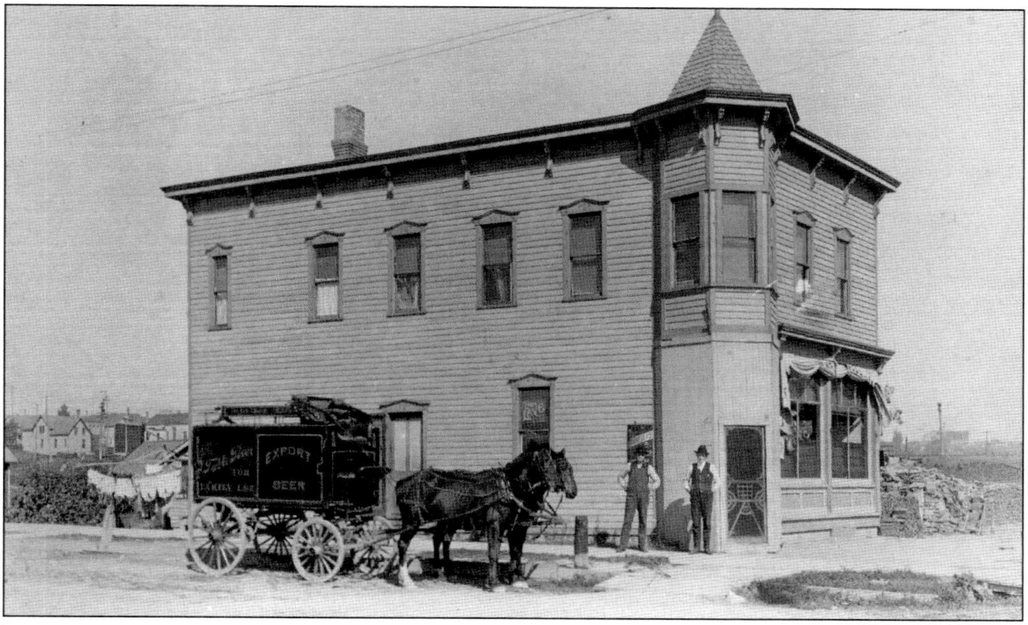

PLANINSCHECK'S TAVERN. Shown here is a Gutsch Beer wagon making a delivery to Planinscheck's Tavern. The sign on the side of the wagon states that this delivery is, "Table Beer for Family Use." There is an advertisement for Schreier's products directly behind the man on the left. Note the old screen door on the tavern. The tavern was located at 1336 Niagara, Sheboygan.

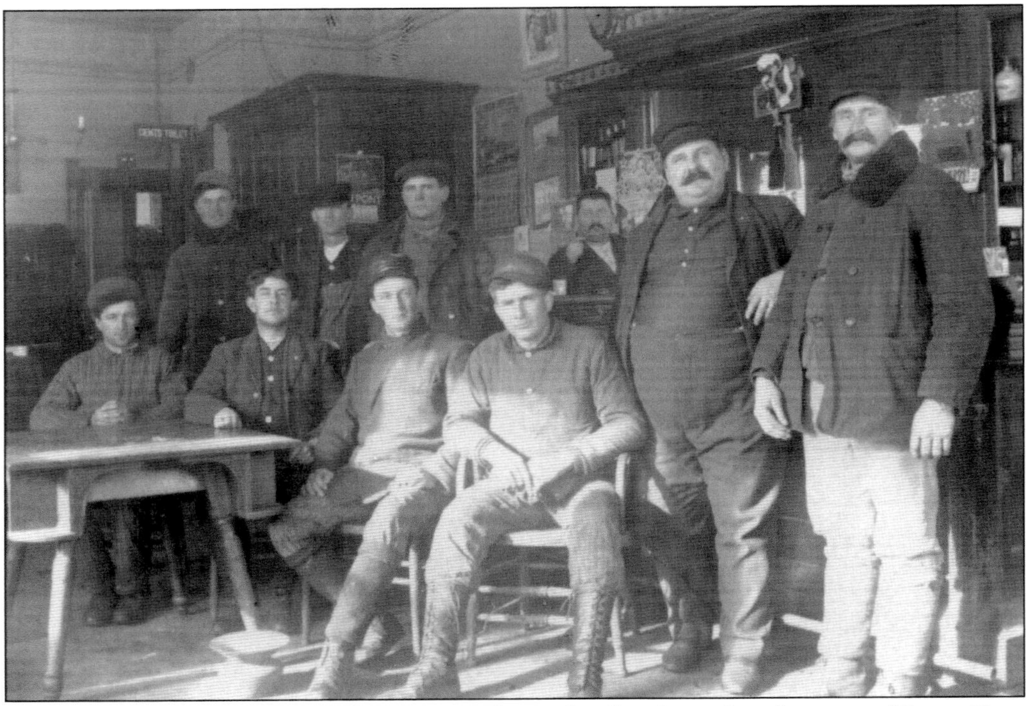

KOCH'S TAVERN. This crossroads tavern was located in Beechwood in the town of Scott. Note the table that held beer mugs on each corner. In this way the beer glasses did not get in the way of card playing, thus minimizing the number of spills. Also, the ever-present cuspidor appears at the foot of the table. This tavern later became known as Tillie Schultz's Tavern.

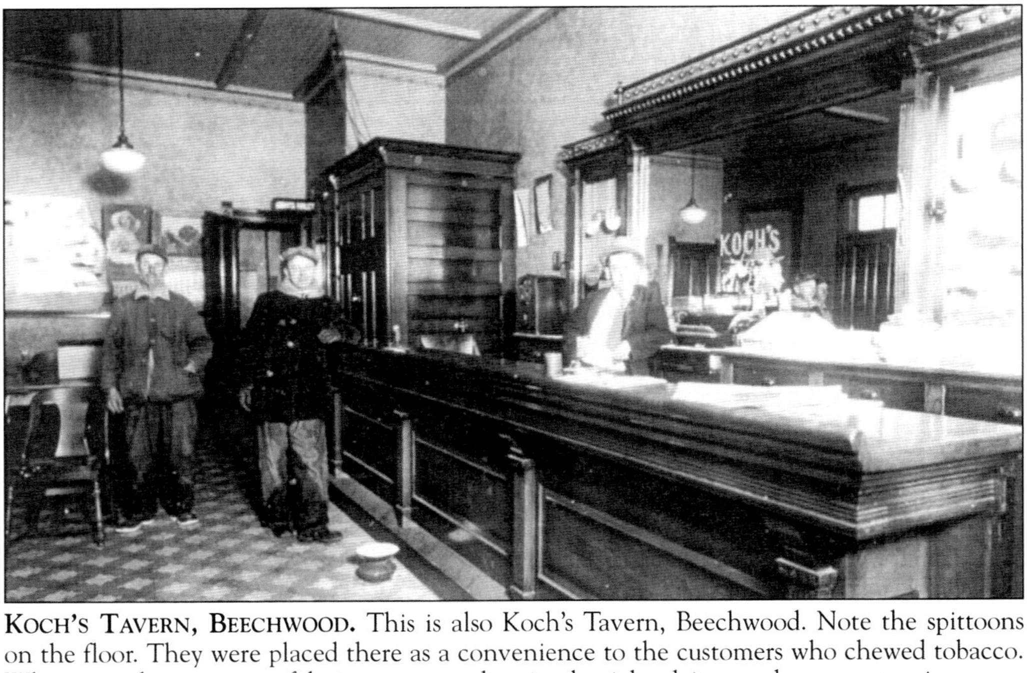

KOCH'S TAVERN, BEECHWOOD. This is also Koch's Tavern, Beechwood. Note the spittoons on the floor. They were placed there as a convenience to the customers who chewed tobacco. Whenever the customer felt it necessary, he simply sighted in on the nearest spittoon or cuspidor, and let fly with a mouthful of tobacco juice.

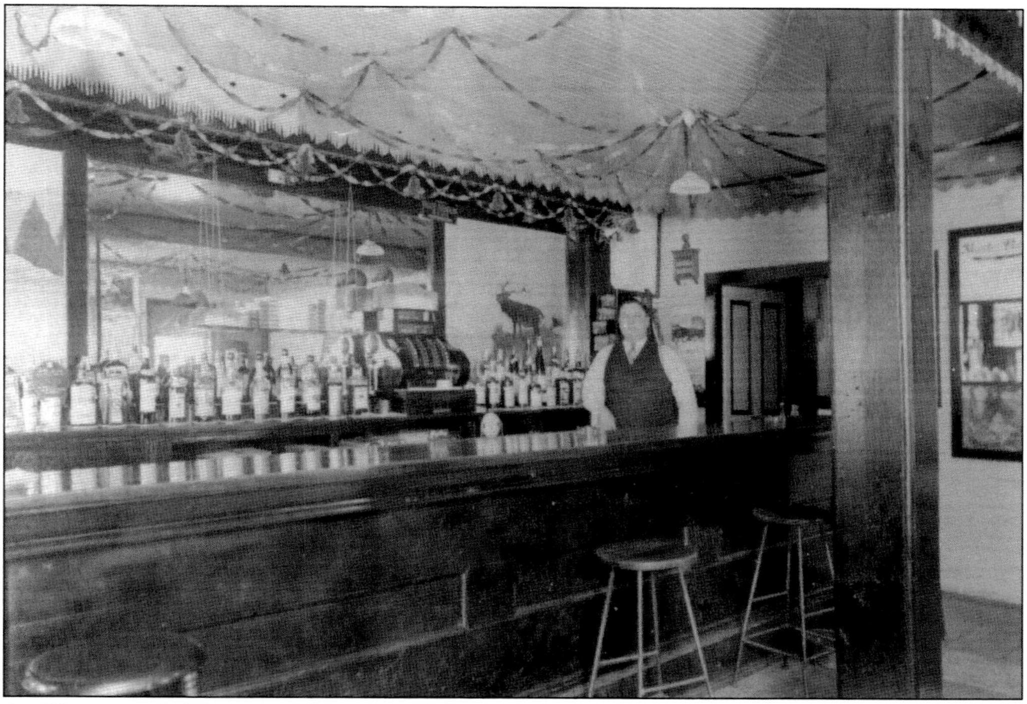

AL HARTMAN'S TAVERN. This view of the Hartman Tavern shows its design in the early days of the saloon.

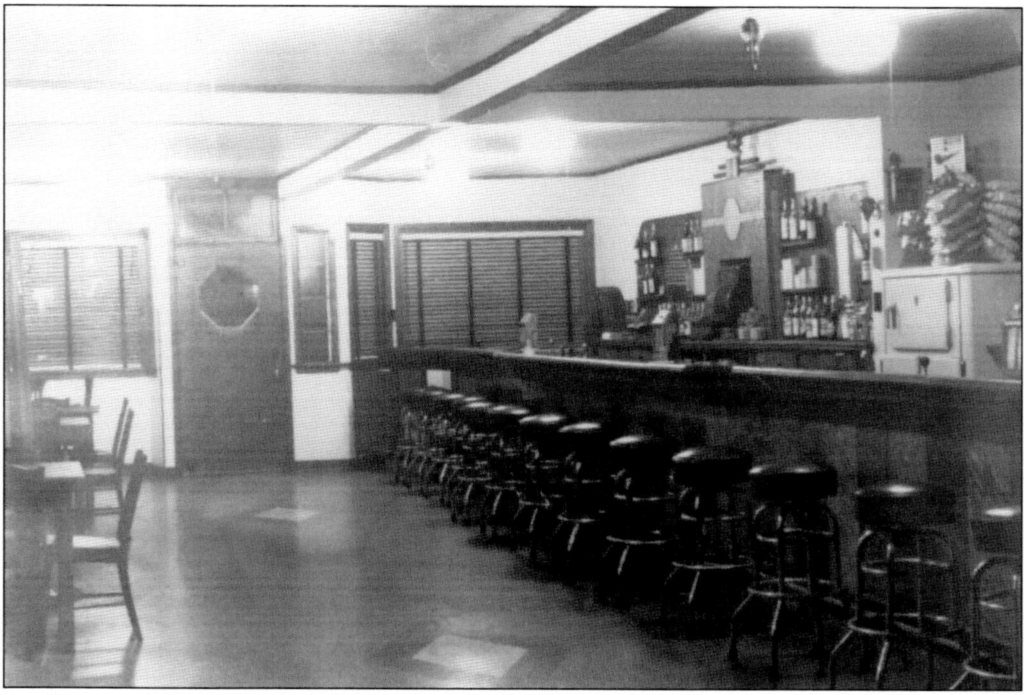

AL HARTMAN'S TAVERN. The Al Hartman Tavern in Erdmann after it was remodeled during WWII. Note that new padded stools replaced the old wooden ones, thereby making countless customers more comfortable.

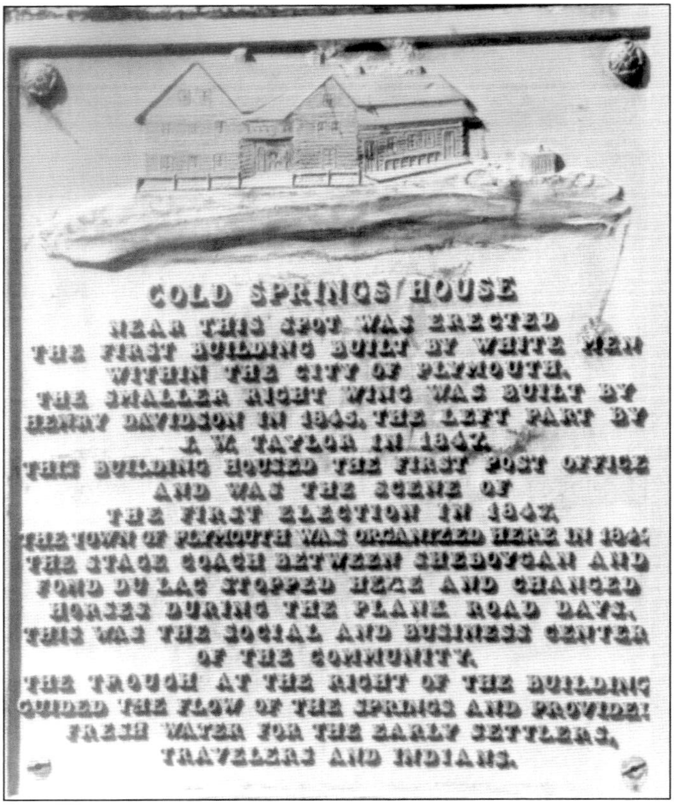

COLD SPRINGS HOUSE. This plaque is all that remains of the Cold Springs House in Plymouth. The first inn and tavern for early settlers, it was located on the site of the Sartori Foods intake at the corner of Main and Western Avenues. The plaque states that "near this spot was erected the first building built by white men within the city of Plymouth. The building housed the first post office and was the scene of the first election in 1847. The stagecoach between Fond du Lac and Sheboygan stopped here for a change of horses during the plank road days. This was the social and business center of the community." A spring provided water for the first citizens of the area.

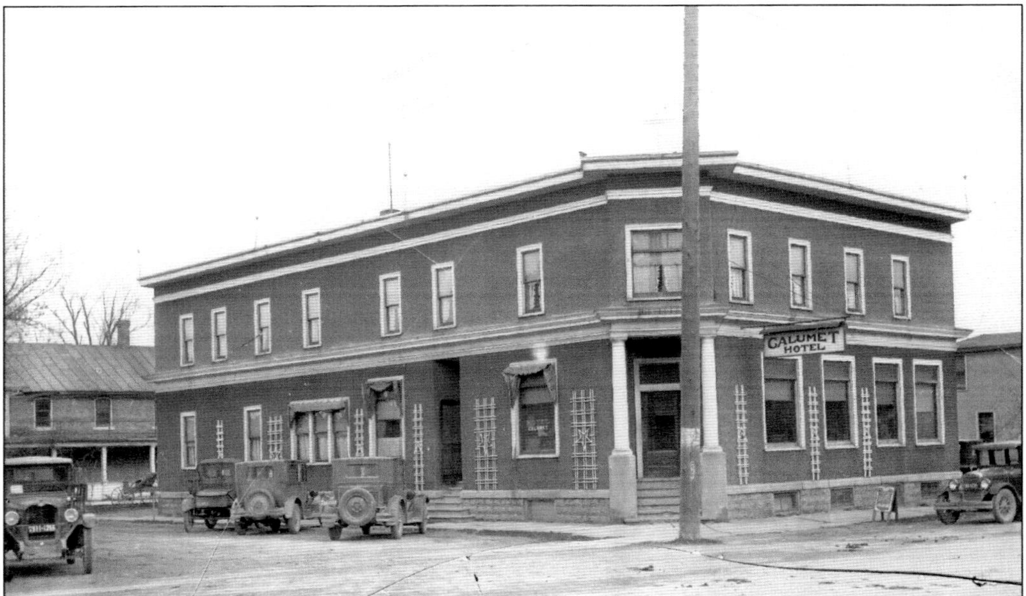

CALUMET HOTEL. Located on Calumet Drive, just south of North Avenue in Sheboygan. The large white building still stands.

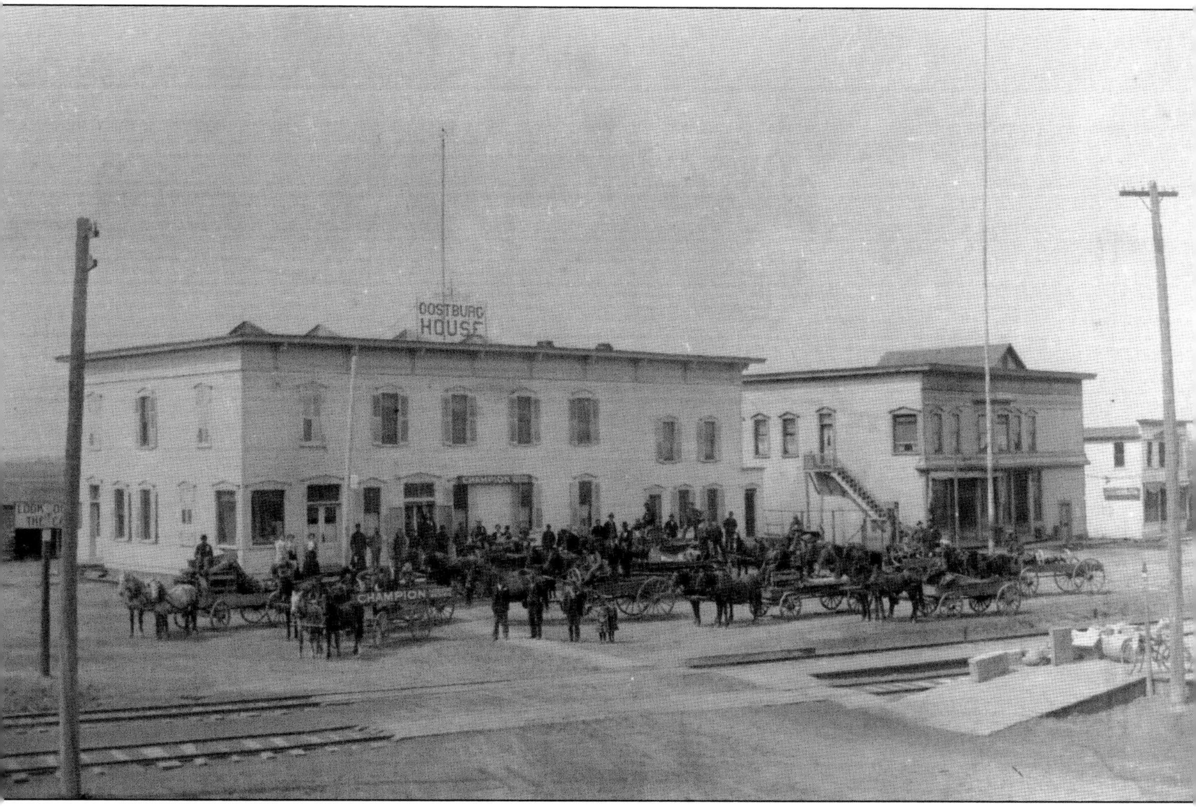

OOSTBURG HOTEL. This photo taken on April 10, 1902, shows wagon teams with Champion harvesting teams. G. Ebbers of Gibbsville received a carload of Champion binders and mowers the week previous to this photo. Local farmers received their binders all at the same time from the dealership. They were treated to a first-class dinner at the hotel, after which a photo was taken of all the wagons loaded with machinery, horses and men. There were fifteen wagonloads delivered that day.

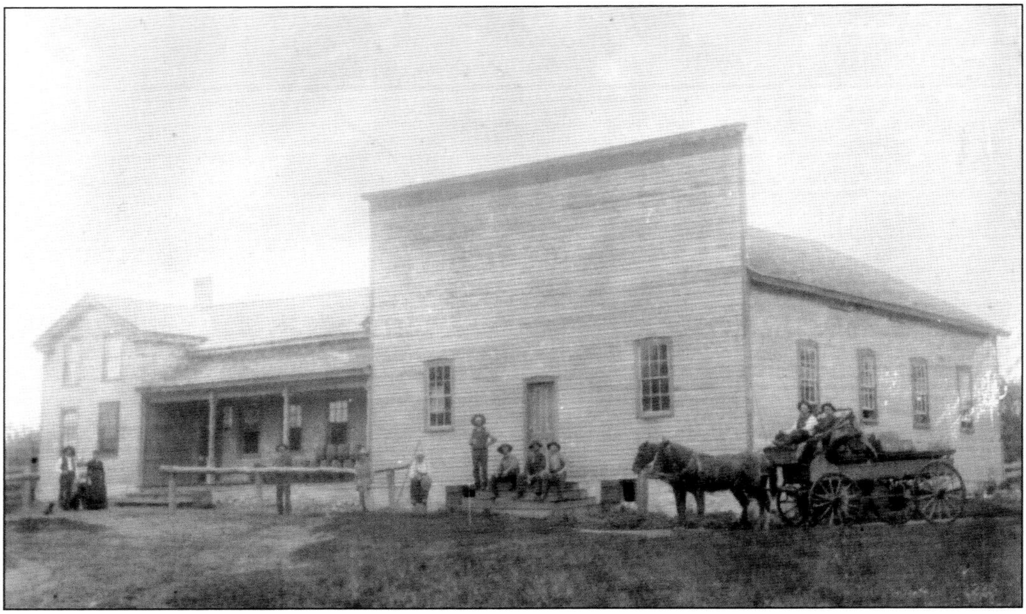

HALFWAY HOUSE. Located halfway between Sheboygan Falls and Howards Grove along the old military road, the Halfway House was an early stopping off point for weary travelers.

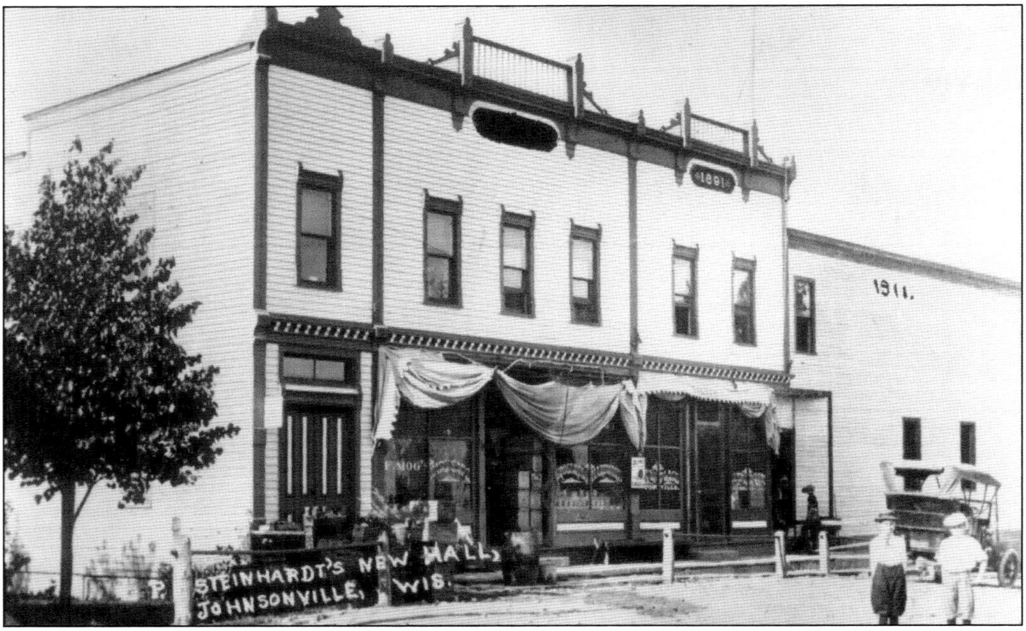

STEINHARDT'S HALL. This large hall in Johnsonville was built in 1856 by Heinrich Wolfe as a saloon after two others failed. They were each a general store and saloon combination. Mr. Wolfe added a grocery store at a later date before passing it to his son. The younger Mr. Wolfe sold it to Hugo Liebner, who in turn sold it to Karl Mauer. The building was purchased by Fred W. "Fritz" Mog, the town's final postmaster, and stayed in business until service ended in July 1903. The town thereafter referred to the store as Mog's. An 1898 history of Sheboygan County described the structure as a "magnificent building which is a credit to the village." Note the presence in this 1911 photograph of a Model T Ford behind the boys in knickers.

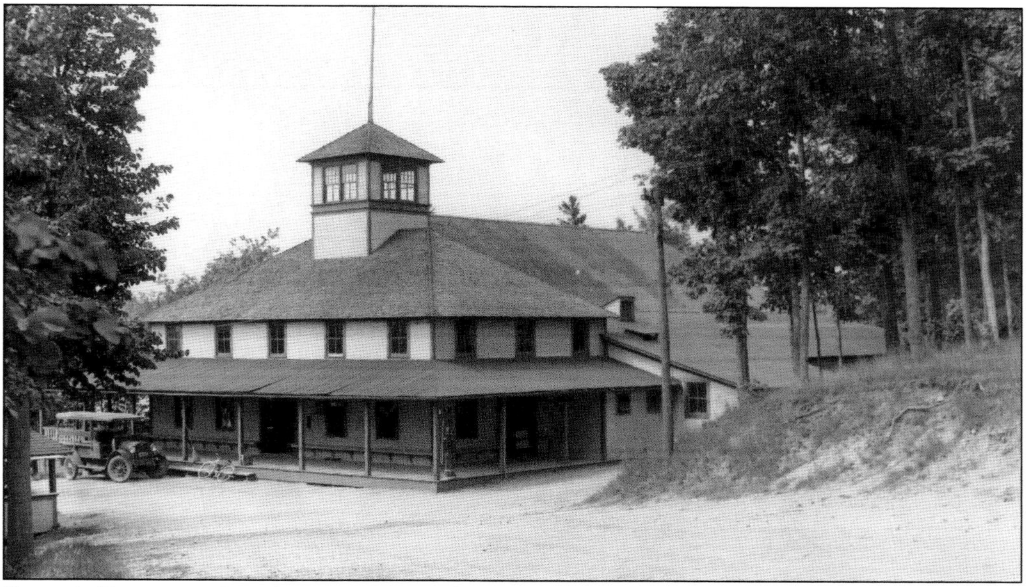

STARK'S PAVILION. Seen here in August of 1926 is Stark's Pavilion at Crystal Lake. Beginning in 1913, the Starks held dances each evening and Sunday afternoon from the last Saturday in June until Labor Day. Students from the University of Iowa provided music. A park once surrounded the pavilion with huge cedar trees, which gave the lake its original name, Cedar Lake. People came on the streetcar from Sheboygan, Kohler, Falls, and Plymouth. A large windmill stood on the hill pumping water for the resort. The bathhouse, beach, and an 18-foot high dive seemed to be the largest attraction at the time. The facility was later known as Crystal Isle Inn. It was popular for big bands and weddings. The entire facility was demolished in 1981.

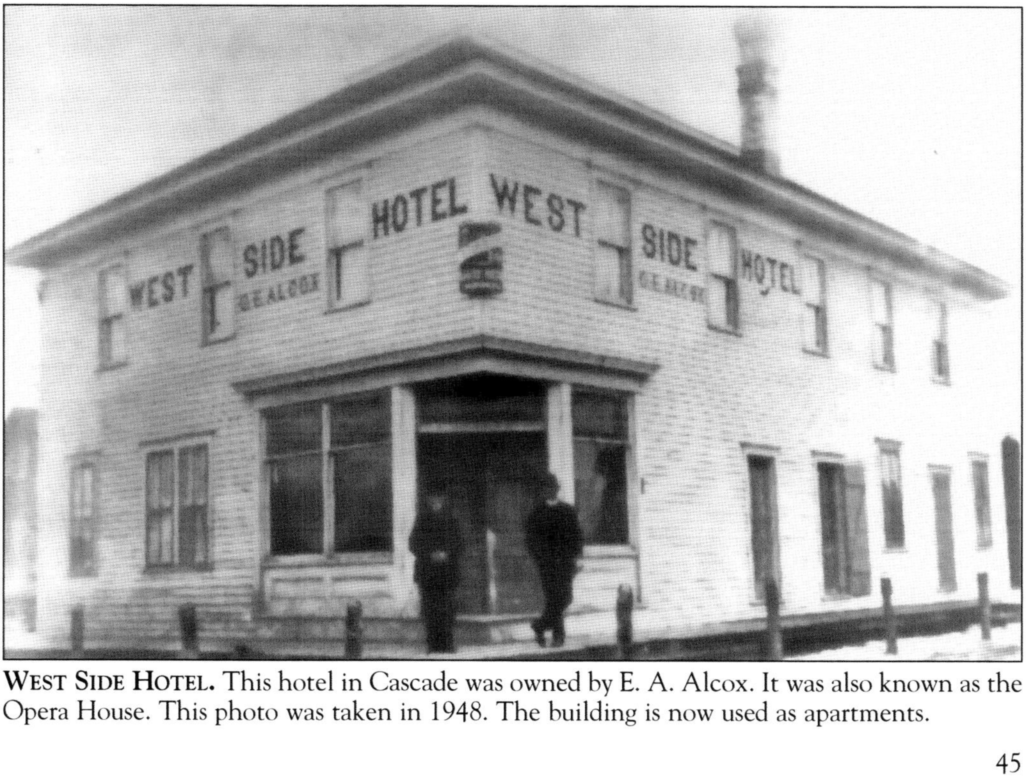

WEST SIDE HOTEL. This hotel in Cascade was owned by E. A. Alcox. It was also known as the Opera House. This photo was taken in 1948. The building is now used as apartments.

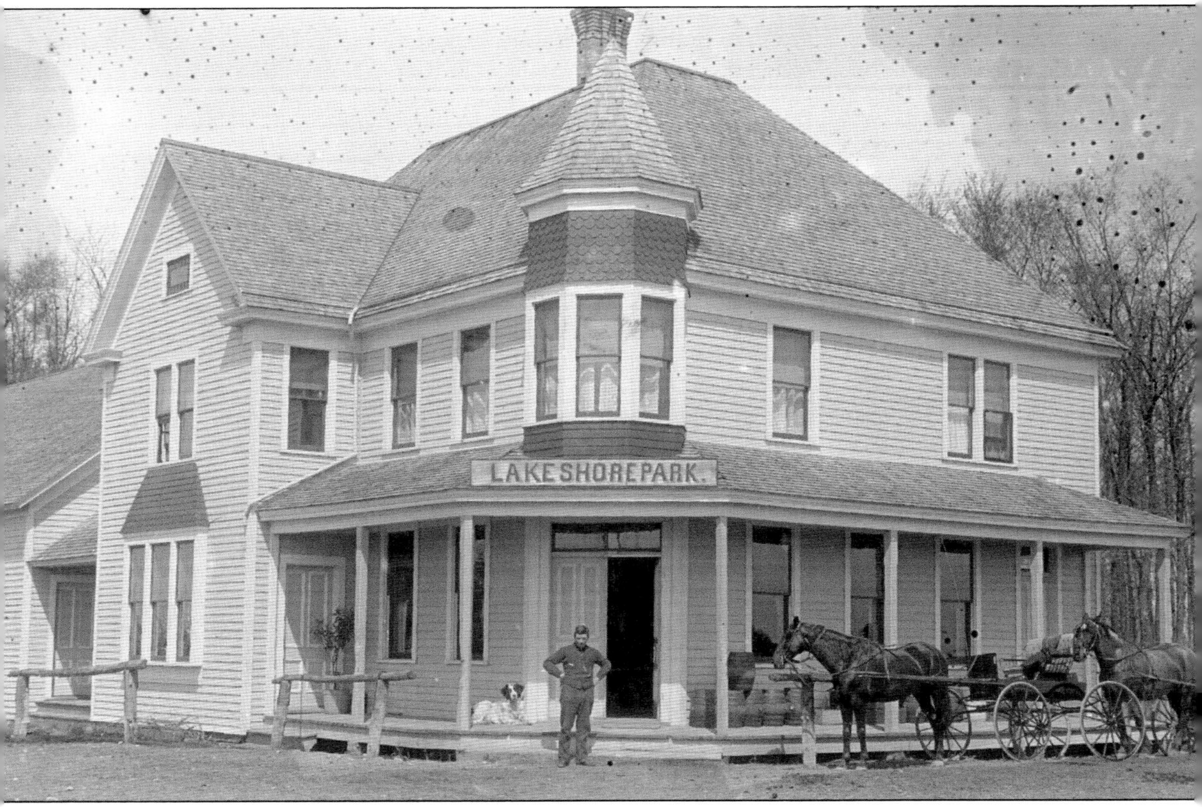

LAKESHORE PARK HOTEL. Built in 1891, the hotel is seen here in a photo taken in 1905. The hotel burned in 1967. It was owned by Carl J. Erdmann and Ida Mog Erdmann. Shown in the photo are Dog Florey and Carl Erdmann. The hotel was located on Lakeshore Road, north of Sheboygan.

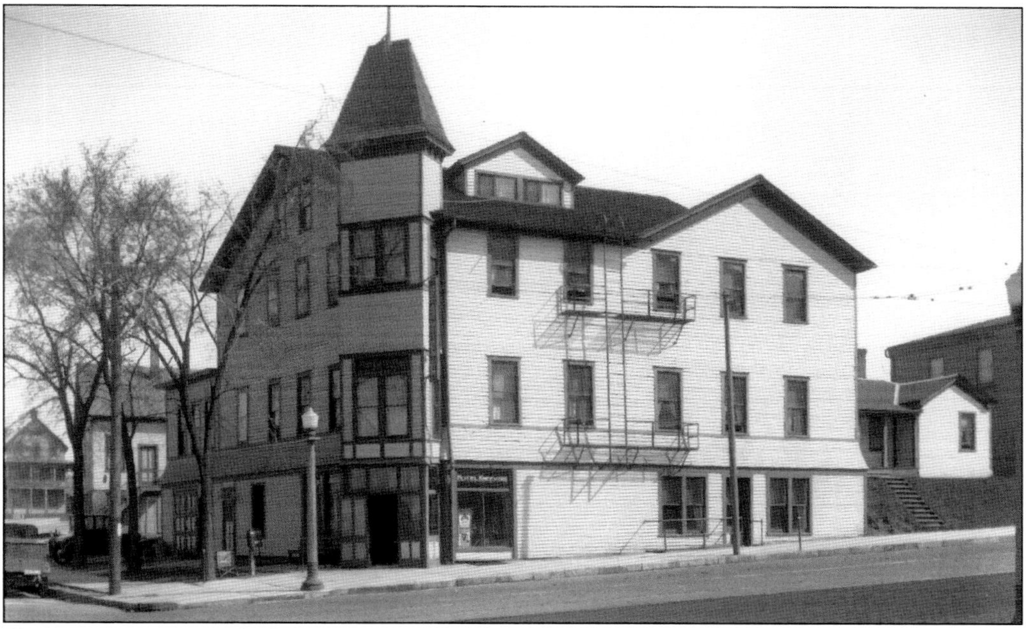

KNEEVERS' HOTEL. The hotel was managed under the Kneevers' name from 1921 to 1978. The old hotel was located at 918 Pennsylvania Avenue, Sheboygan, prior to a fire, which destroyed it in 1978. Kneevers' "claim to fame" was its food. It was known for its good, hearty food at an affordable price. This photo was taken in 1929.

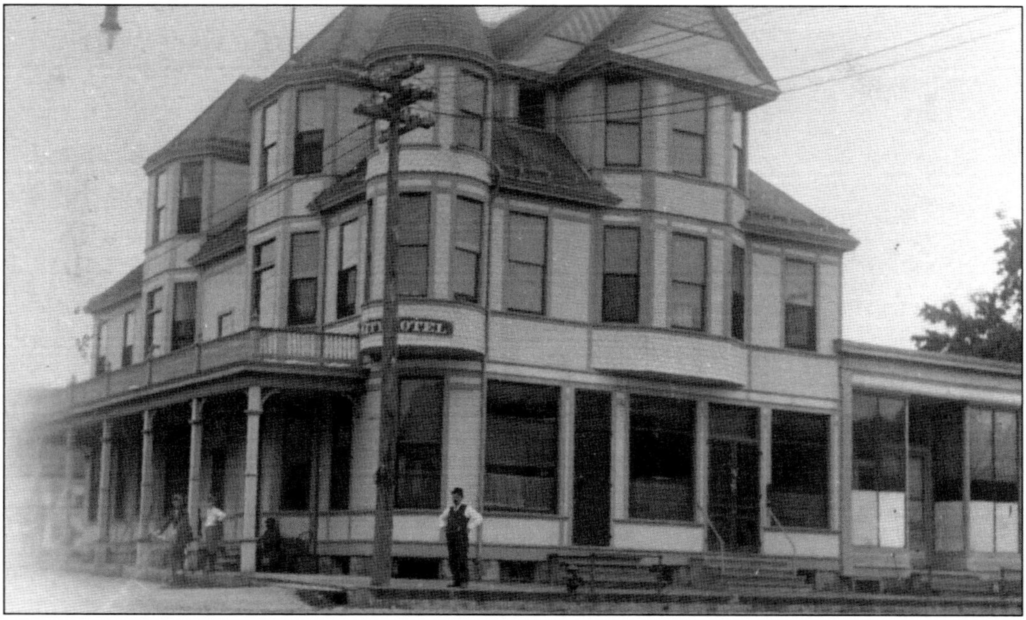

CITY HOTEL. Louis Ballschmider built City Hotel of Sheboygan Falls during the summer of 1892. It was located on the site of the Sheboygan Falls Post Office at the corner of Broadway and Maple. It cost more than $10,000 to construct. A Saturday night treat for men and their wives was to gather in the City Hotel's side room and enjoy a bowl of chili and a glass of beer. Mrs. Schreiner made the chili in huge copper boilers. Weisse tannery workers would cross the street for beer, carried away in two-pound lard pails, to enjoy with their lunch. The beer cost ten cents per pail.

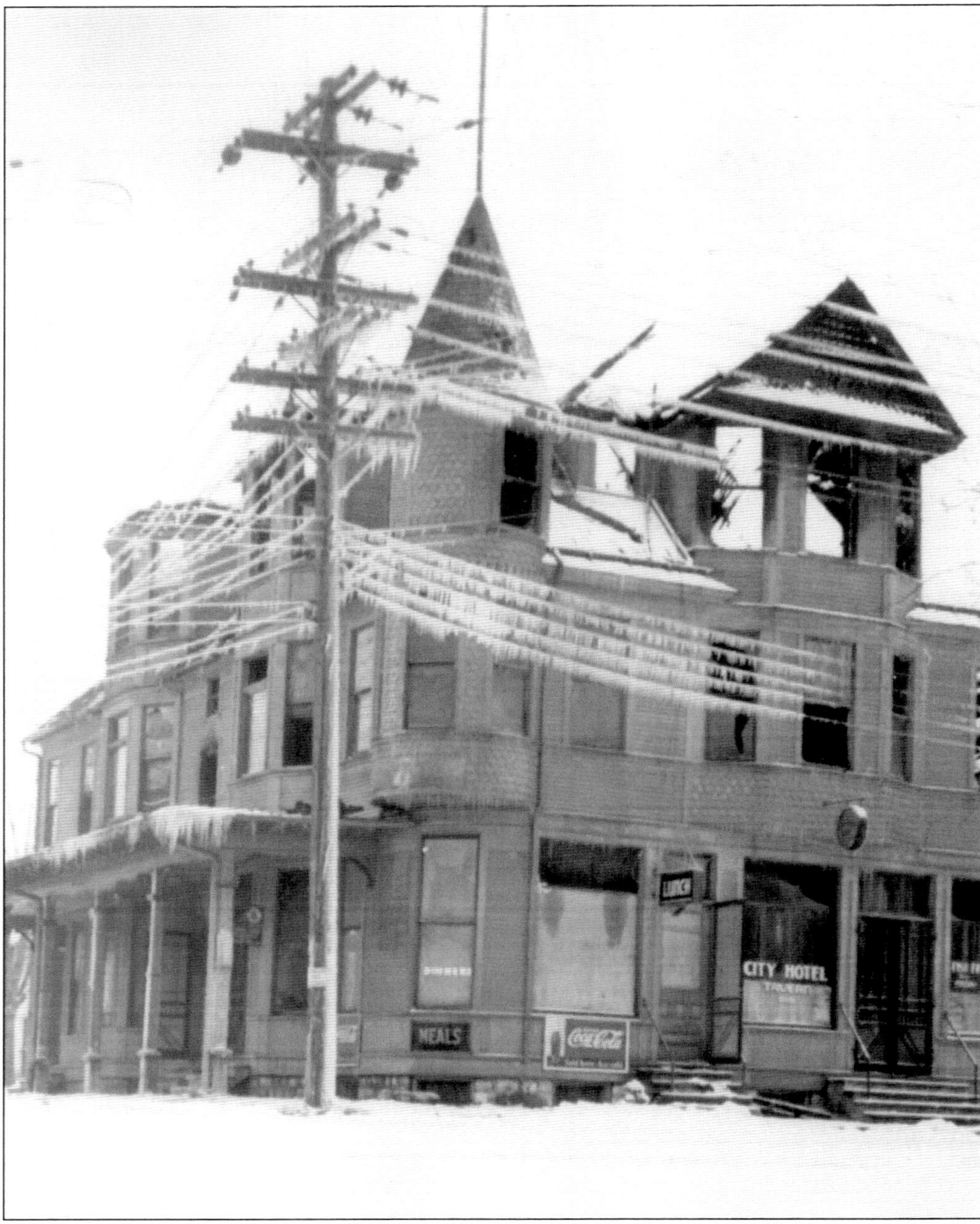

CITY HOTEL. The hotel had a history of fire. In 1908, the roof of the hotel caught fire. The fire department used such a heavy pressure hose that it knocked firefighter Herman Boldt from the peak of the building. He slid down the length of the roof, and luckily his clothing caught on the eaves, saving him. Another fire broke out at about 3 a.m., December 19, 1937. When it was all over the City Hotel was a charred ruin. Water was poured on the blaze at a rate of 1300 gallons per minute by 10 hose lines. Water froze on all surrounding wires, and formed a solid sheet of ice on the ground. Two men were fined $4.51 each due to their driving their cars across the fire hoses on Broadway during the fire emergency.

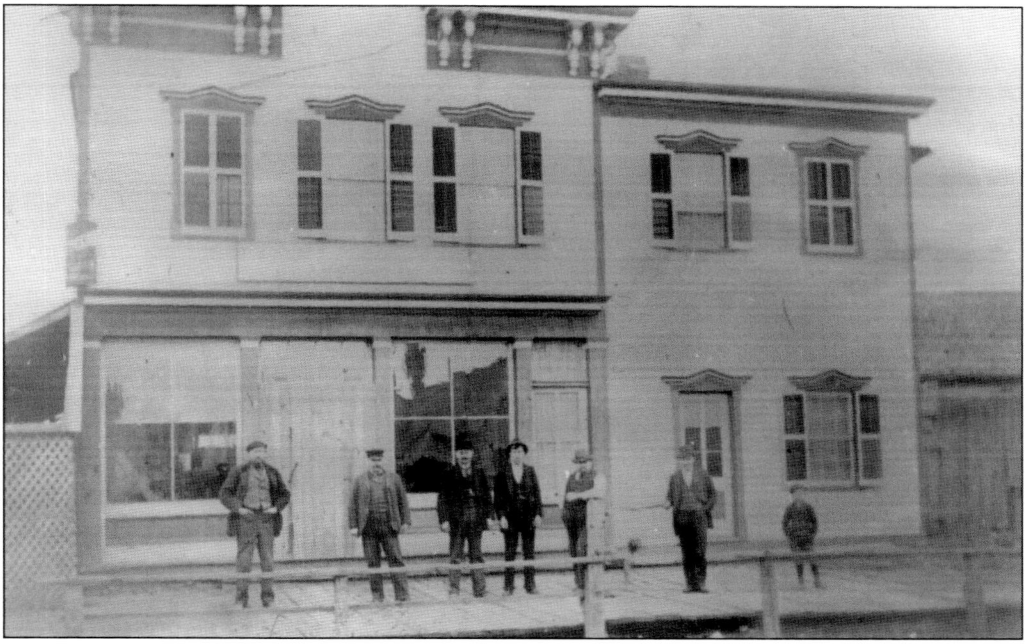

FRANKLIN HOUSE. Located in Sheboygan Falls, the Franklin House was one of the earliest hotels in the area. This one-and-a-half story plaster house dates from before the Civil War. It was first used as a saloon and meat market. Shown here in 1894, from left to right are ? Visser, Mike Kane, John Schwartz, Sylvester Patrick, John Bauernfeind, John Roska, and Al Bauernfeind.

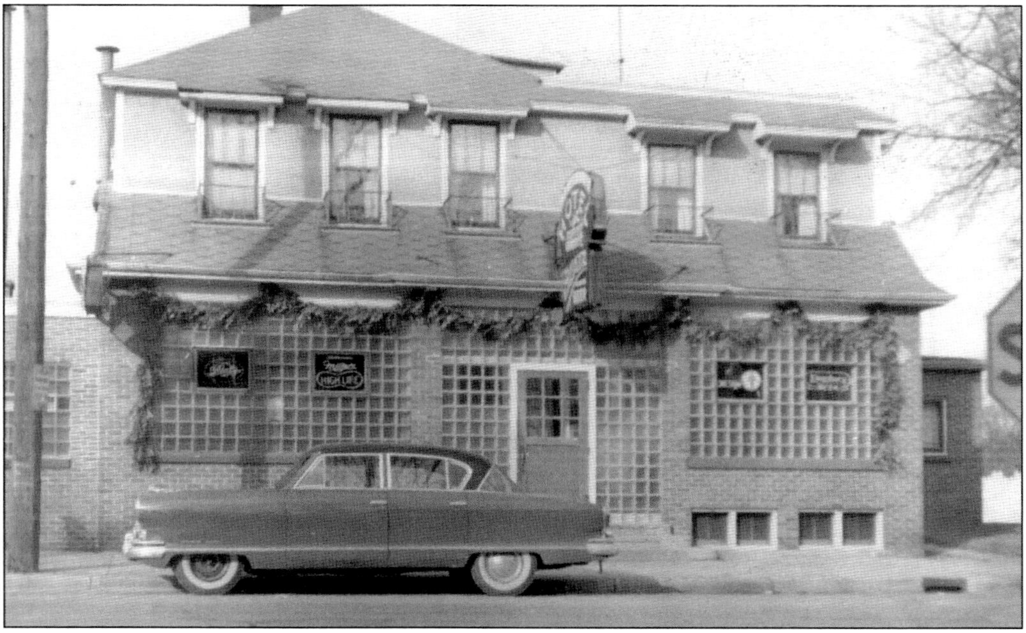

FRANKLIN HOUSE. In 1926, Julius Heus bought the building. It had been changing over a period of years. Each new owner seemed to enlarge the building and added new features to modernize the premises. Heus, too, remodeled the place in 1931. A coffee shop was added and there were more rooms for boarders. A favorite activity for the men was for them to sit on the steps on warm summer nights to girl watch.

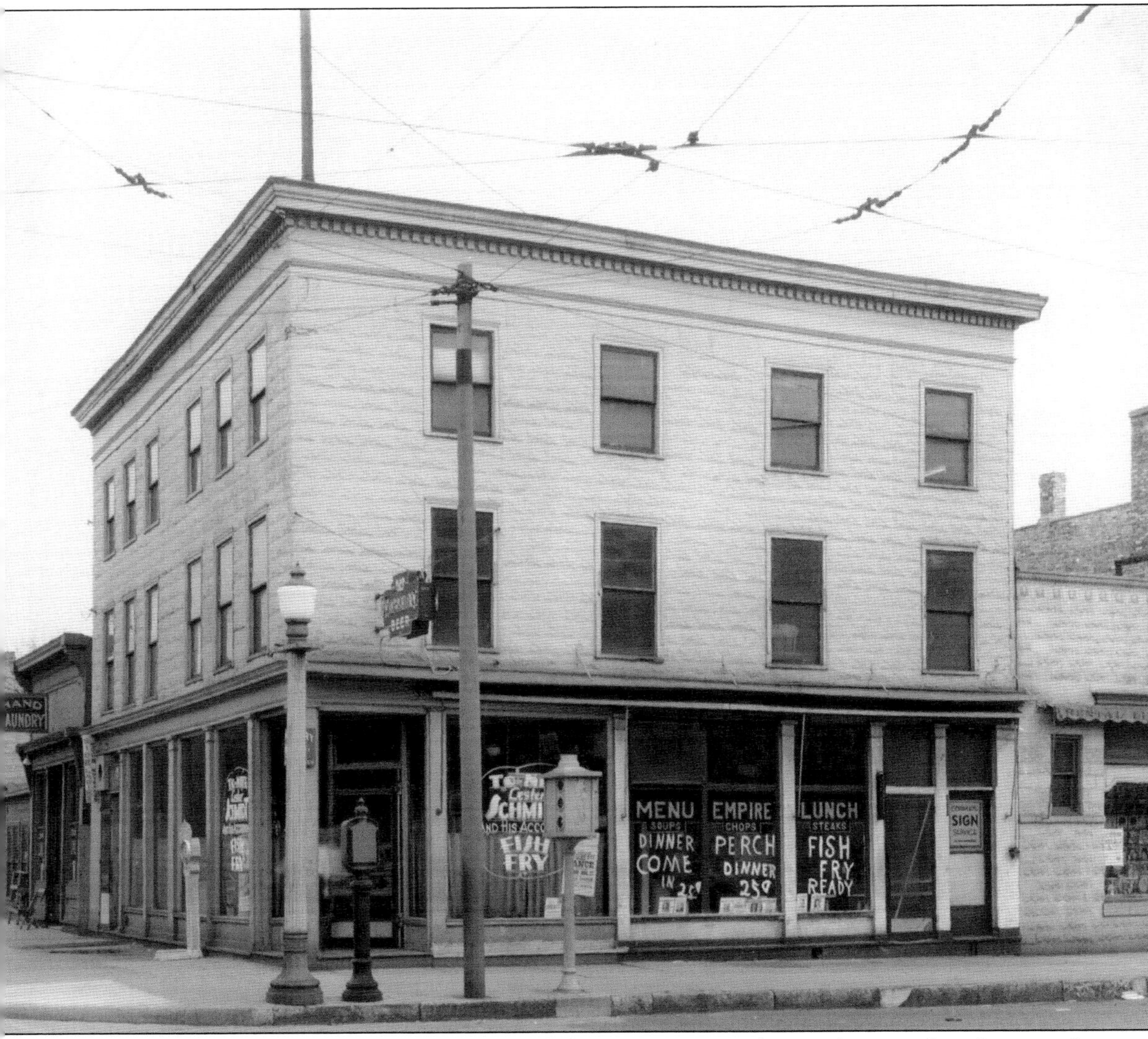

EMPIRE TAVERN. Located at 431 North Eighth Street at Pennsylvania Avenue, this photograph of the Empire Tavern was taken c. 1930s. Friday Fish Fry ads note that 25 cents will buy the Perch Dinner.

HOTEL LAACK. Located on the southwest corner of Stafford and Mill Streets in Plymouth, this hotel was originally known as Laack's Hotel. It later became the Mitchell Hotel after its new owner. Today it is 52 Stafford, an Irish bed-and-breakfast.

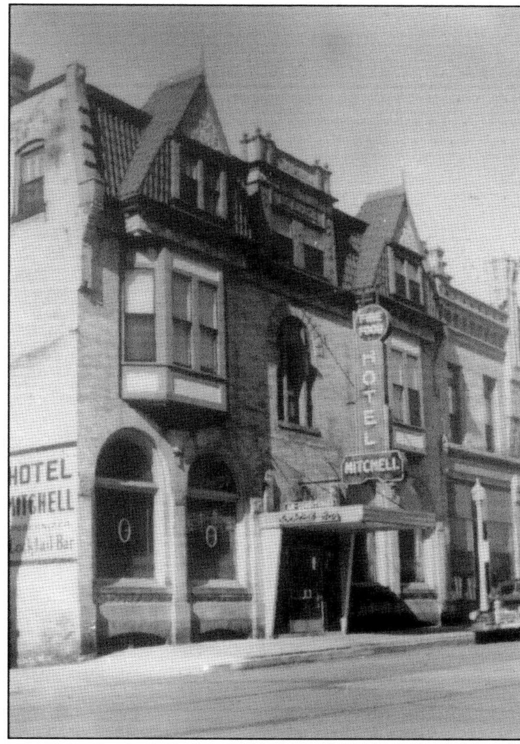

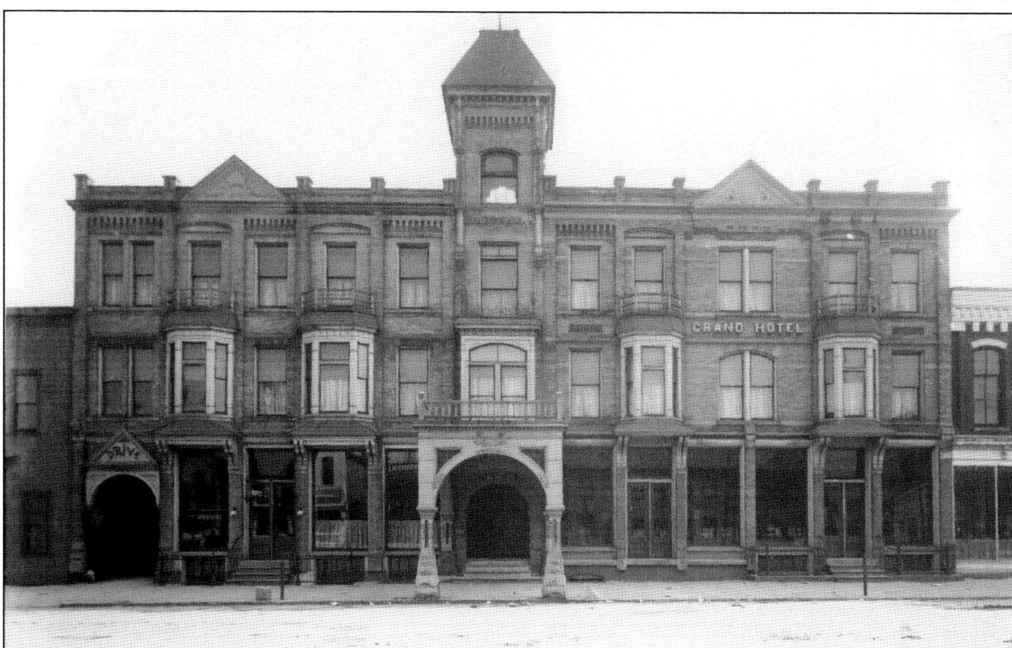

GRAND HOTEL. Demolished in 1964 to make room for a more modern hotel, the Grand Hotel was once the queen of the many hotels and rooming houses that stood on Center Avenue in Sheboygan. Eleven of them stood on Center Avenue and housed the first immigrants to come to Sheboygan. The first rooming house on the site was built in 1849. Julius Zimmerman erected the imposing brick structure that became the Grand Hotel in 1890.

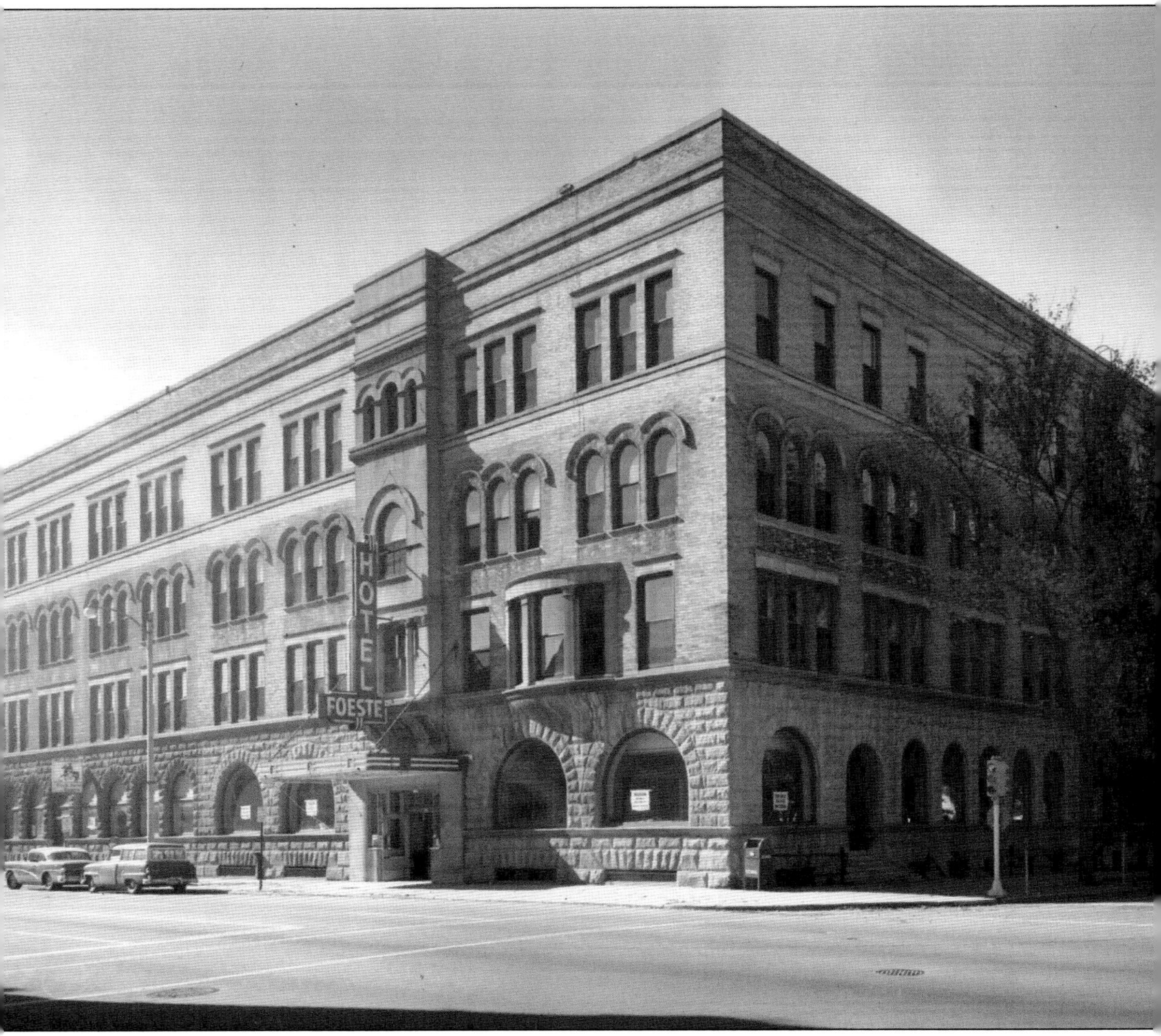

HOTEL FOESTE. In 1881, Henry Foeste built a hotel on the southwest corner of Eighth and Ontario. The 153-room Foeste was a landmark in Sheboygan for years. The massive stone and brick structure was razed in 1960 to make way for the new Fountain Park Hotel.

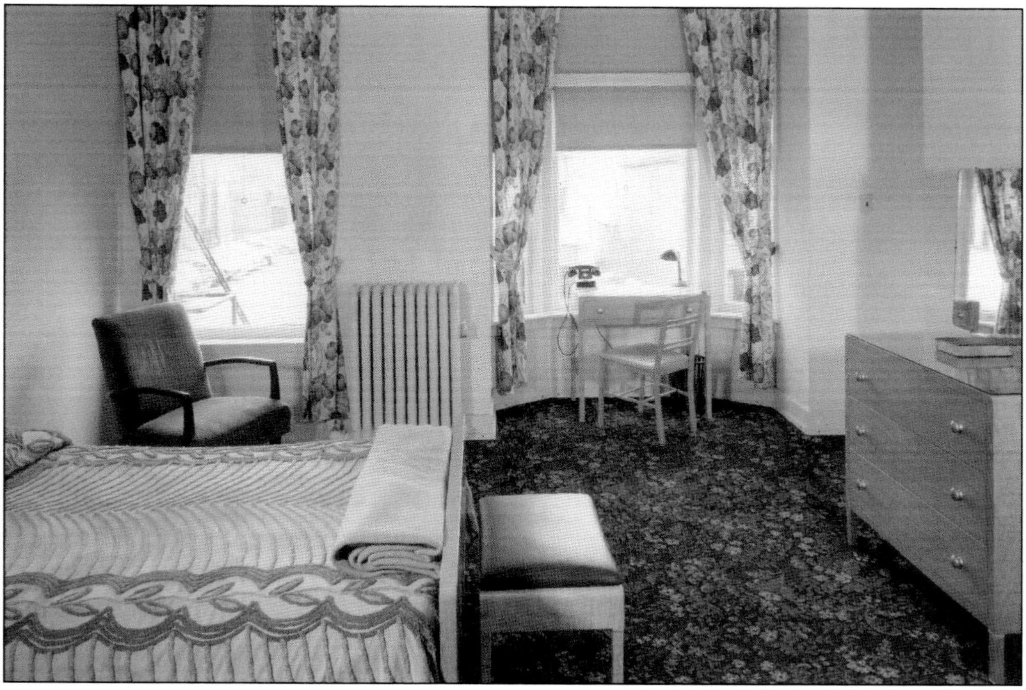

GRAND OLD LADY OF CENTER AVENUE. Louis Ballschmider became the next owner of the building. An avid historian and Lincoln aficionado, Ballschmider organized the "Lincoln Corner," which was situated in the northwest corner of the lobby. It held a bust of Lincoln and other mementos of the President. The hotel was completely renovated in 1924 and again in 1946. This shot shows the interior of a room after the 1946 renovation.

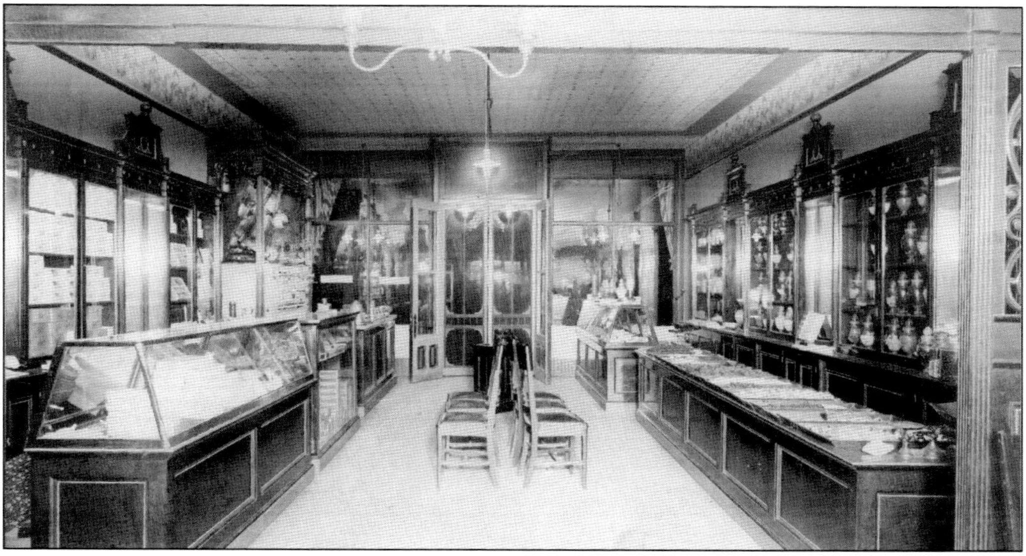

KALLATT'S ICE CREAM PARLOR. Note the multitude of delicious candies waiting to tempt the customers. Notice that the tables and chairs were placed at the back of the store. This meant that the customer was tempted twice—once on the way in and once on the way out. This was a marketing tactic used by many ice cream parlors. The buildings that housed these parlors were usually long and narrow. Kallatt's Parlor was located at 816 N. 8th in Sheboygan.

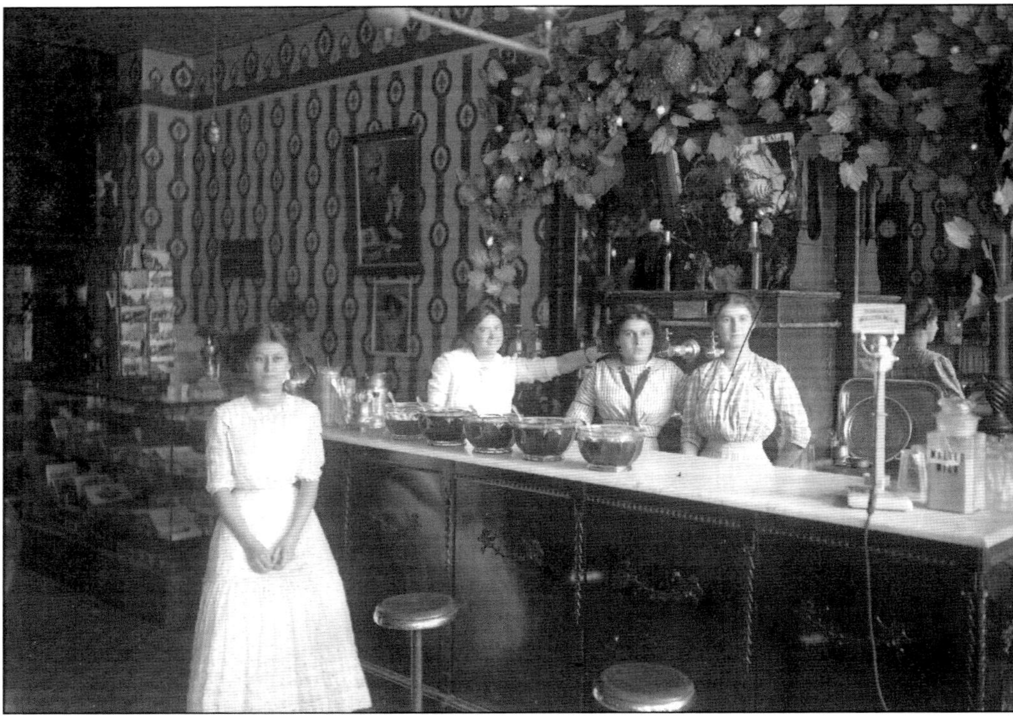

Dressler's Ice Cream Parlor. This interior view of Dressler's Ice Cream Parlor, 504 N. 8th Street, Sheboygan, shows the soda fountain. Note the new Horlick's Malted Milk Mixer on the right front of the fountain, complete with a container of Malted Milk. Undoubtedly, the owners were very proud of their new electric mixer as its usual place would be on the back counter, not on the fountain itself.

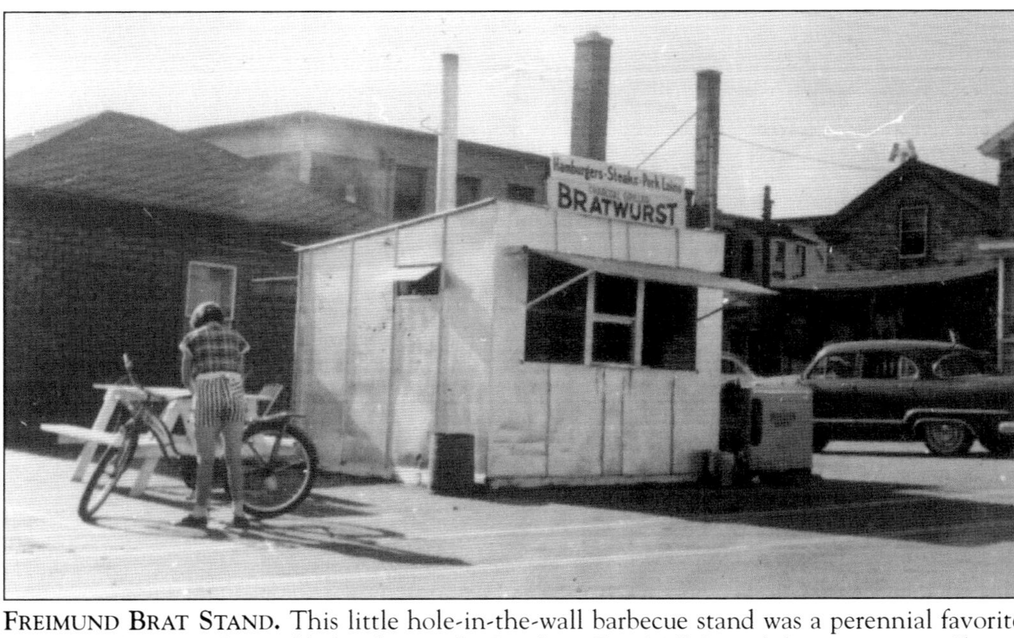

Freimund Brat Stand. This little hole-in-the-wall barbecue stand was a perennial favorite in Plymouth. It was located behind Kretsch's Bar (401 East Mill Street) for many years. Shown here at the brat stand is Glen Freimund. This photo was taken in August of 1957.

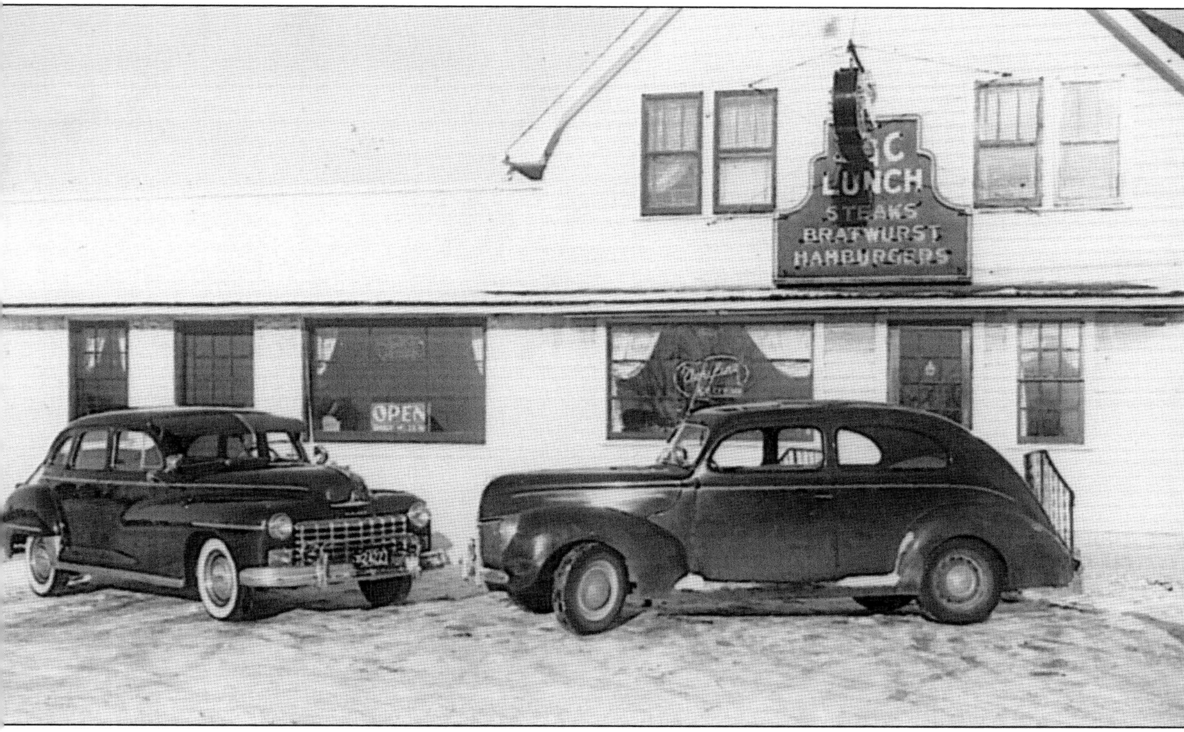

SCHETTER LUNCH. This eatery was established in 1936 by Cordelia and Joe Schetter on the corner of North Avenue and Calumet Drive in Sheboygan. It was built as a hamburger stand to satisfy the crowds returning home after a weekend outing in the Pine Woods (Evergreen Park). The business was originally named C & J Lunch for Clarence Schetter and John, a friend who worked at Miesfeld's. John only stayed involved for a short time. The business expanded and lasted until 1957. The building was converted into Schetter's Furniture. In 1966, the building was moved across Calumet Drive and the original land sold. Today the restaurant building is still standing on North Avenue just across the street from the Northside McDonald's. Burger King and Country Kitchen restaurants now stand on the land that was once Schetter's Lunch.

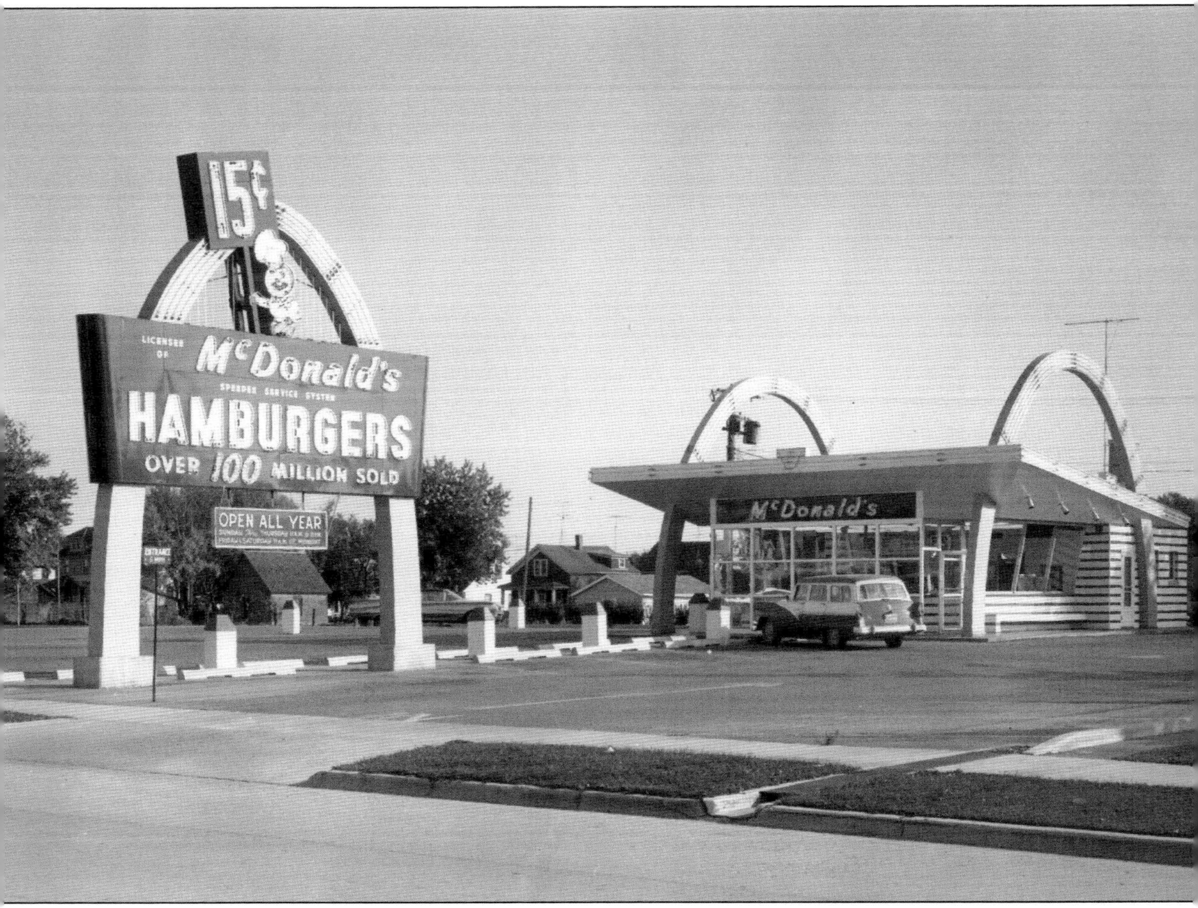

McDONALD'S NORTH SIDE. This is a photo of the Golden Arches located on North Avenue in Sheboygan. It was the first of four McDonald's to eventually be built in Sheboygan. The photo was taken during the 1950s. Remember when it was just a drive-in with no special orders, before the Big Mac, the McRib, and Supersized everything?

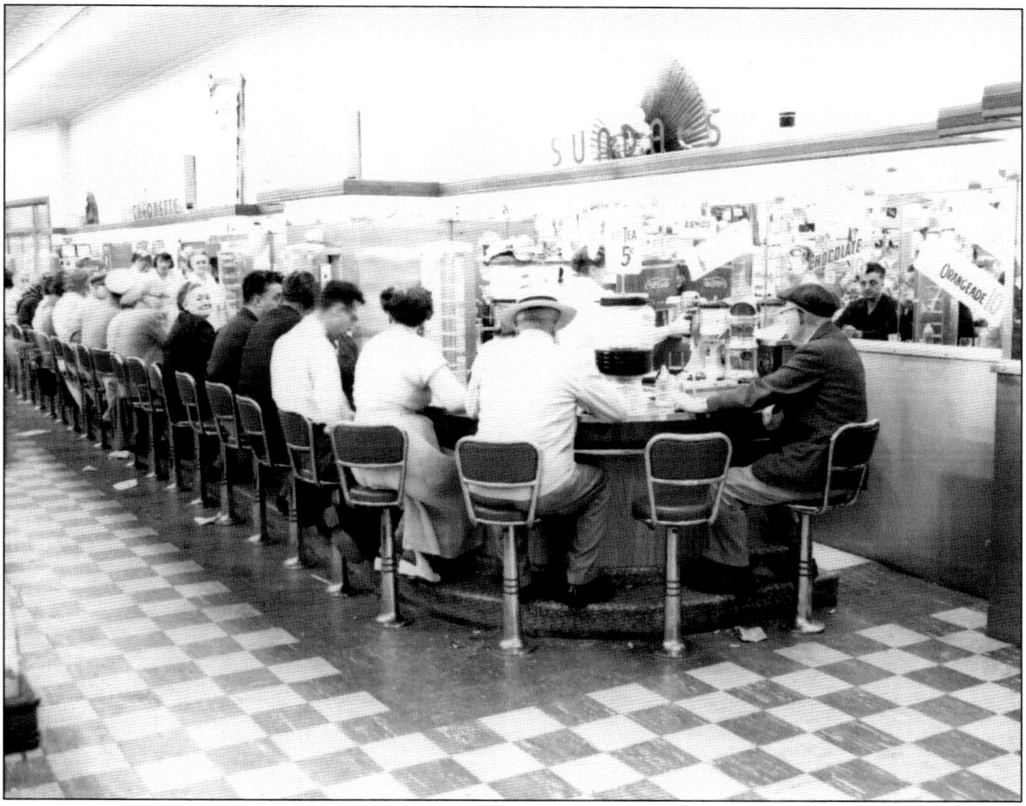

KRESGE'S LUNCH COUNTER. Lunch counters were found in many dime and drug stores throughout the 1940s and 1950s. Pictured here is the counter at the Kresge store on Eighth Street in Sheboygan. The year is 1953. In the 1960s, Kresge became K-Mart.

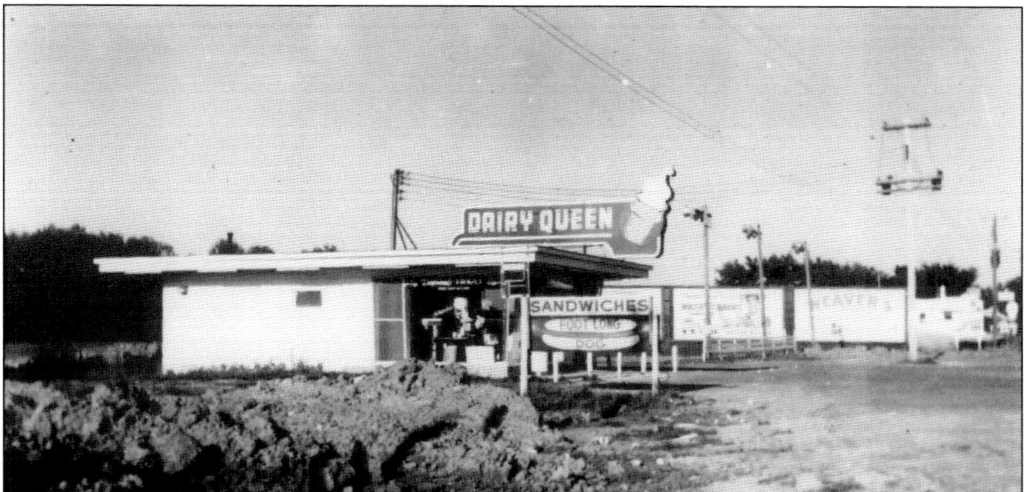

DAIRY QUEEN. This is the one and only Plymouth Dairy Queen Drive-In on the city's east side near Highway 57 as it appeared in 1956. Remember the giant chocolate and vanilla plaster ice cream cones that framed the order window? The Dairy Queen has been operated by the Schuette family for many years.

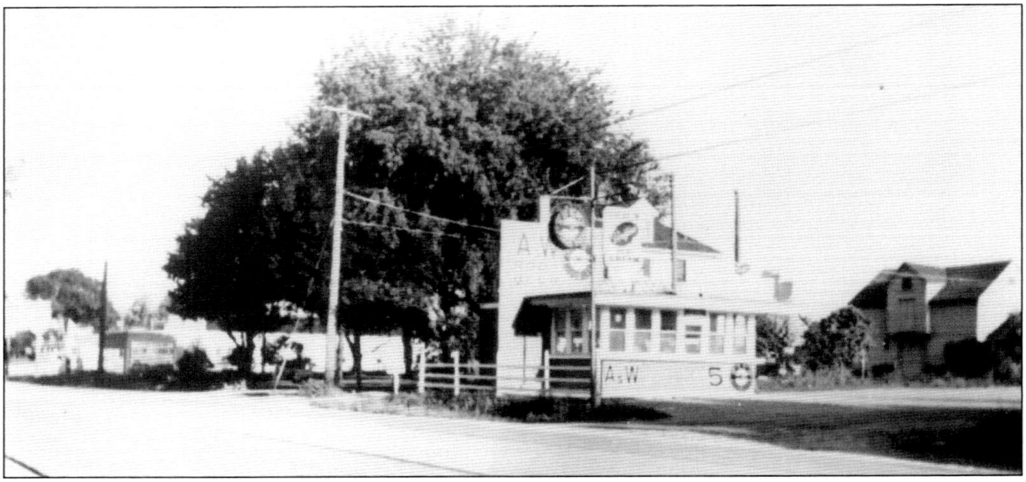

A&W Drive-In. Shown is the A&W Drive-In on Eastern Avenue in Plymouth in 1956. Note the amount of open space surrounding the business. This A&W was recently renamed Chester's and ceased to be an A&W. The Richards family has operated it for decades.

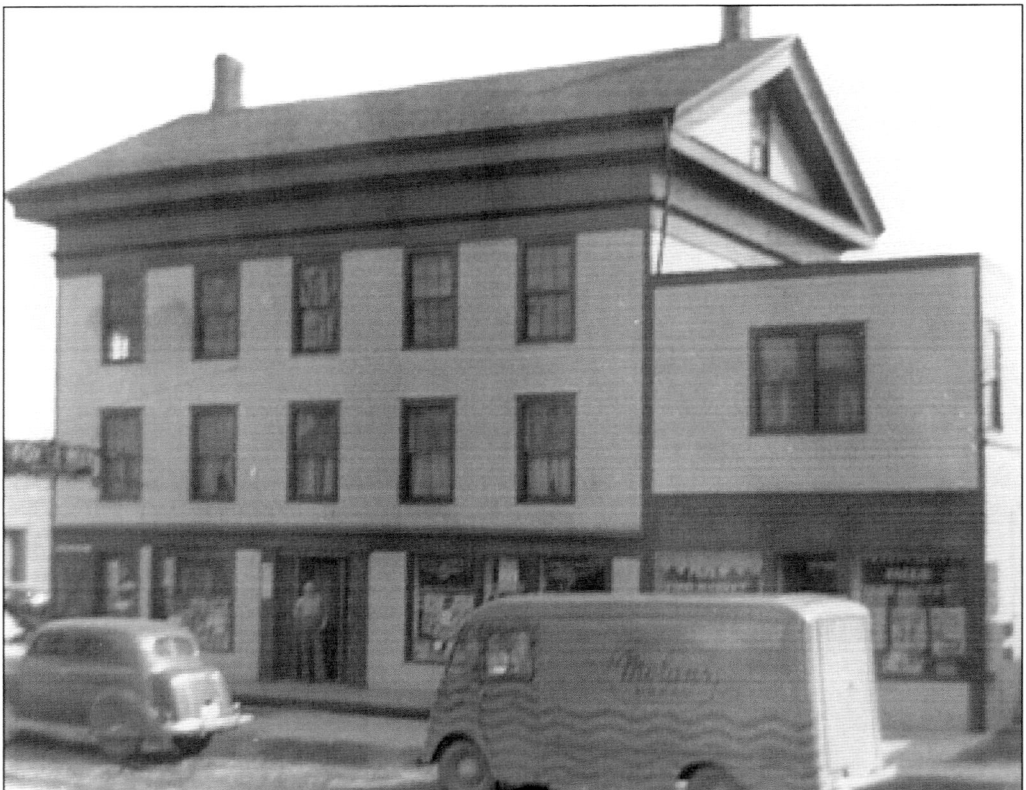

Thorpe Hotel. Originally the Thorpe Hotel, this three-story Greek Revival structure was built in 1846. It was the first hotel built in Sheboygan Falls. During the mid-1800s, the hotel was run on a strict temperance basis. Much of Sheboygan Falls was a part of the temperance movement led by Yankee settlers. The building is now home to Richard's Restaurant of Sheboygan Falls. The structure is located at 510 Monroe Street.

Three

Gambling and Vice

Over the years Sheboygan County has had its share of businesses that engaged in illegal gambling and prostitution. Many of these businesses were taverns that engaged in legitimate moneymaking activities, but sought alternative ways to increase their legal trade as well as earning a little extra "on the side." Periodically, the Law would conduct raids in which it would confiscate gambling equipment, or occasionally an individual would be arrested for keeping a house of ill fame. After a short time everything would be back to business as usual. It was not until the 1950s that there was any real crack-down on gambling or prostitution. With the election of a new, aggressive district attorney, the process of cleaning up the county had begun.

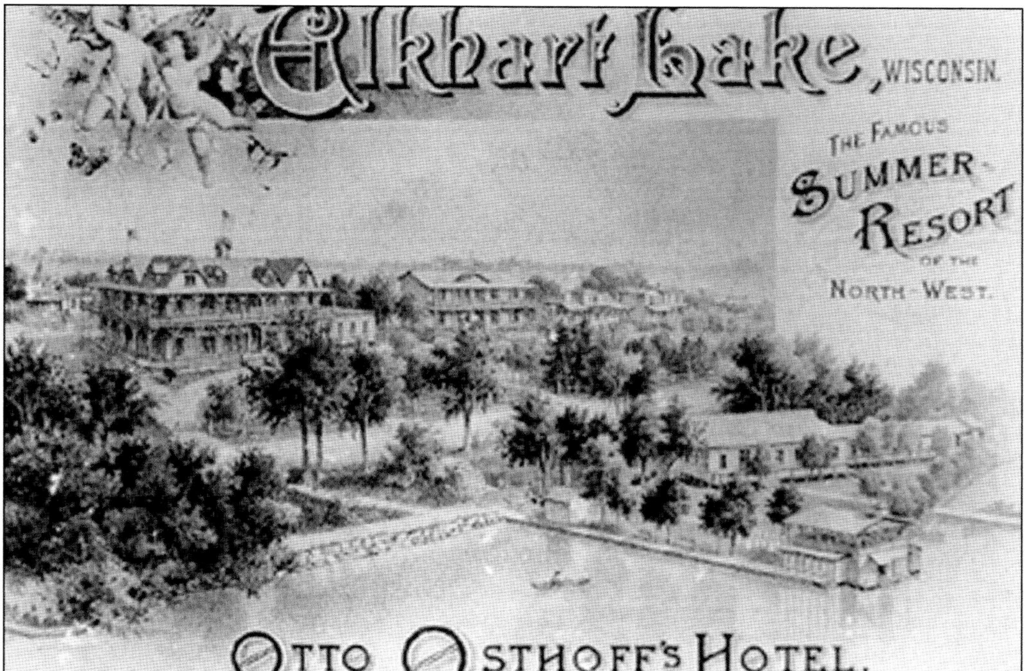

Osthoff Resort. Osthoff Resort was rumored to be conducting extracurricular activities in the 1930s.

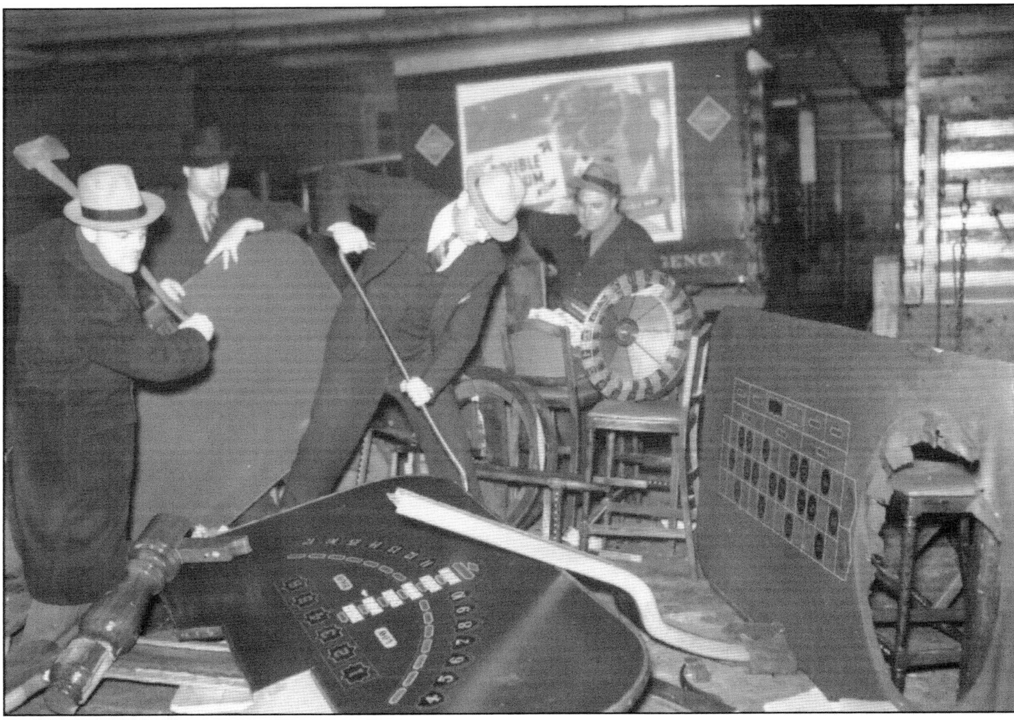

DESTRUCTION OF GAMBLING EQUIPMENT. Sheriff Joe Dreps and aides destroy confiscated gambling equipment taken from the Paddock Club in Elkhart Lake in the early 1930s.

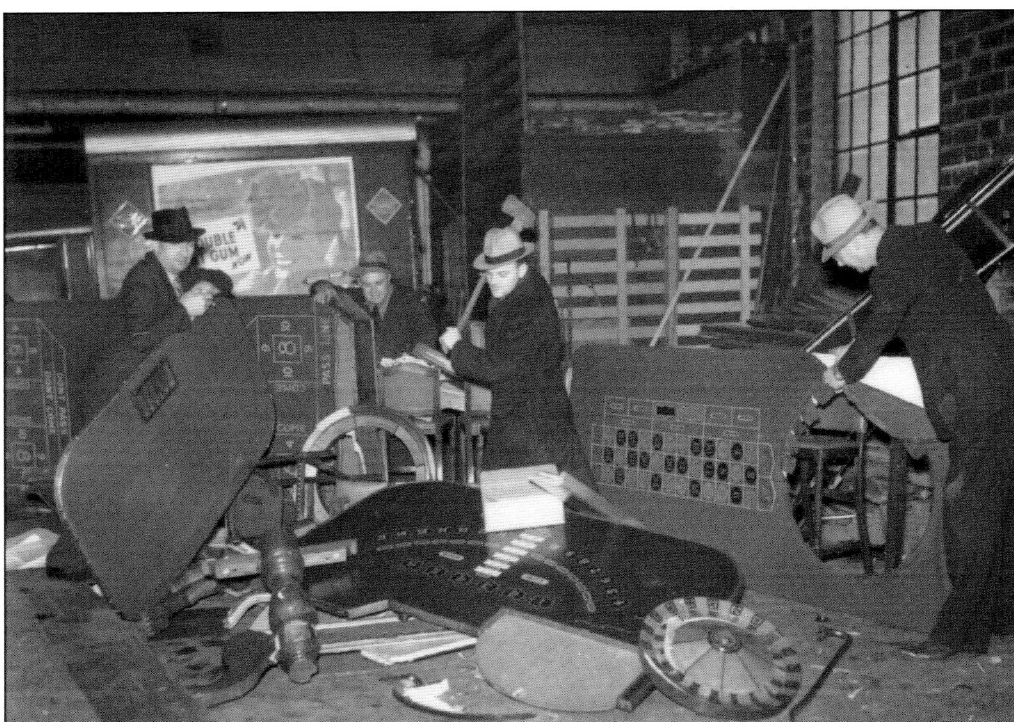

A GAMBLER'S NIGHTMARE. More equipment from Elkhart Lake is destroyed.

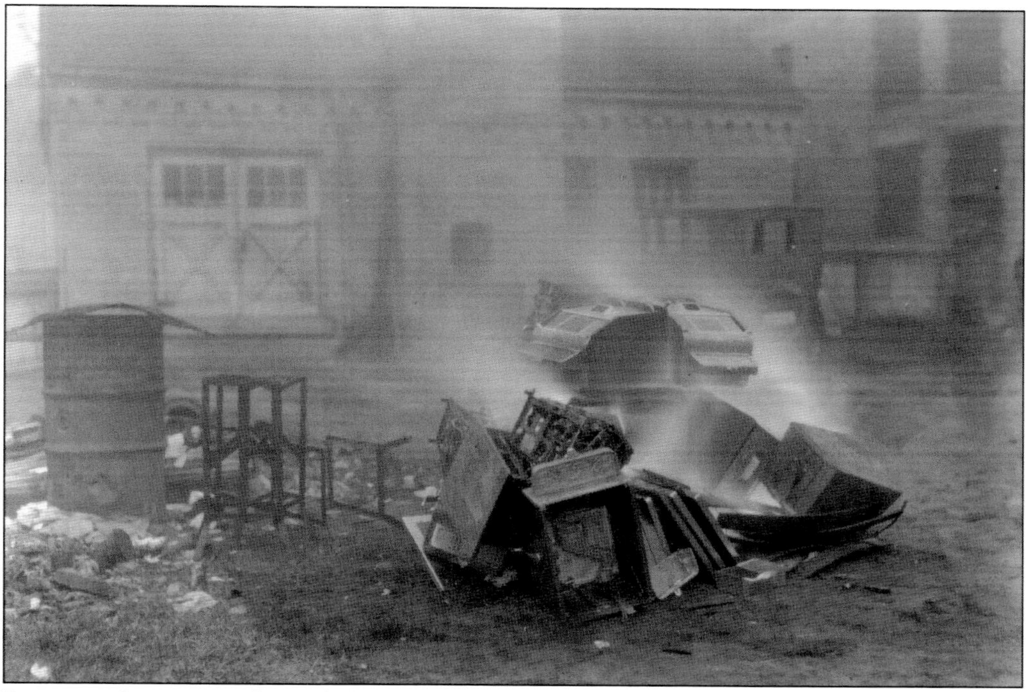

Burning Slots. Confiscated slot machines and other gambling paraphernalia are burned in April of 1930 in Elkhart Lake.

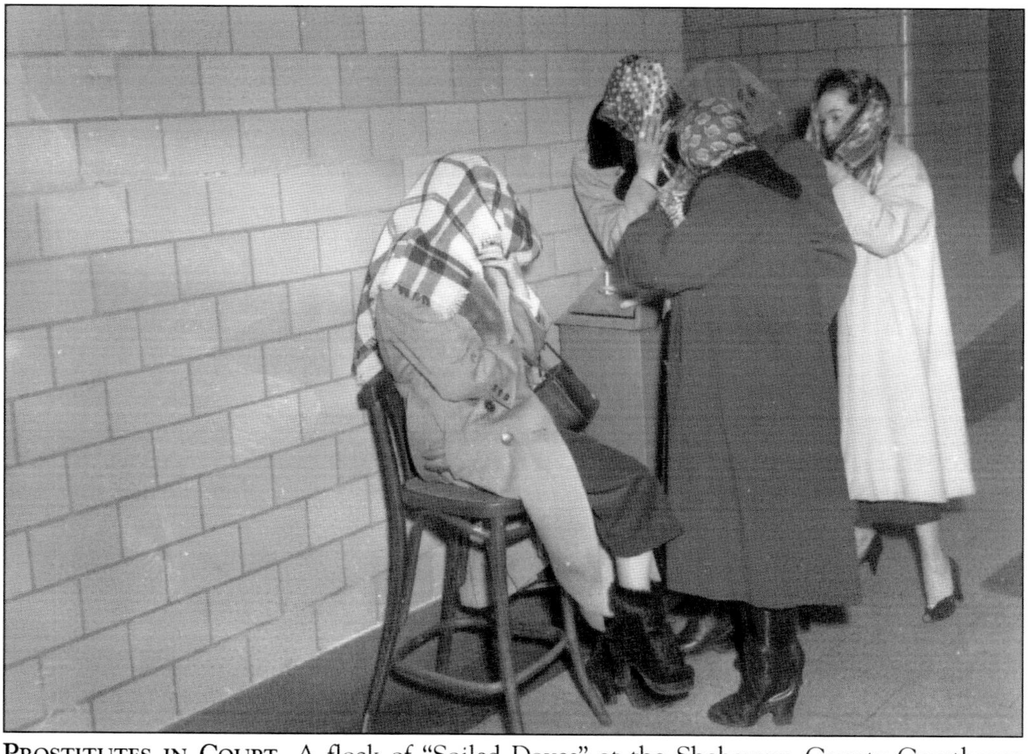

Prostitutes in Court. A flock of "Soiled Doves" at the Sheboygan County Courthouse awaiting their appearance before the judge in December of 1951.

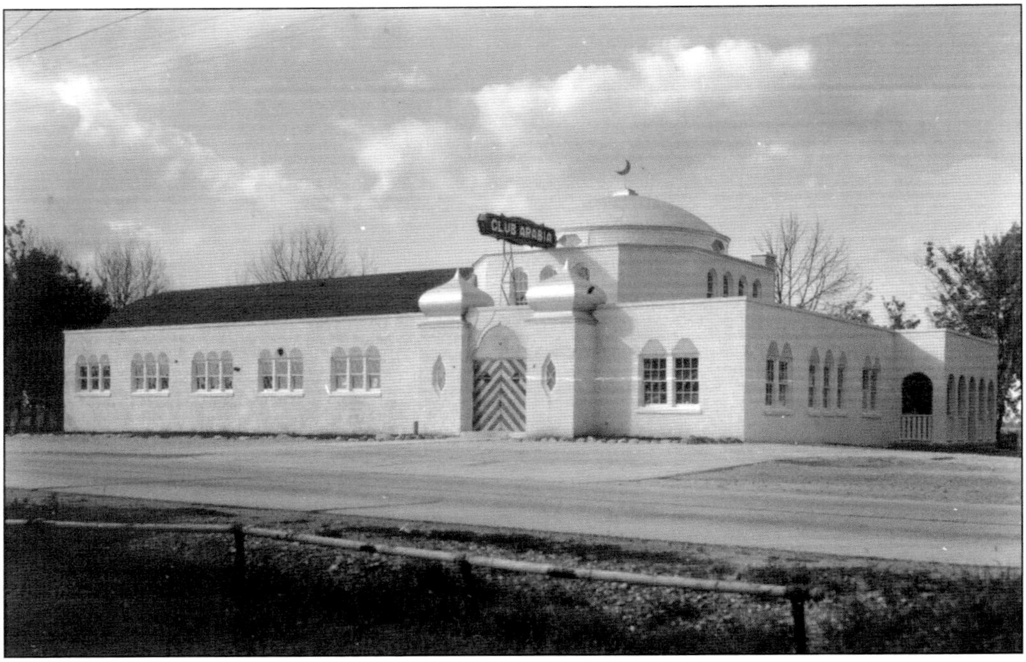

CLUB ARABIA. This brothel later became the Flamingo Supper Club. It was located on Calumet Drive in Sheboygan. This photo shows its exterior in 1933.

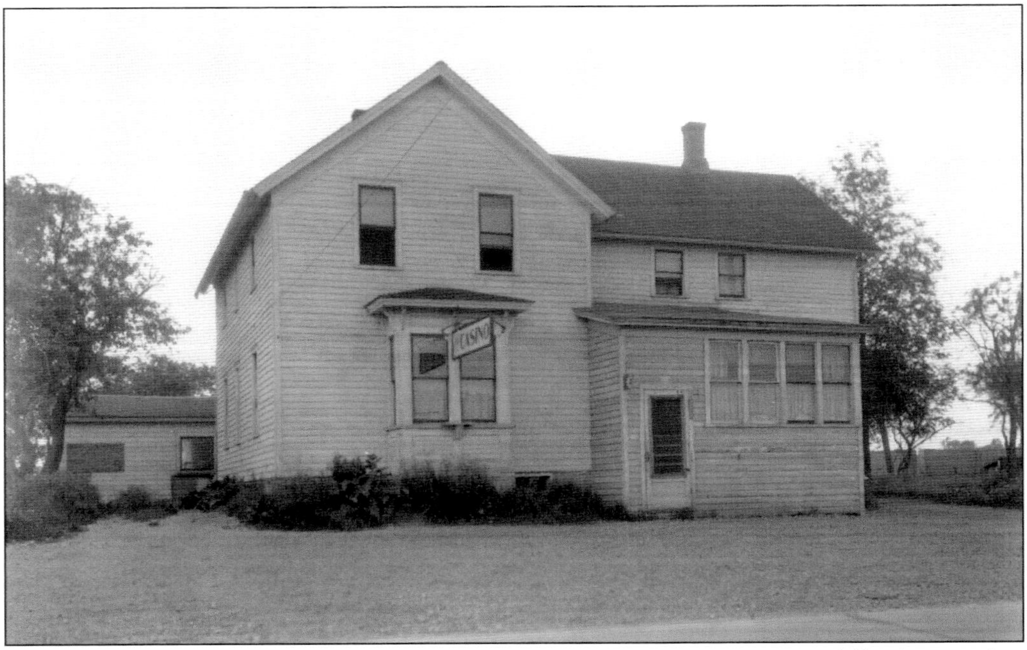

CASINO ROADHOUSE. This photo shows the establishment in 1929. It is difficult to gather specific information about businesses of this type. There are accounts of delivery boys who got a glimpse of the house, or the memoirs of doctors who treated the girls, but customers are reluctant to speak out. It is interesting to note, however, that while many men have no "first hand" knowledge of the places, they possess a remarkable ability to describe interiors in great detail.

Four

Specialty Manufacturing

Sheboygan County with its locally heavy German population became the home to many specialty industries. Breweries were one example. In addition to having a ready market for sales, the county had pure well water for the brewing process. It had a harbor that was useful in the transportation of raw materials and the finished product. It had abundant forests and logging mills, as well as skilled labor for the brewing and barrel making processes. Finally, the climate was favorable, and growing conditions for a wide range of agricultural products was good. These elements were advantageous to all industry, not just breweries. Each ethnic group brought its own flavor to industry.

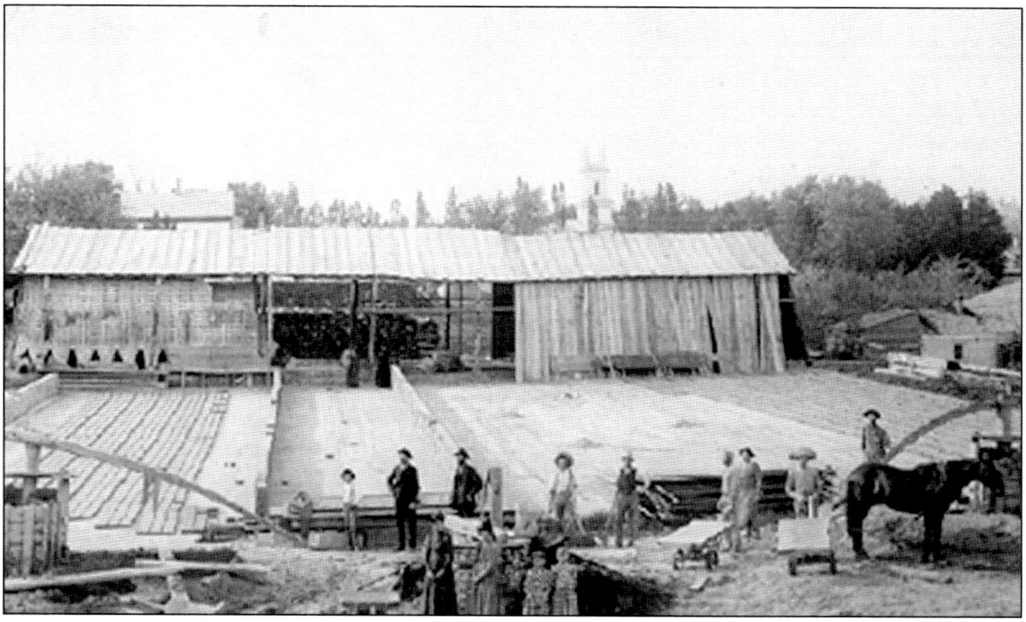

Brickyards. Shown here is Ramaker Brickyards of Sheboygan Falls. This was one of the yards supplying the beautiful Cream City Brick to the area.

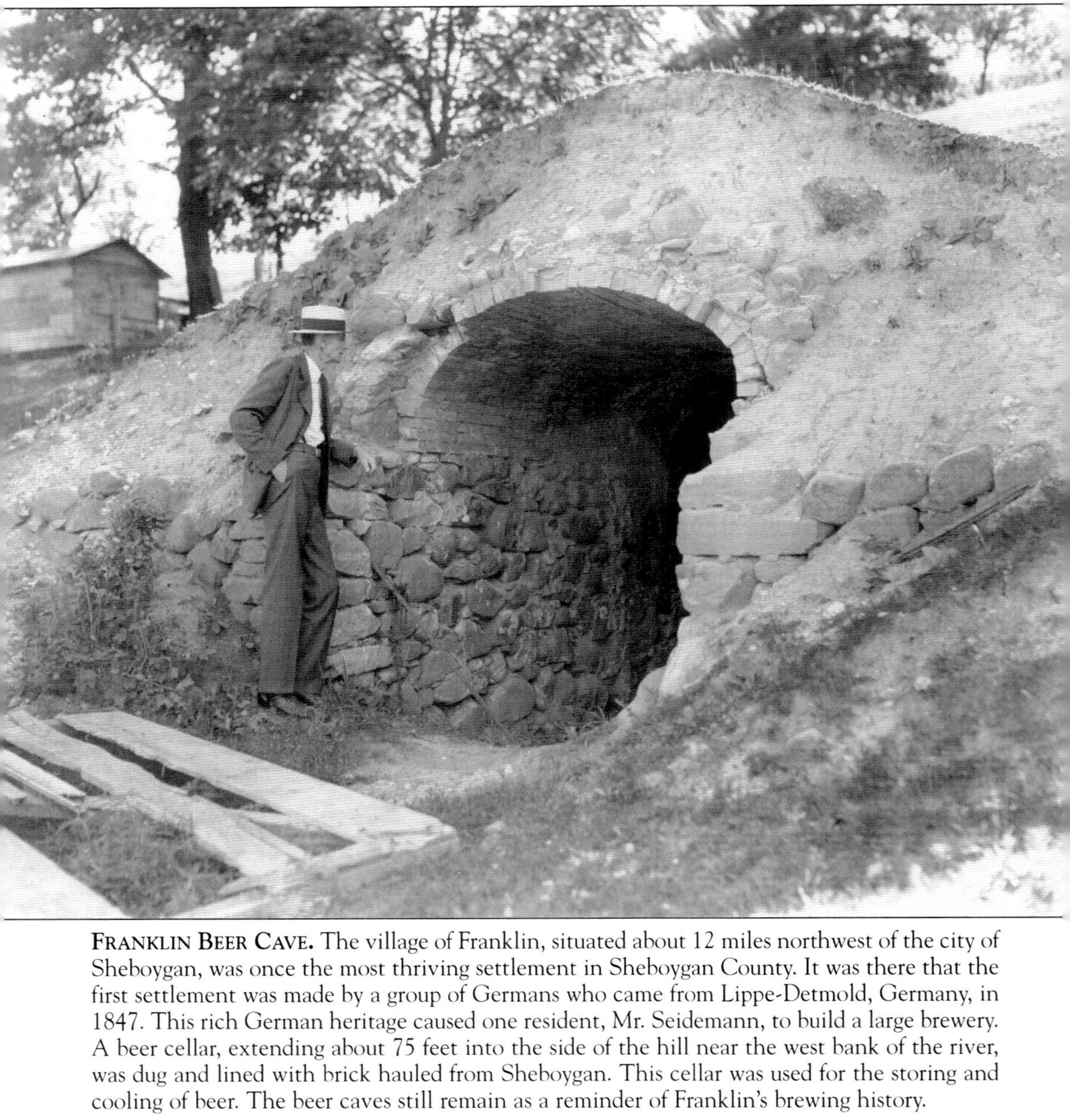

FRANKLIN BEER CAVE. The village of Franklin, situated about 12 miles northwest of the city of Sheboygan, was once the most thriving settlement in Sheboygan County. It was there that the first settlement was made by a group of Germans who came from Lippe-Detmold, Germany, in 1847. This rich German heritage caused one resident, Mr. Seidemann, to build a large brewery. A beer cellar, extending about 75 feet into the side of the hill near the west bank of the river, was dug and lined with brick hauled from Sheboygan. This cellar was used for the storing and cooling of beer. The beer caves still remain as a reminder of Franklin's brewing history.

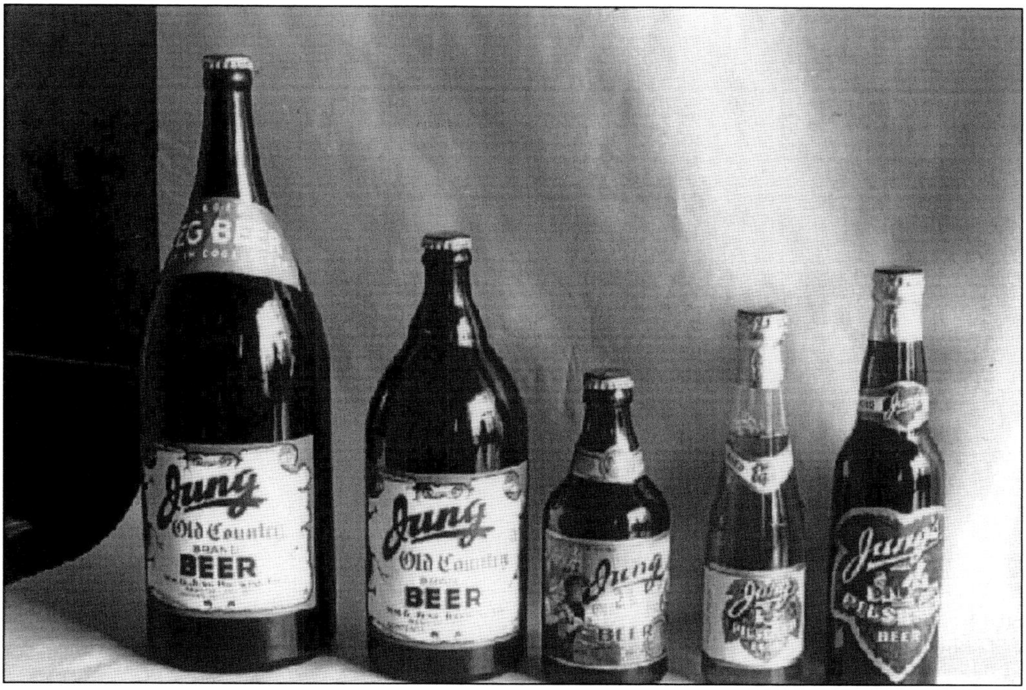

JUNG BEER BOTTLES. The William G. Jung Brewing Company was a part of Random Lake's history from 1933 to 1958. The company operated on Carroll Street from 1921 to 1933 producing soda and near beer until the end of Prohibition. After Prohibition, Jung began producing beer with great success. Jung Brewery produced 20,000 barrels of beer at its peak. This display of various products shows different sizes to accommodate different tastes. Brands included Old Country, Lager, Jung Pilsner and Jung Beer.

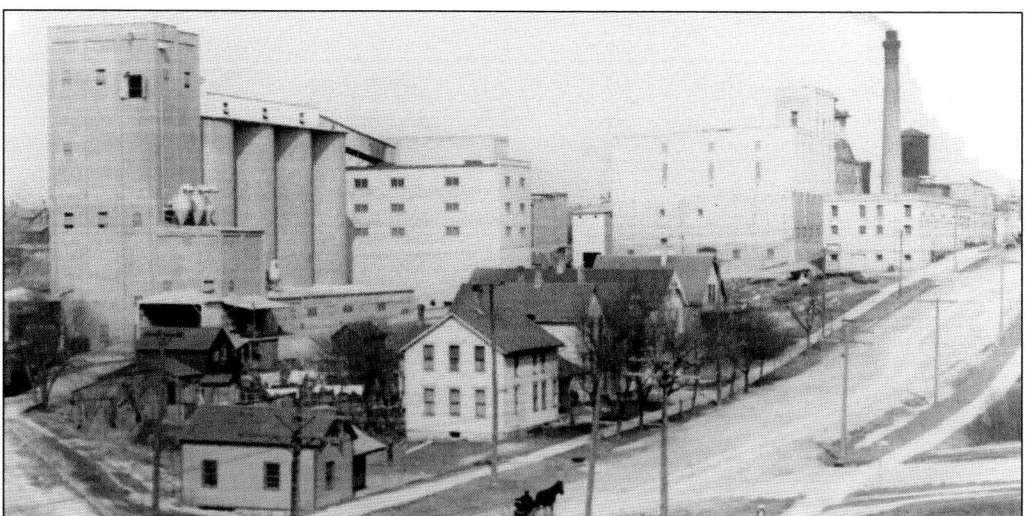

SCHREIER MALTING COMPANY. This photo of Schreier Malting is shown looking east up New Jersey Avenue in Sheboygan. The year is 1911. Konrad Schreier and S. Schlicht established the company in 1856. It was destroyed by fire and rebuilt with Schreier as sole owner. During prohibition, the company made soda water, brown bread and Schreier Wis. Rye Flour. In 1933, malting was resumed.

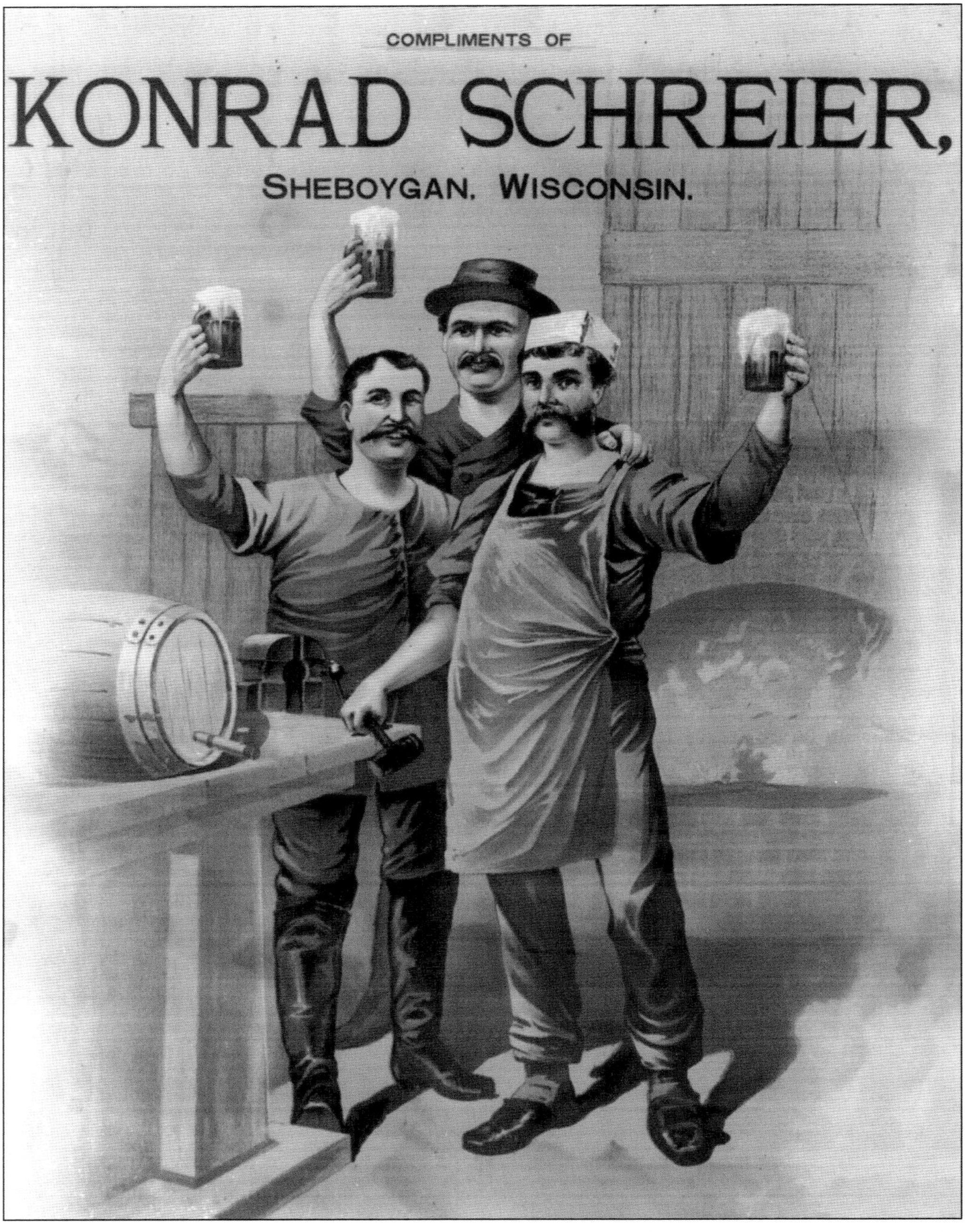

KONRAD SCHREIER BEER POSTER. Posters advertising various breweries were common in the late 1800s and early 1900s. This poster, advertising the Konrad Schreier Brewing Company of Sheboygan, was one of the last of its type, being issued in 1933.

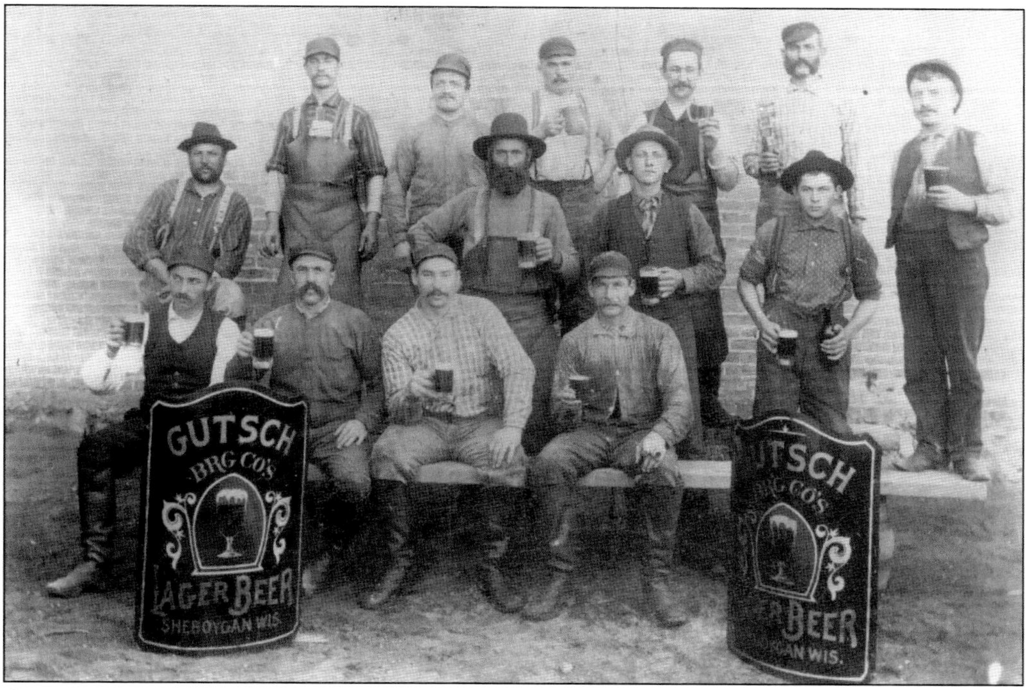

GUTSCH BREWERY EMPLOYEES. A group of Gutsch employees pose outside the brewery in 1889. Each employee is holding a full glass of beer. It was common practice for brewery employees to drink while on the job. Eventually, this "perk" was limited, and then eliminated due to safety concerns.

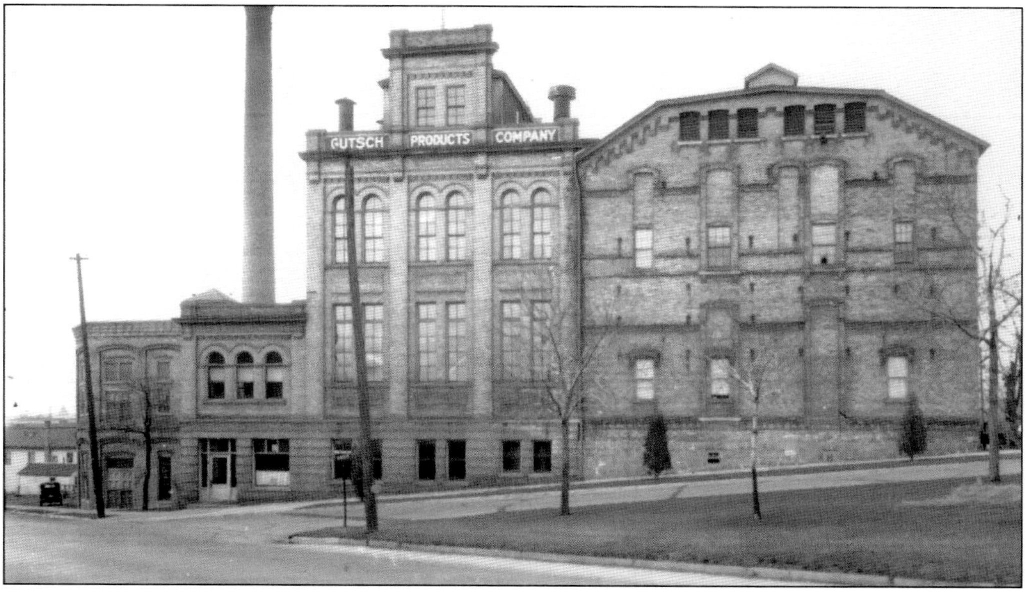

GUTSCH BREWERY. This photo was taken in November of 1932. Twin brothers Leopold and Franz Gutsch established the business in 1847. It was situated on the northeast corner of New York Avenue and Water Street in Sheboygan. In 1926, the firm was sold to the Manitowoc Products Company. Its corporate name was changed to Kingsbury Breweries Company in 1933. Eventually it was sold to G. Heilemann of La Crosse and closed in the 1970s.

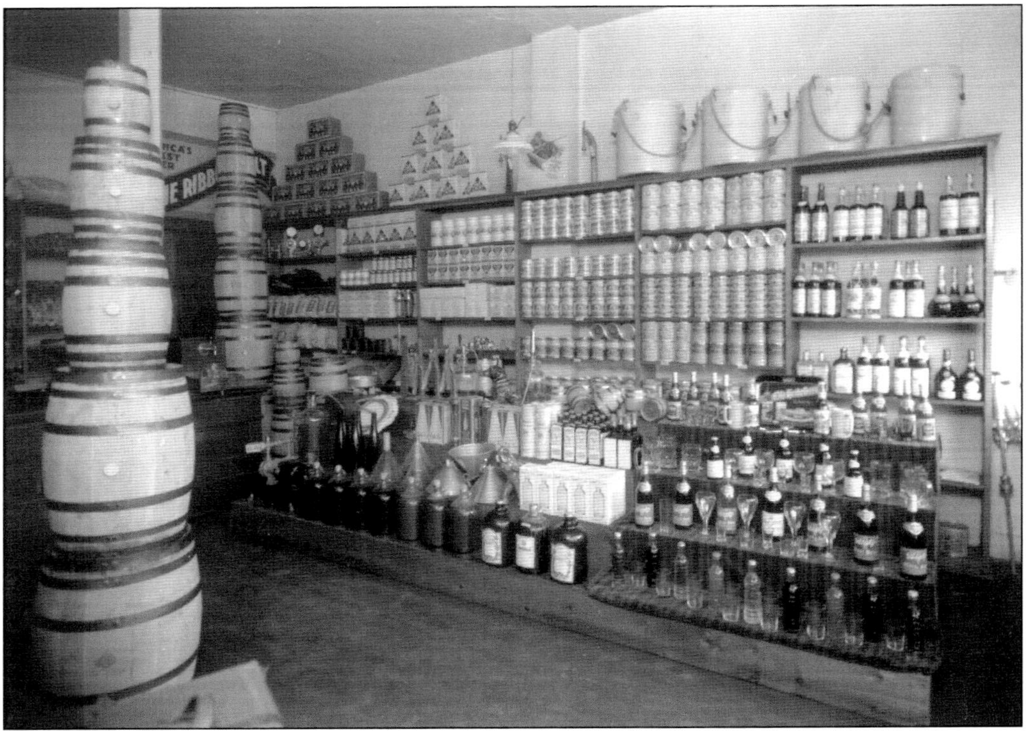

SHEBOYGAN MALT PRODUCTS. This store was located at 415 North Eighth Street, Sheboygan. It is now Cesar's. The photo was taken in October of 1932 during Prohibition.

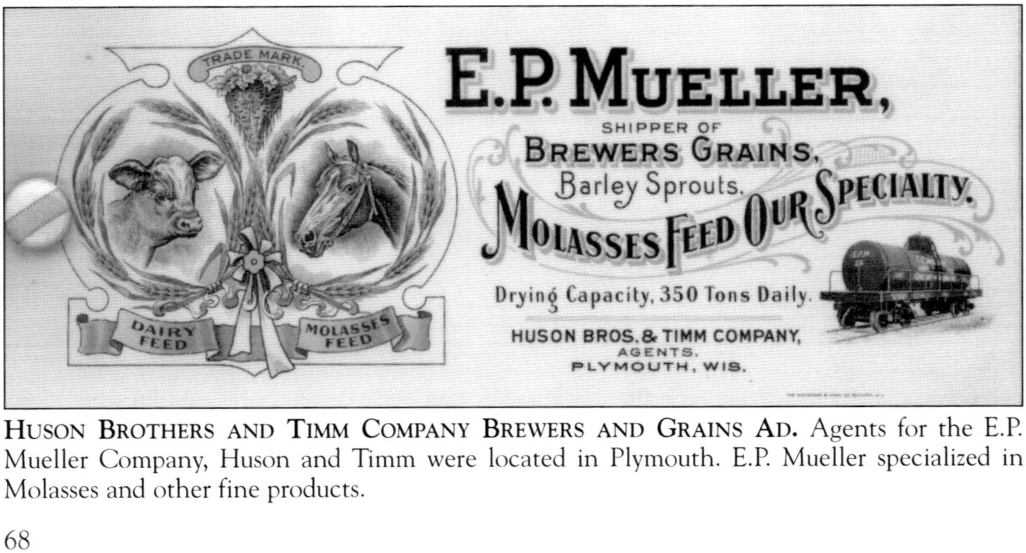

HUSON BROTHERS AND TIMM COMPANY BREWERS AND GRAINS AD. Agents for the E.P. Mueller Company, Huson and Timm were located in Plymouth. E.P. Mueller specialized in Molasses and other fine products.

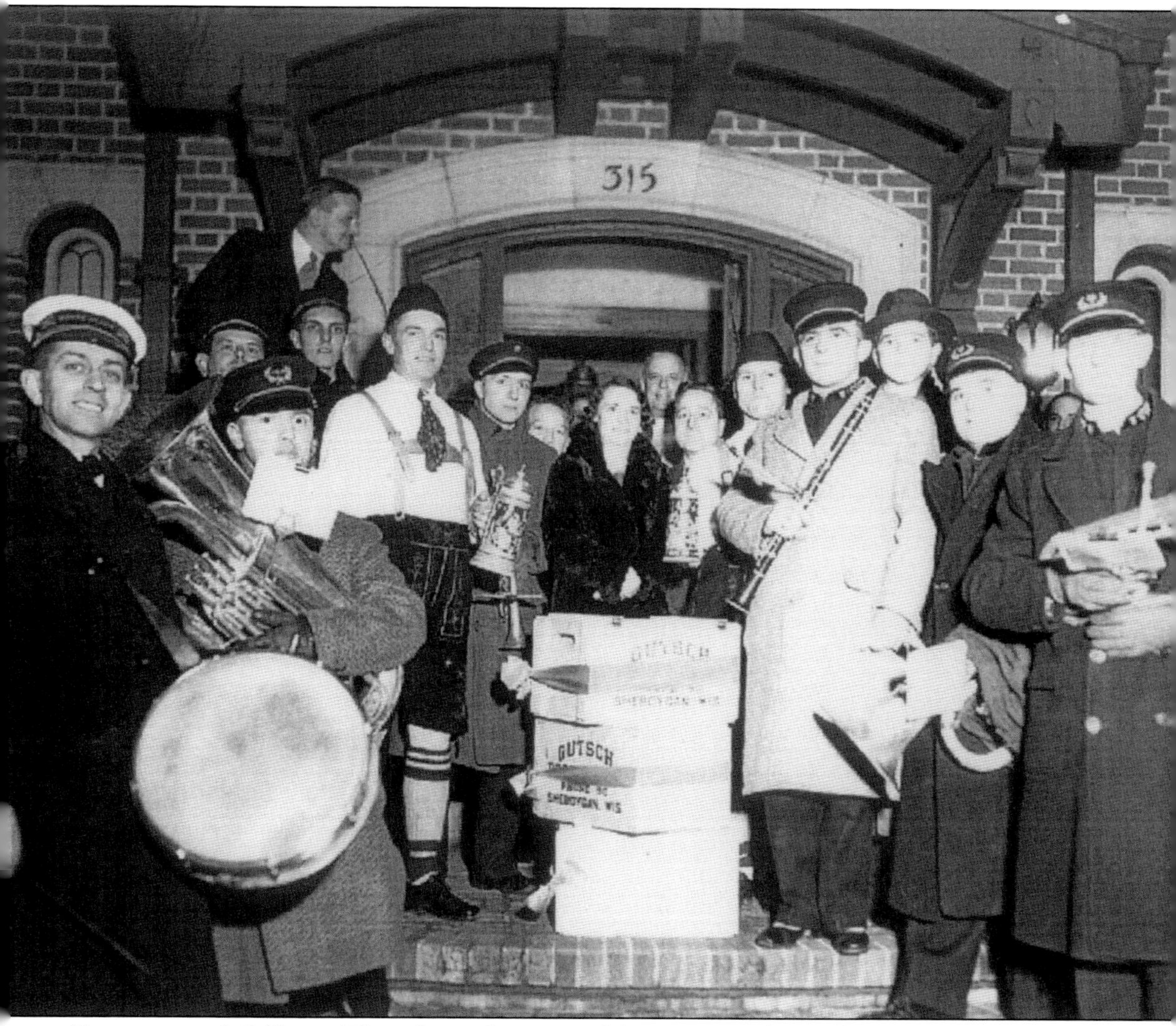

RETURN OF 3.2 BEER. This photo shows a celebration, involving three cases of Gutsch Beer and a German Band, at the home of *Sheboygan Press* publisher Charles Broughton. The celebration took place on April 7, 1933, and was inspired by the end of Prohibition and the return of 3.2% beer. Prohibition in the United States was a measure designed to reduce drinking by eliminating the businesses that manufactured, distributed, and sold alcoholic beverages. The Eighteenth Amendment to the U.S. Constitution took away license to do business from the brewers, distillers, vintners, and the wholesale and retail sellers of alcoholic beverages. The leaders of the prohibition movement were alarmed at the drinking behavior of Americans, and they were concerned that there was a culture of drink among some sectors of the population that, with continuing immigration from Europe, was spreading. In the spring of 1933, Franklin D. Roosevelt made "real beer" exempt from the 18th amendment. By December of the same year, Utah was last necessary state to ratify the 21st amendment—repeal of prohibition—and on December 5th, alcohol was legal once more.

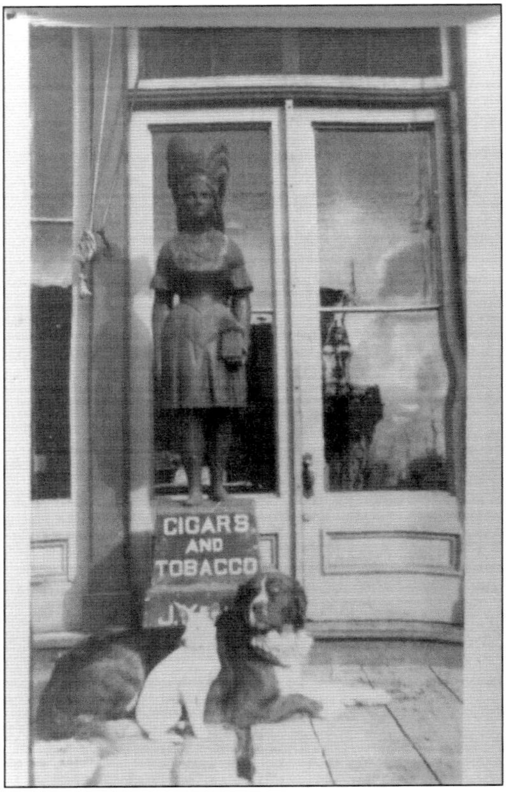

KEHL CIGAR STORE. This wooden cigar store Indian that stood in front of the Frank Kehl Cigar Store advertised the production of fine tobacco products. It was located in Sheboygan Falls in 1900. A local brand produced here was named Frog.

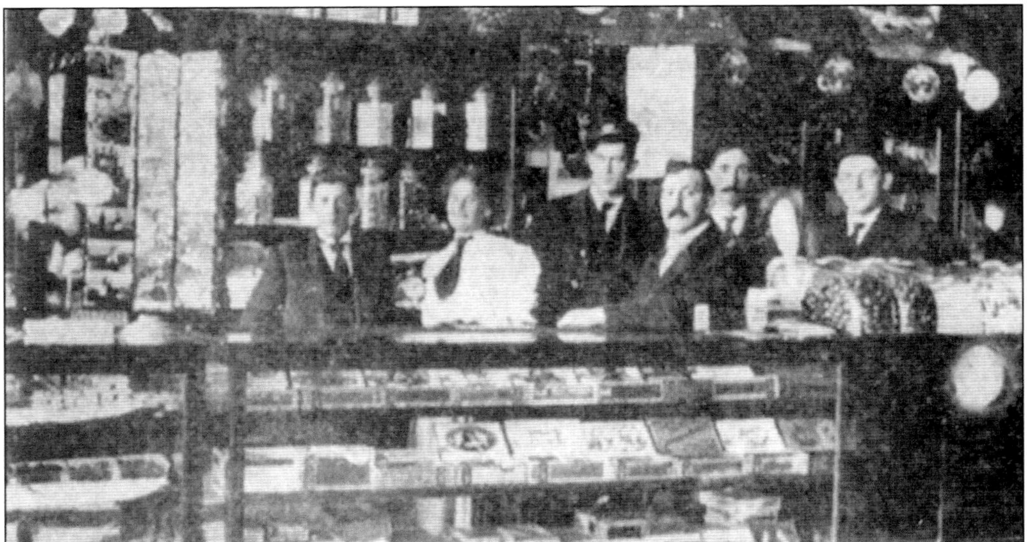

MOOSE DIPS AND BARRISTERS. "Moose Dips" and "Barrister" were two brands of cigars available at the tobacco and candy counter of the Milwaukee Northern Depot in Sheboygan. The photo is dated about 1916.

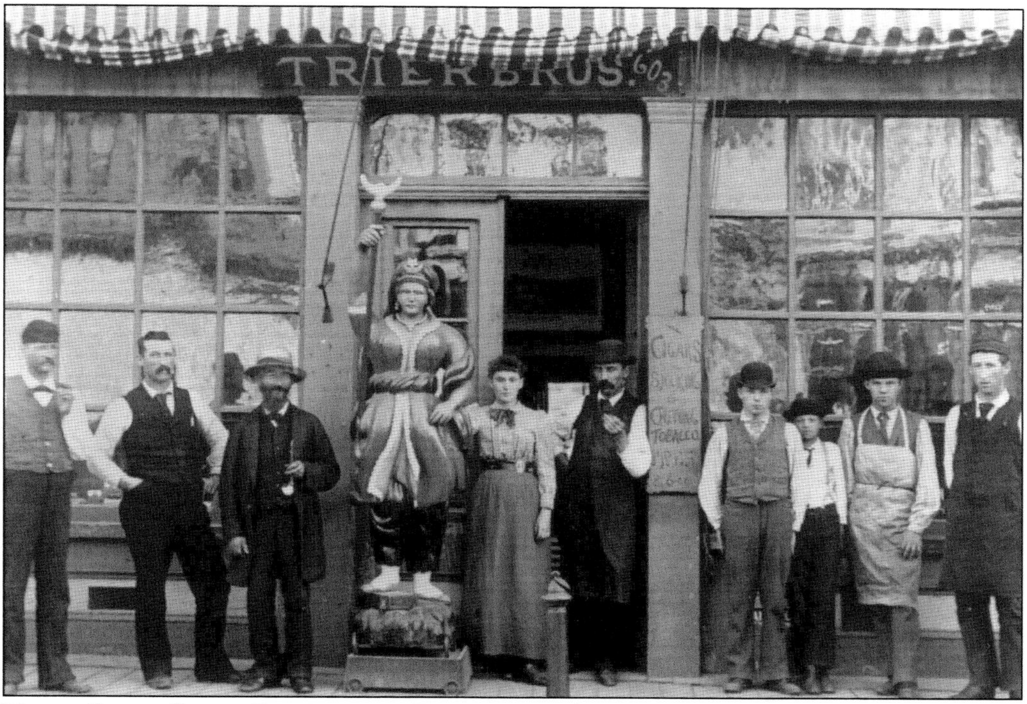

TRIER CIGAR STORE INDIAN AND EMPLOYEES. The cigar makers and clerks at the Trier Brothers Tobacco Shop pose with the wooden Indian. Note, too, the hitching post. Customers would tie their horses to the post while transacting business in the store.

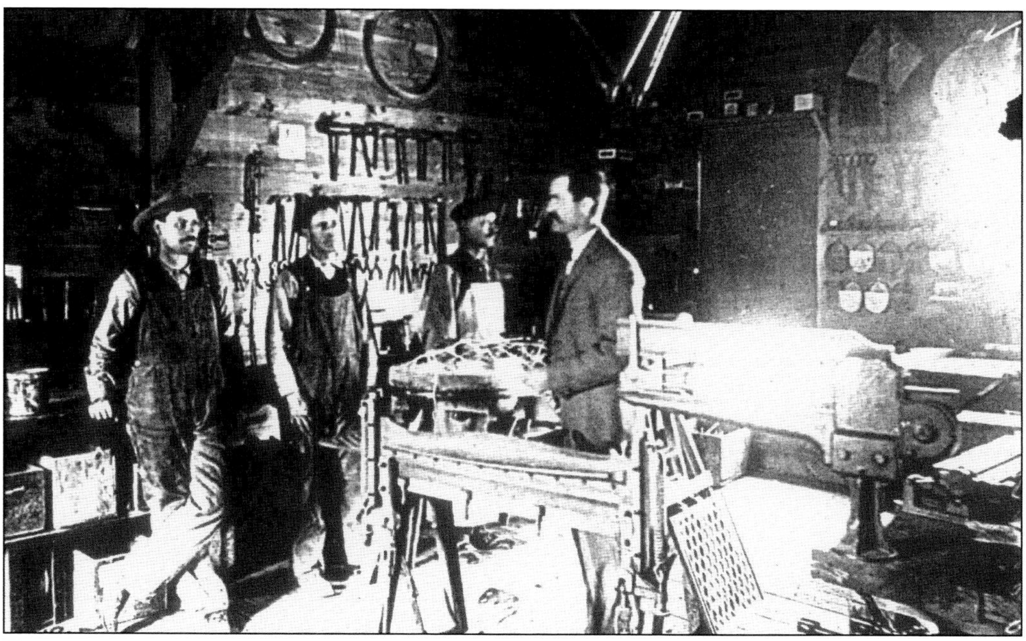

TIMMER TIN SHOP. The tinsmith, also known as a whitesmith, has passed from the scene. Today a tinner is known as a sheet metal worker. Note the array of machinery used by the tinsmith in molding his creations. Important goods produced were ladles, pails, and milk cans. Henry Timmer, the owner of the shop, stands in the center.

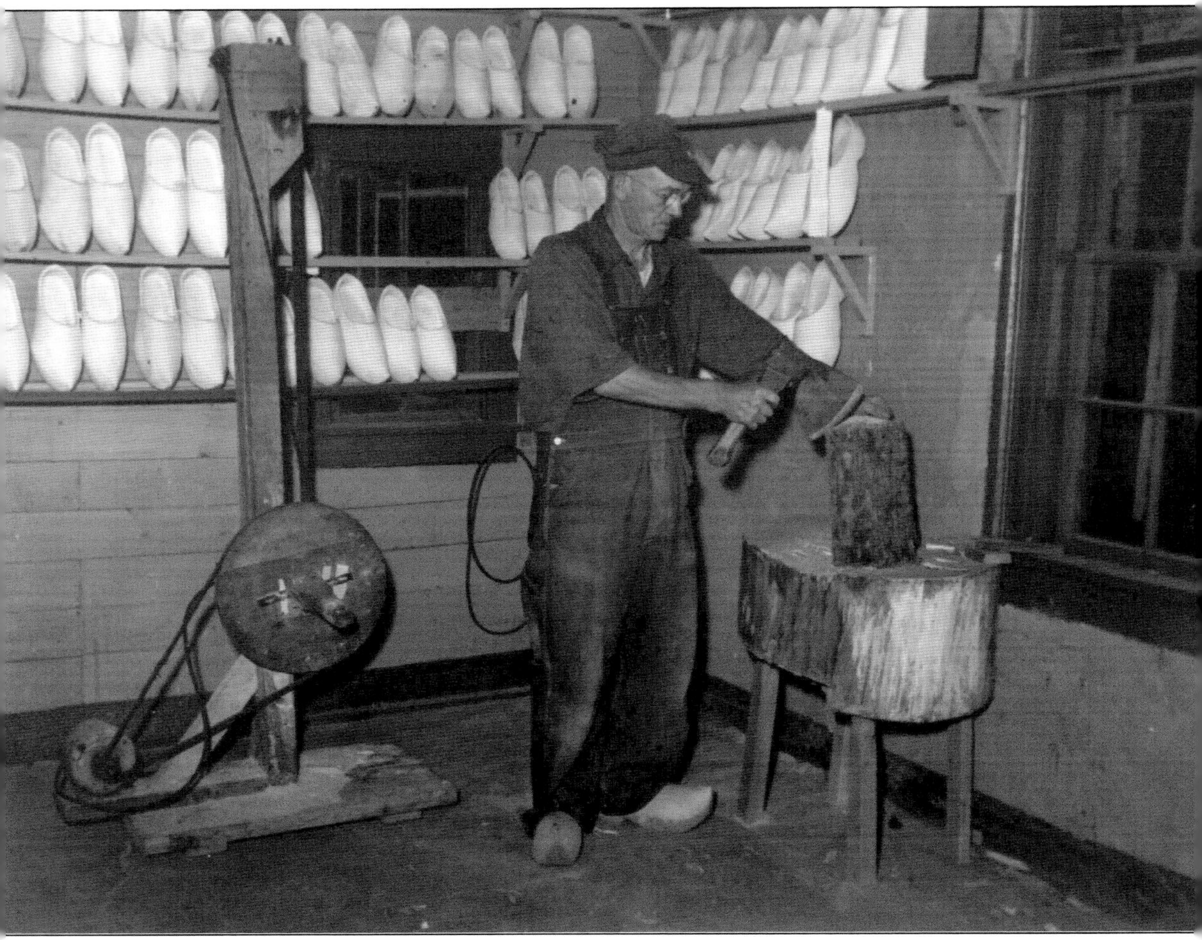

WM. KLOMPENHOUWER. Wm. Klompenhouwer of Oostburg was one of the county's last remaining wooden shoemakers. He is shown in his workshop during July of 1952. His father spent two years in Holland learning the trade. The elder Mr. Klompenhouwer was capable of making more than 400 pairs in a winter, or four pairs per day. Each sold for 25 cents. Even the Klompenhouwer name reflects the trade. It means wooden shoe hewer. A newspaper reported that in 1920 the Theune Brothers of Oostburg commenced making wooden shoes in a new facility. Southeastern Sheboygan County remains heavily Dutch to this day. Another Dutch settlement, Cedar Grove, maintains its Holland Fest the last Friday and Saturday of July each year. The streets are scrubbed and Klompen dancers remember their heritage.

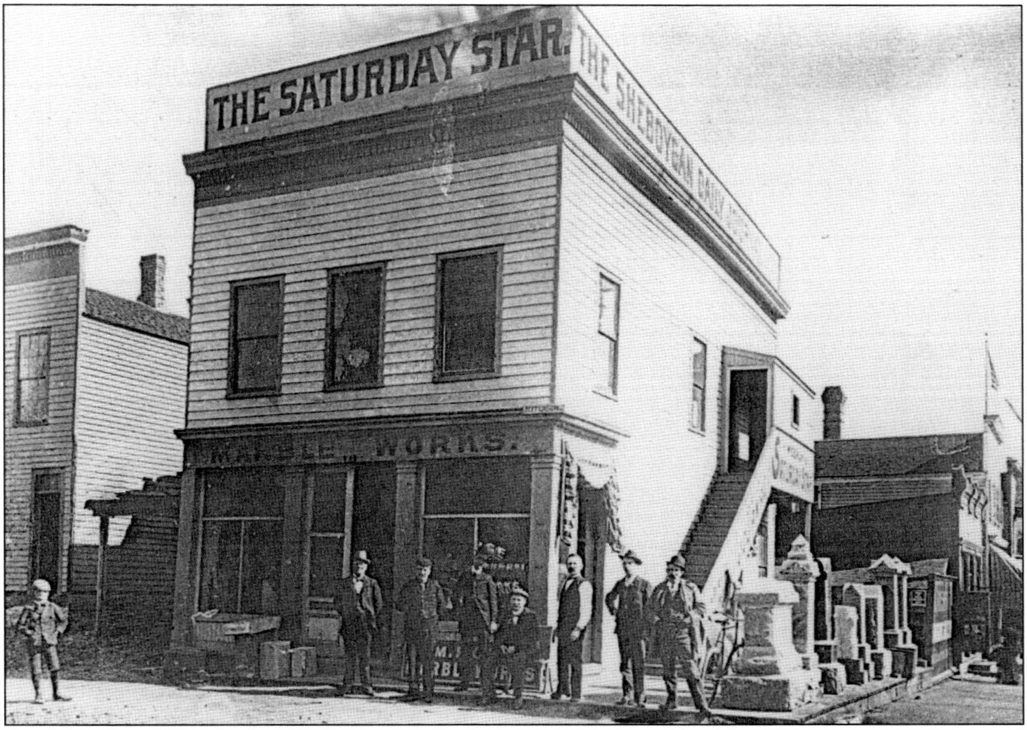

WILBUR ROOT'S MONUMENT SHOP. Located at 733 Jefferson Avenue in Sheboygan, this 1896 photo shows examples of Mr. Roots' work along the walkway at right. Above the marbleworks was The Saturday Star office, a short-lived weekly newspaper. Root began his career in his father's cooperage in Plymouth. He was a Civil War veteran and became commander of the local G.A.R.

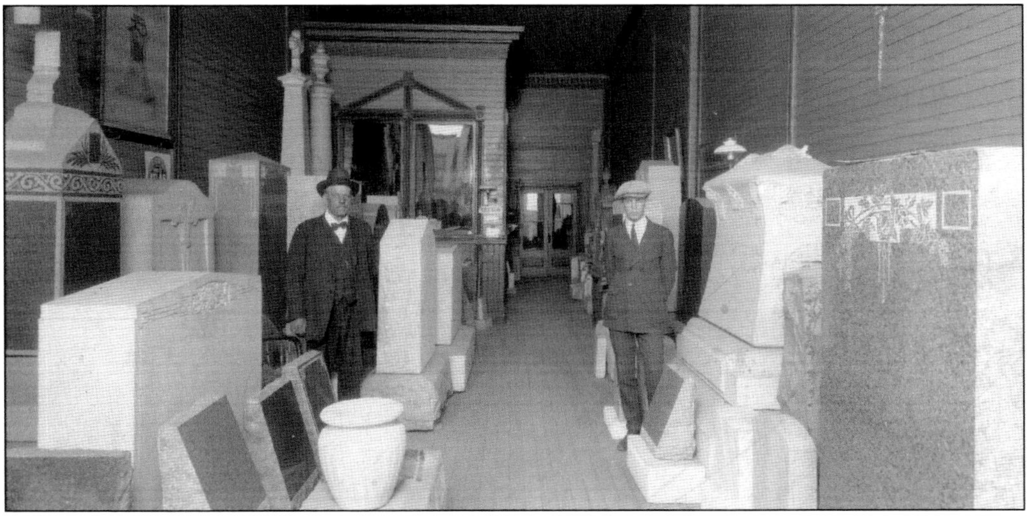

SCHEELE MONUMENT WORKS. Henry Scheele, an immigrant from Nindorf, Germany, arrived in Sheboygan in 1848. He originally earned a living as a cabinet-maker and house moving contractor. He entered the marble business in 1871. His business, shown here in 1922, was located at 712 N. Eighth Street in Sheboygan. The exterior of the Scheele building was unique in that it was topped by a four and one-half foot, 500-pound statue of Hope, clothed in a long, flowing robe with her right hand supporting an anchor and her left holding a laurel branch.

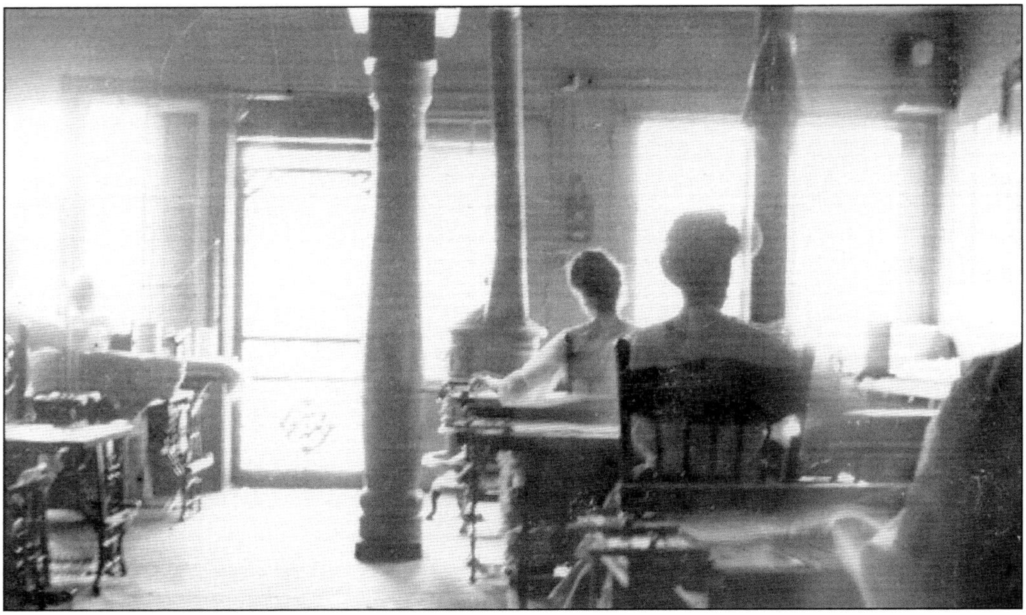

SEWING CHEESE BANDAGES. The Lumsden Bandage Factory of Sheboygan Falls made cheese bandages at their plant at 504 North Water Street. A cheese bandage was used to wrap the cheese prior to the invention of paraffin or tin foil. Here we see a room full of women about the year 1887 sewing the pieces of cheesecloth into appropriate bandage sizes.

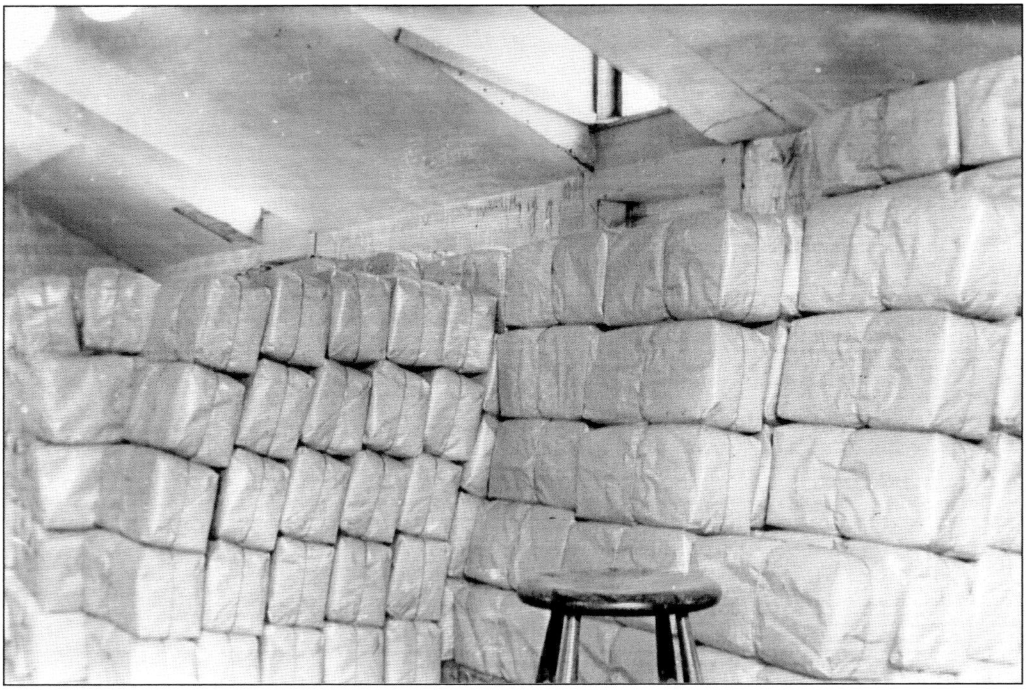

STACK OF CHEESE BANDAGES. Alexander J. Lumsden, the owner of the plant, invented an automatic cheese bandage cutter. His obituary stated that "Lumsden's ready-made cheese bandages are widely known and sought after by cheese makers throughout the world." Here we see a stack of his product.

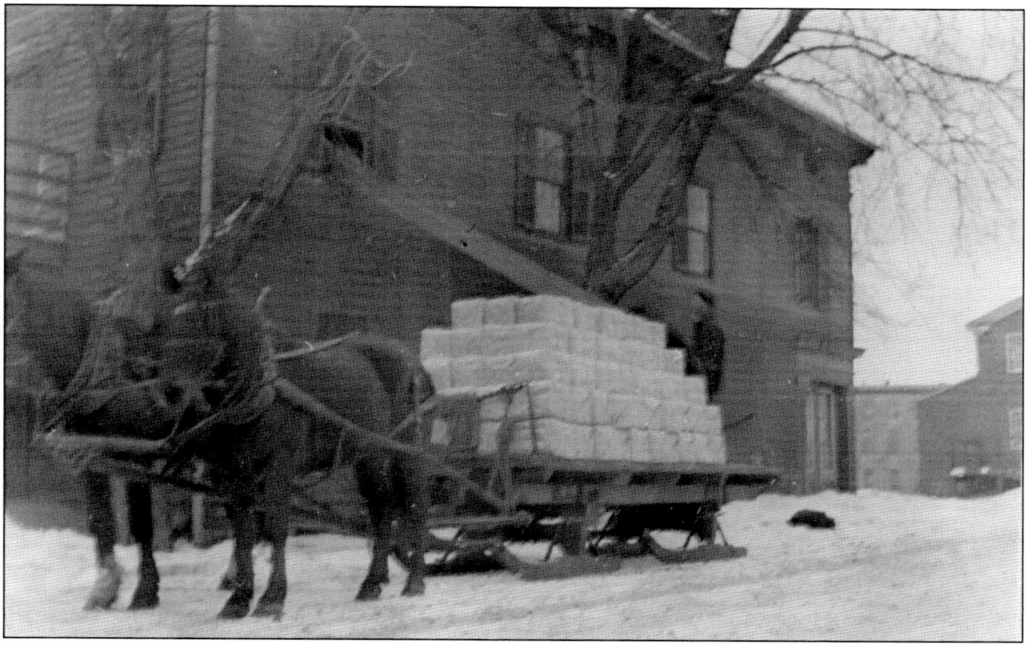

CHEESE BANDAGES ON SLED. This winter scene shows the method of transport for the season. After Lumsden's death, the factory was run by his son-in-law, Almon Leavens. The business ended just before the start of WWI. The building today houses the Rochester Inn, a beautiful bed and breakfast.

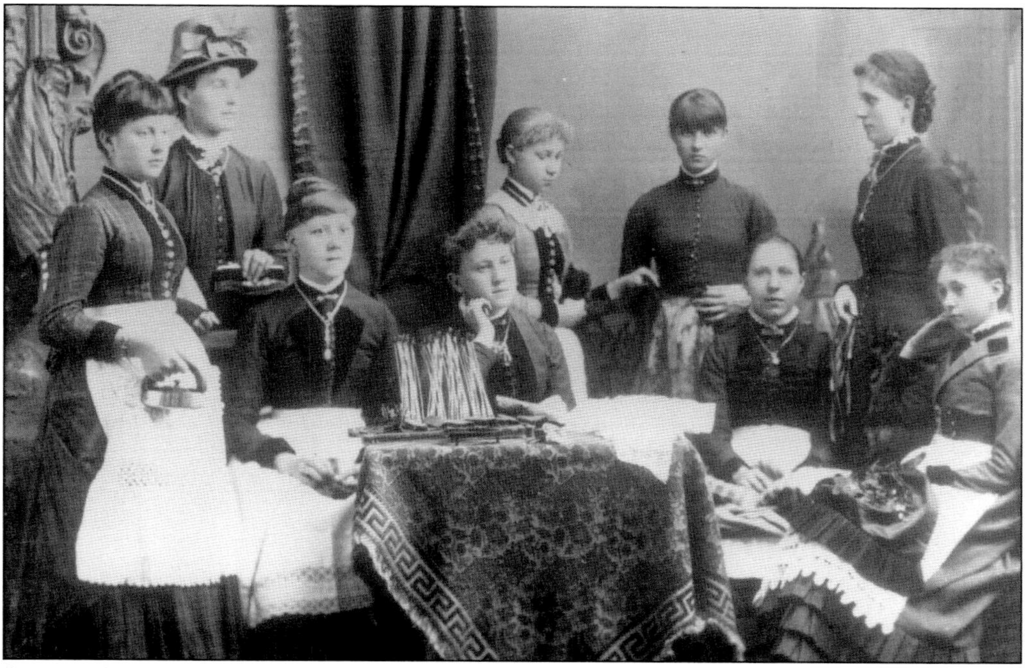

SEWING CLASS. A group of nine women is shown posing with a pleating machine, used to make folds in skirts and pants. The experienced dressmaker would work with the young ladies of the neighborhood to teach the basic elements of sewing. Every respectable female needed to know how to make and mend clothing for her family.

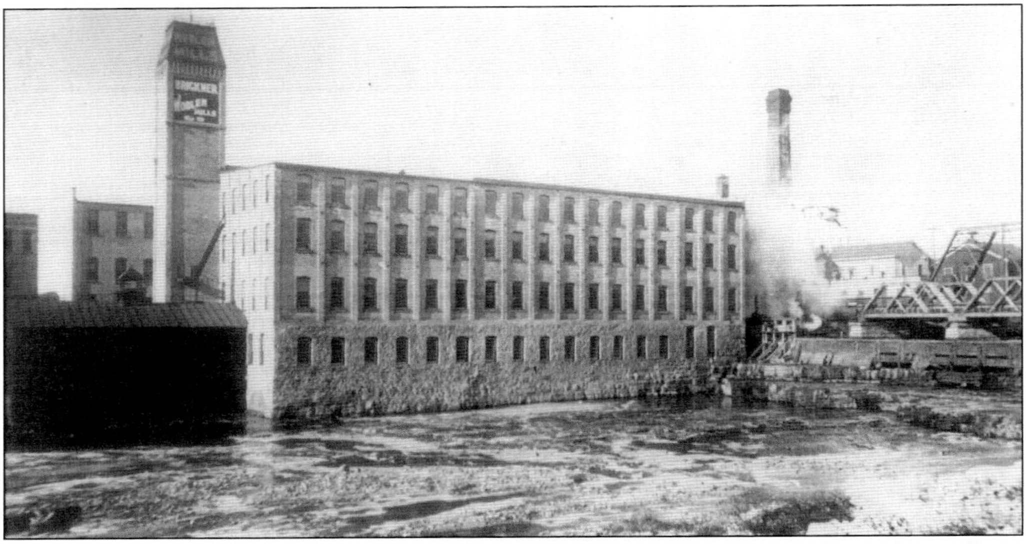

Brickner Woolen Mills. The Brickner family has been associated with woolen mills in Sheboygan County since 1862. The present cream city brick factory on Monroe Street in Sheboygan Falls was built in 1879. The company ceased operations in the 1930s. This mill employed 80 to 100 people making blankets, flannels, and dress goods. The factory had 27 broad looms with 2050 spindles.

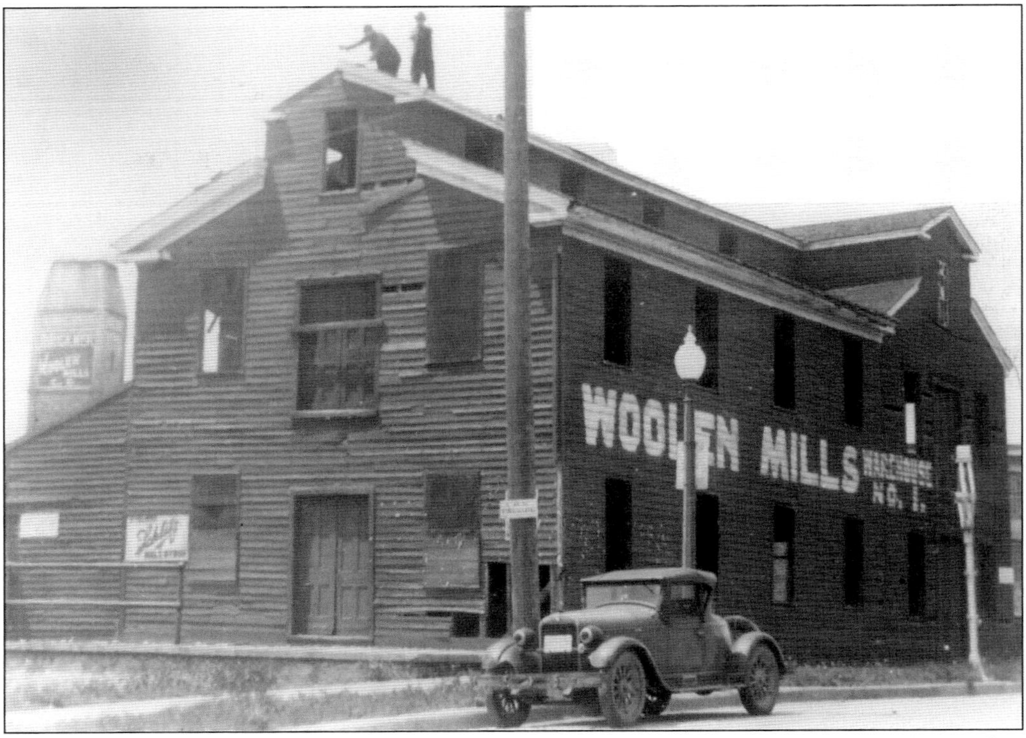

Woolen Mills Warehouse. This photo shows the Brickner Woolen Mills Warehouse that was once located on the east side of the river in Sheboygan Falls at Monroe Street. Sheboygan Falls Mutual Insurance Company is now on that site.

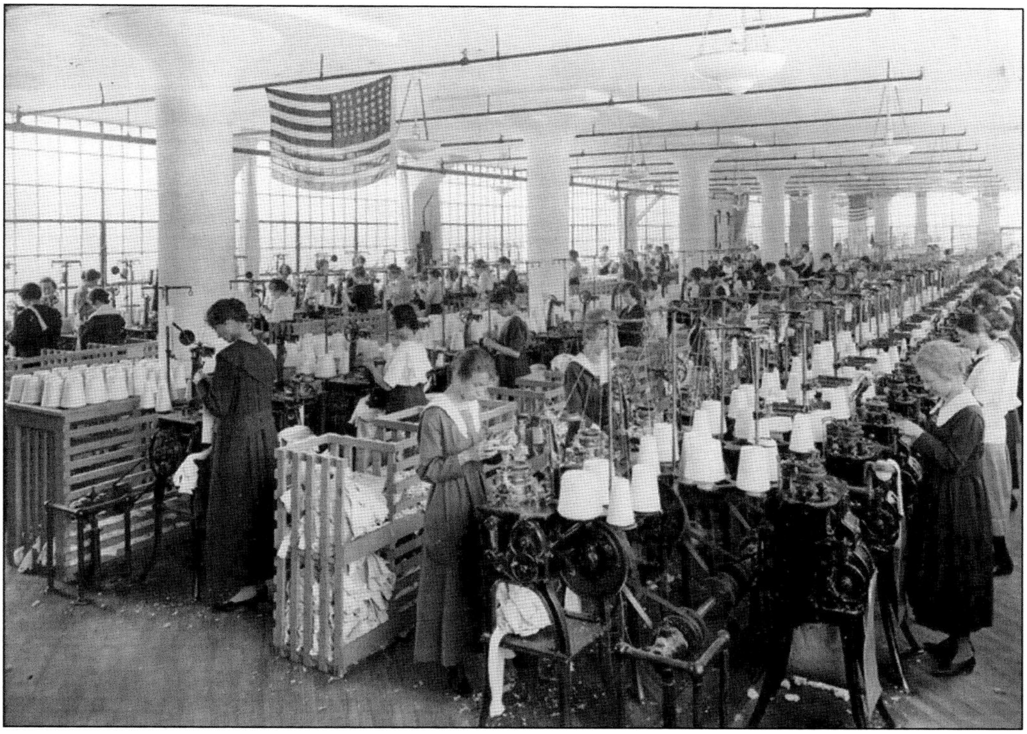

BLACK CAT HOSIERY COMPANY. Hundreds of women were employed at this sock factory. This photo depicts a huge workroom filled with dozens of small machines engaged in the production of socks at Black Cat Hosiery Company, located at 509 S. 9th in Sheboygan. The building is surprisingly airy and bright for a turn of the century factory.

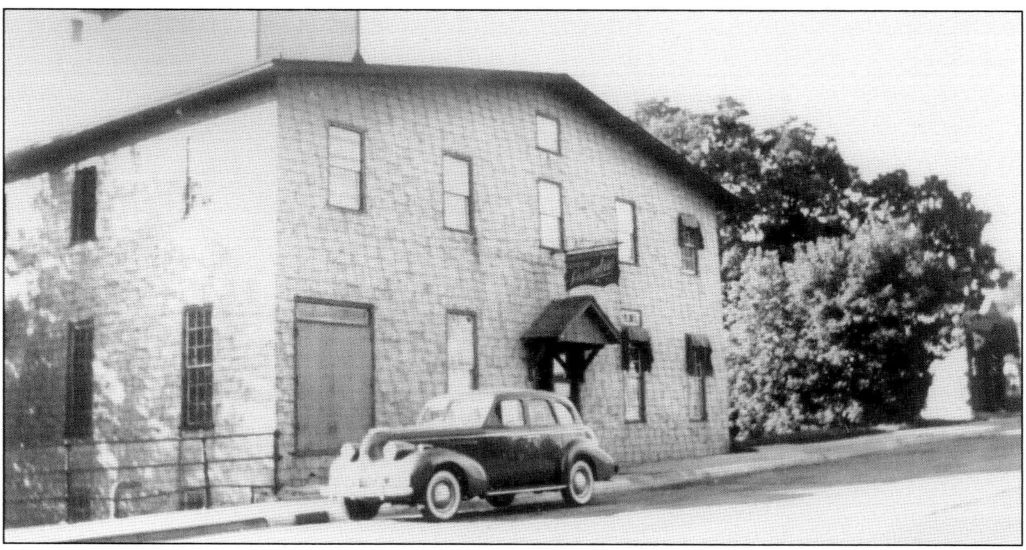

PLYMOUTH LAUNDRY. Located at 19 Stafford Street on the south side of the Mullet River, this building originally housed a mill. Laundries were very successful business enterprises before the days of the home washer and dryer. Another factor that led to their downfall was the advancement in detergents as well as clothing materials. Better materials made home washing easier and more likely to be successful.

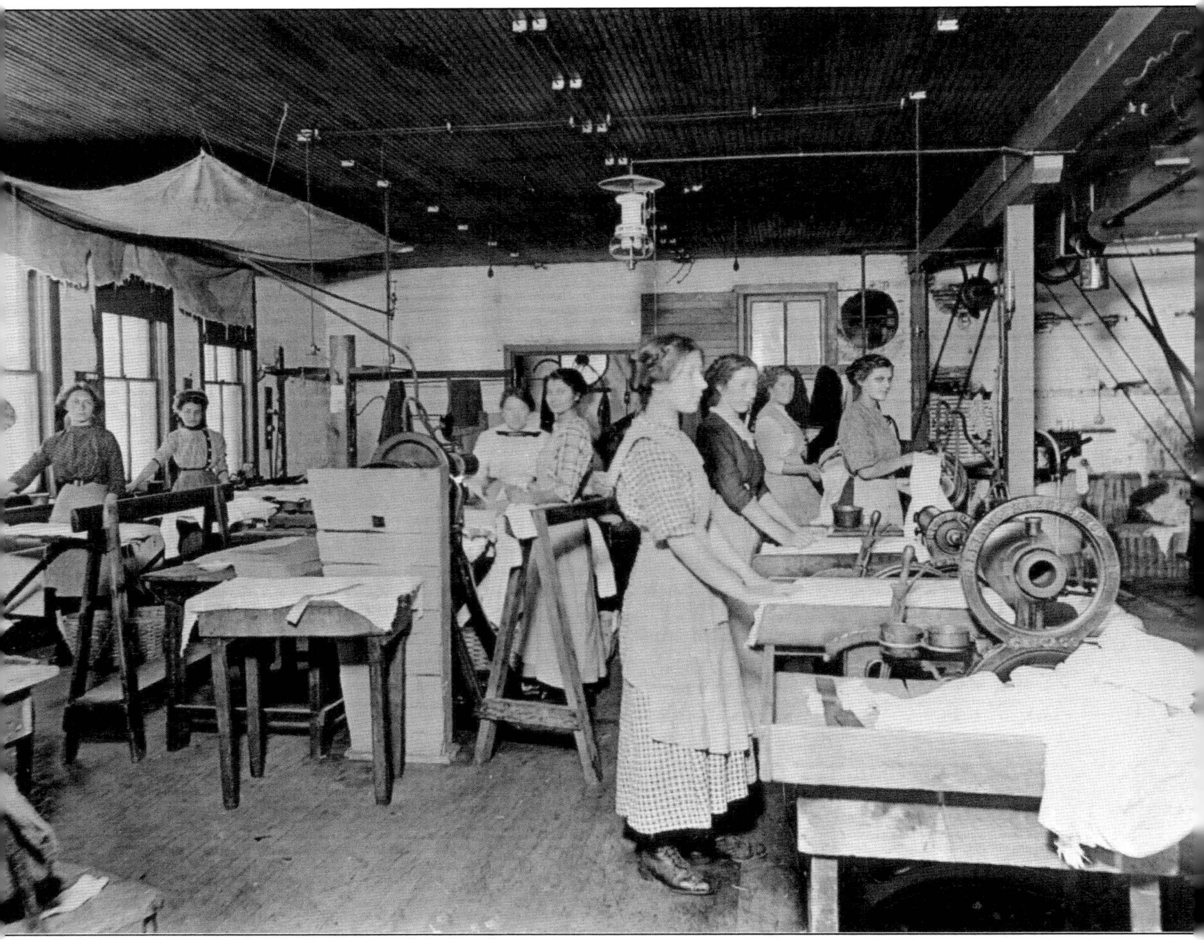

EXCELSIOR LAUNDRY. This photo was taken around the turn of the last century. The laundry was located at 1113 Georgia Avenue in Sheboygan. The employees were young women who were "working out" during their years between schooling and marriage. While laundry work remained essentially unchanged until the middle of the nineteenth century, the simultaneous development of machines for washing clothes combined with an emerging Victorian ethic which emphasized cleanliness brought about revolutionary changes in the way washing was done. Entrepreneurs and capitalists opened large commercial laundry facilities that resembled factories in their structure and organization of labor.

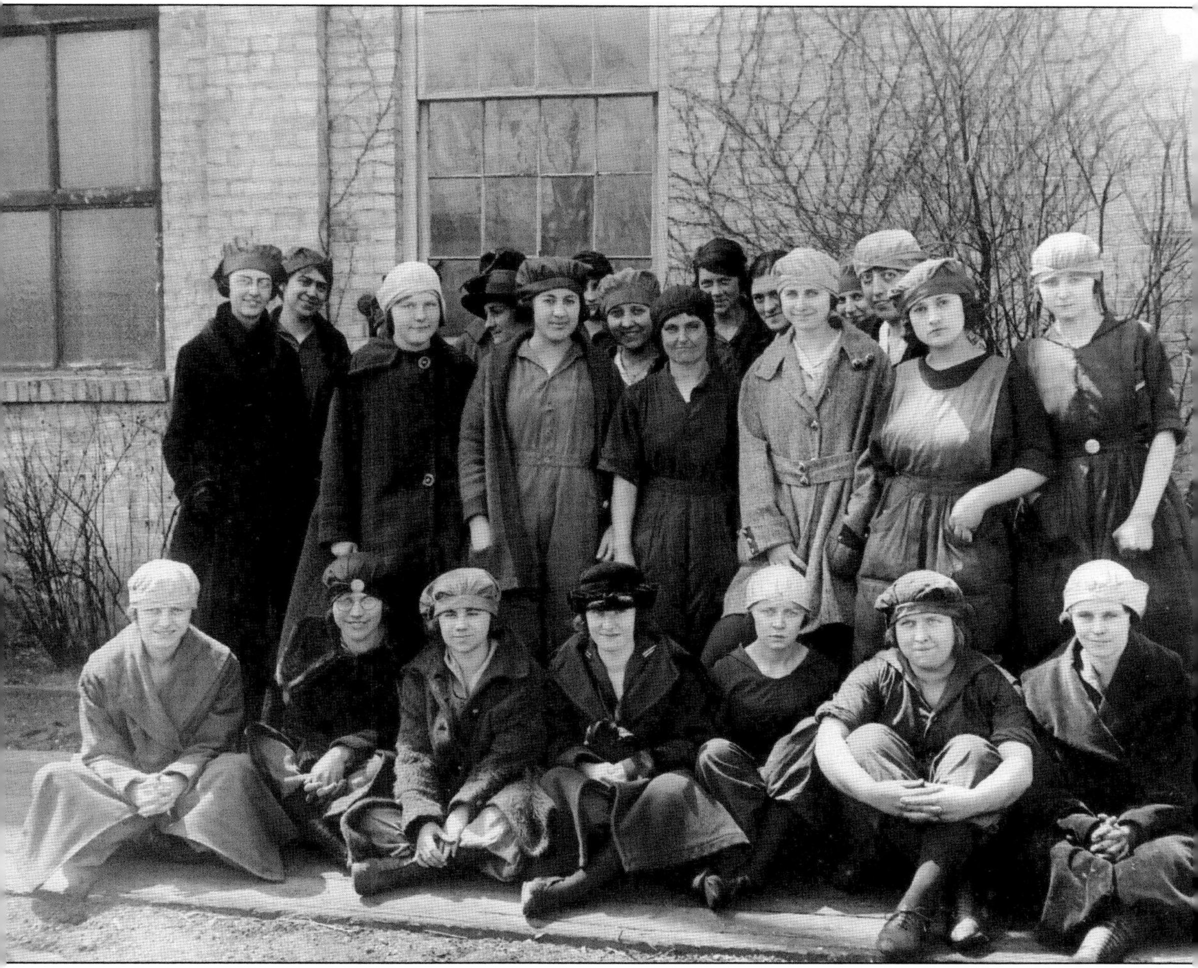

FALLS MOTOR COMPANY. One of the largest employers in Sheboygan County, during its existence, was the Falls Motor Corporation. During its peak production over 700 workers were employed. The streetcar tracks were laid to pass the plant to transport the men to work. In the spring of 1916, the firm incorporated as Falls Motor Corporation. It was originally the Falls Machine Company. The woodworking machinery line was sold at this time. The Falls Motor Corp. built only a limited number of cars itself, but it produced engines by the thousands, which powered Elgin, Velie, Apperson, Maibohn, and Dort automobiles. During WWI automobile engine production was nil. During the spring and early summer of 1924, most of the existing automobile manufacturers, outside of Ford, GM, Chrysler, Hudson, Studebaker, Nash, and Auburn went out of business, causing Falls Motors to go into bankruptcy. The factory was located in the manufacturing plant that is now the home of Kohler General. Pictured here in the 1920s is part of the female workforce.

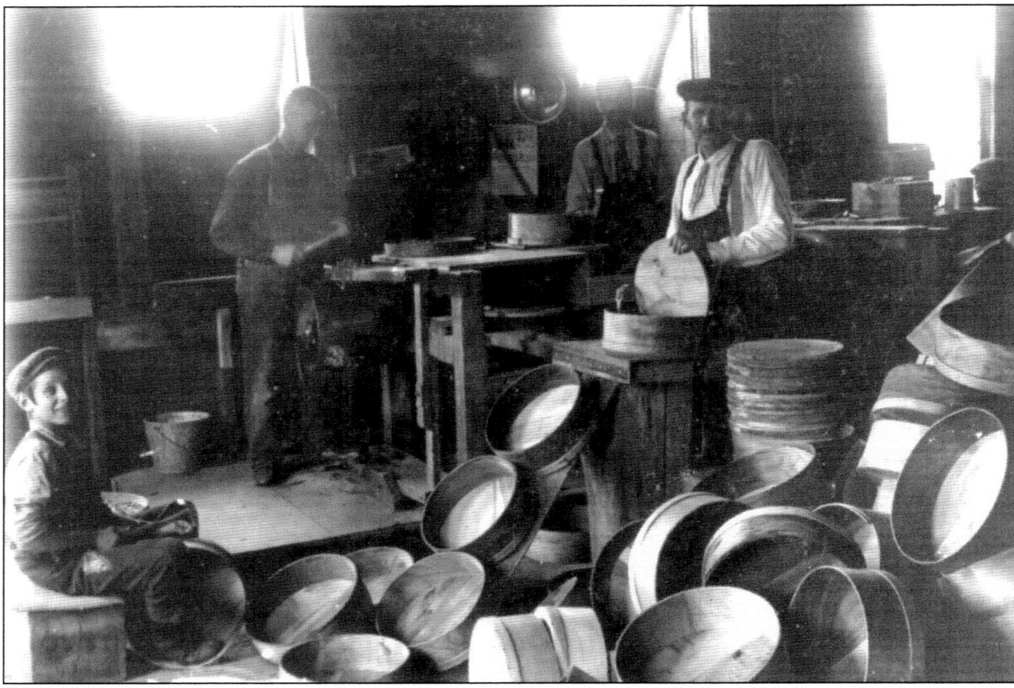

MILLERSVILLE BOX COMPANY. Shown here is an interior view of the Millersville Box Company. This large pile of cheese boxes was produced to store and ship cheese from local cheese factories.

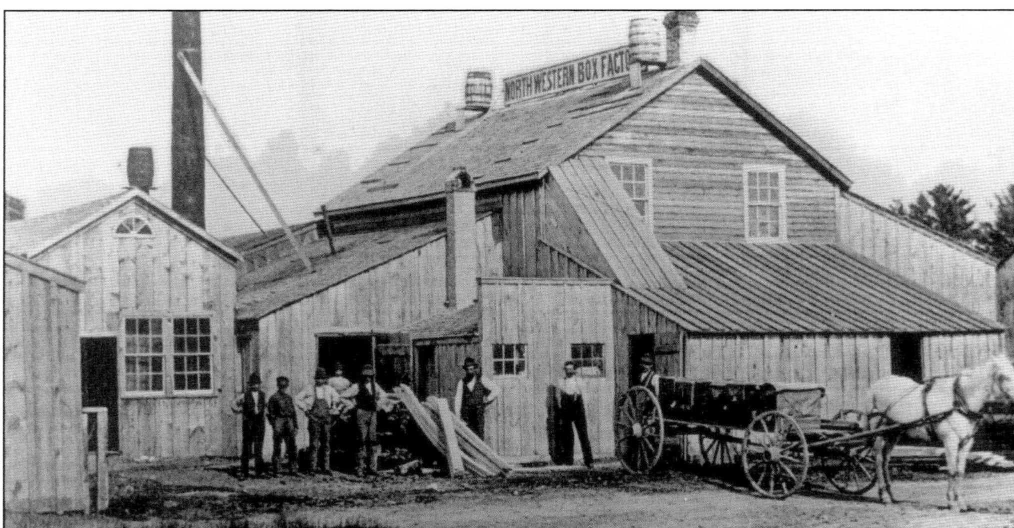

NORTHWESTERN BOX FACTORY. This is a picture of the old Northwestern Box factory before it was destroyed by fire in 1880. The photo was taken in 1876 and appeared in one of the Sheboygan papers. At that time, the Kohler Foundry was located on the site of the present Turner Hall. Kohler as a village did not yet exist. The box factory was situated on the alley back of the Kohler Company in Sheboygan. The plant employed about 20 men in the planing mill and cigar box factory. Note the water barrels on the roof for fire prevention. It seems apparent that they didn't work.

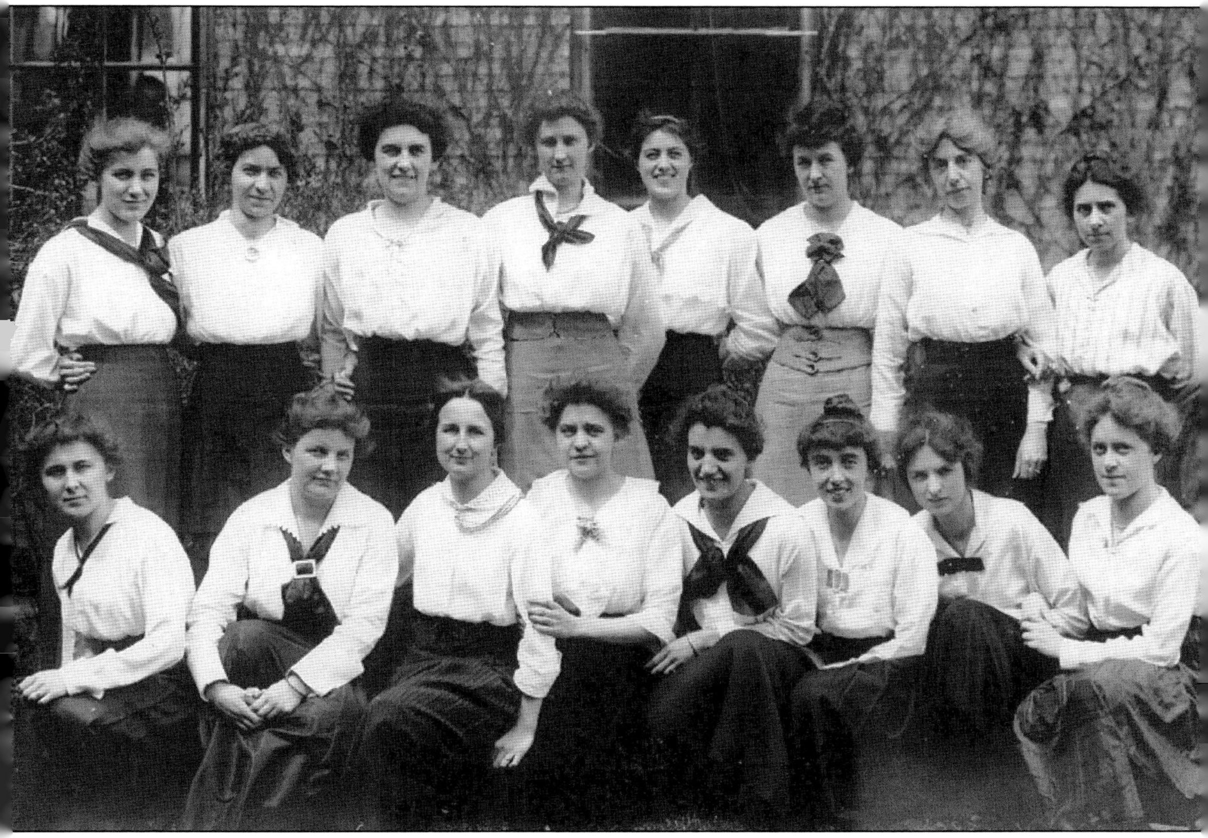

NORTHERN FURNITURE COMPANY WORKERS. On November 28, 1904, the Mattoon Manufacturing Company changed its name to Northern Furniture. Between 1919 and 1926 the company rebuilt the entire factory on Commerce Street, just south of the Sheboygan River in Sheboygan. Pictured here in 1916 is a portion of the female workforce. In 1942, the name of the company was changed to R-Way Furniture Company. Northern was the pioneer of furniture showrooms throughout the United States. The company manufactured bedrooms and dining room suites, which were sold through dealers only.

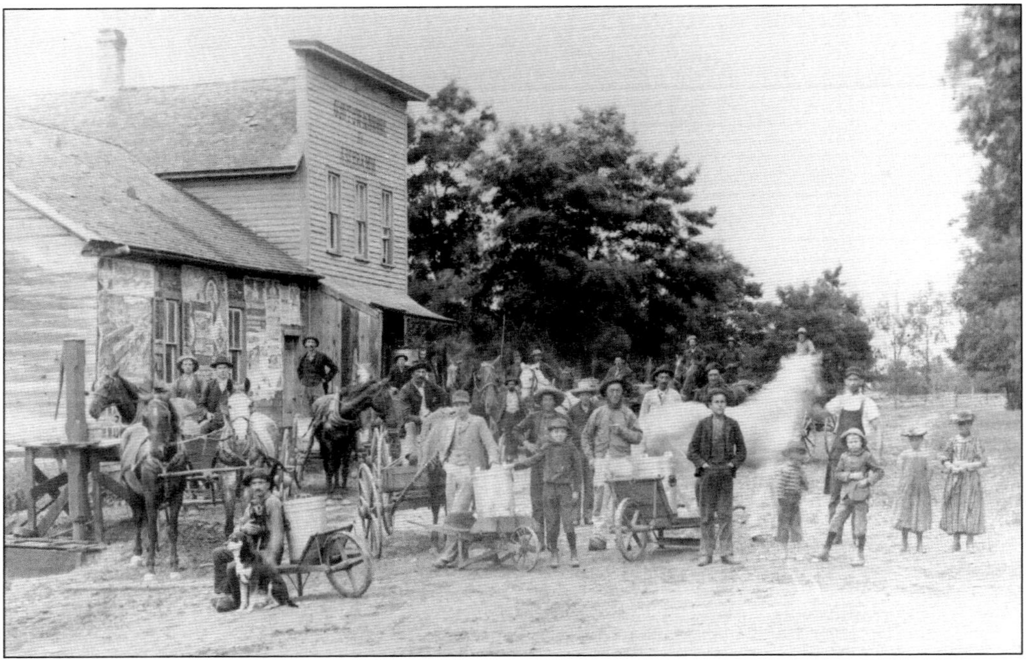

OURTOWN CHEESE FACTORY. The daily gathering of farmers was a pleasant opportunity to exchange views on crops and weather, or just catch up on local gossip. This photo was taken in 1892 when Fred Boldt was the cheesemaker. Posters on the wall at the left advertise the Ringling Brothers circus. In those days, if a farmer had more than one can of milk, he would probably transport it to the factory in a wagon pulled by a team of horses, but it was just as likely that the farmer would use a wheelbarrow, particularly if he had only one can.

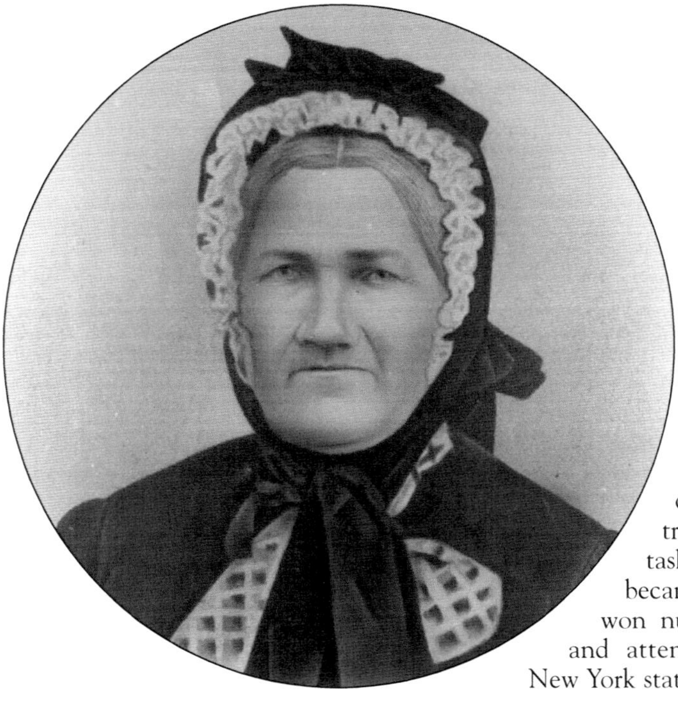

KATHERINE FELDMANN. Katherine Feldmann was Sheboygan County's first female cheesemaker. She learned the trade from her son, when the daily tasks of farming and cheesemaking became too much for one man. She won numerous cheesemaking awards, and attended cheesemaker's school in New York state.

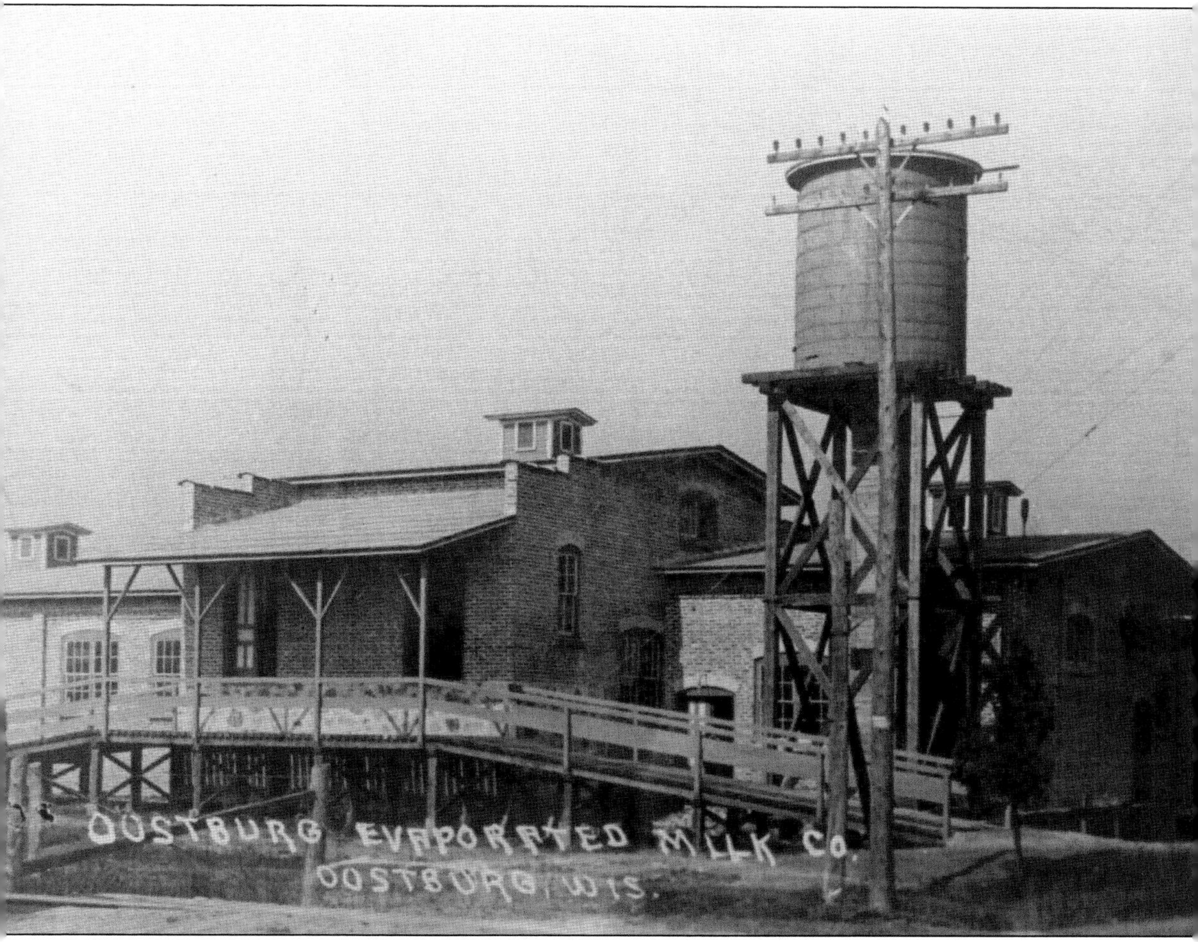

OOSTBURG EVAPORATED MILK PLANT. Sheboygan County is a place defined by its dairy heritage. It has had dozens of cheese factories, creameries, whey plants and dairies. It has had hundreds, even thousands of dairy farms. But Oostburg has the distinction of having the only evaporated milk plant in the county. Evaporated milk is fresh homogenized milk with 60% of its water removed by evaporation. It contains 7.9% milk fat. It is used extensively in baking. This building in Oostburg no longer exists.

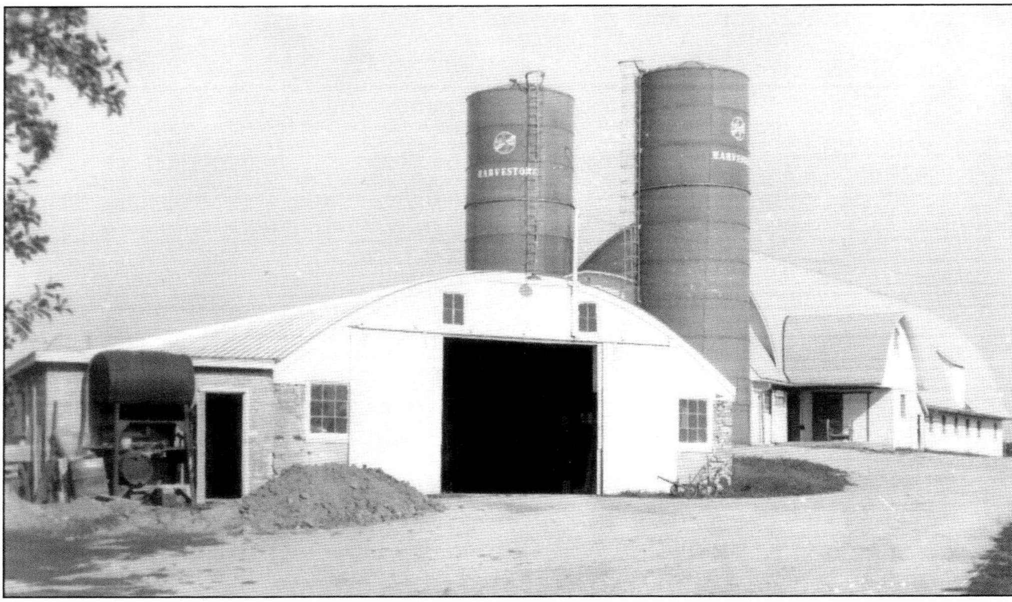

MILEY DAIRY. The Miley dairy was in business in Sheboygan Falls for 39 years. Operated by owners Alfred and Marjorie Miley, the milk from the dairy's "Golden Guernsey" herd was a staple for the children of Sheboygan Falls and Kohler. The Miley Farm was also a dairy bottling facility. It continued in business until Alfred's death in 1964. The farm was located on Upper Falls Road at the east end of Sheboygan Falls.

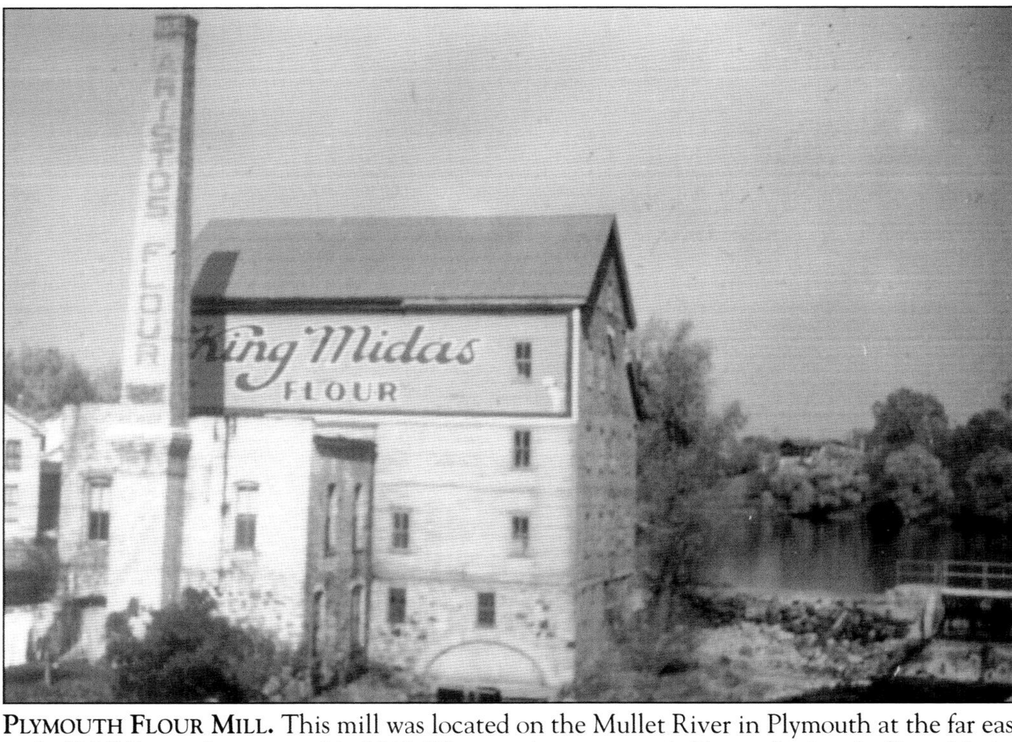

PLYMOUTH FLOUR MILL. This mill was located on the Mullet River in Plymouth at the far east end of Mill Street. It was razed in 1966. The area is now occupied by professional offices. Notice the King Midas and Aristos Flour advertisements on the side of the building.

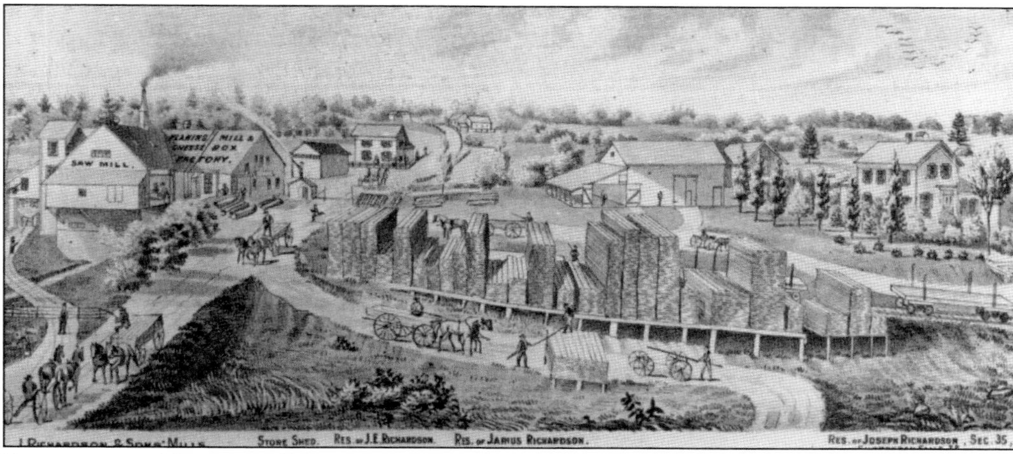

RICHARDSON MILL AND RESIDENCES. In 1848, Joseph Richardson founded the J. Richardson Sawmill. When Joe and Carrie Richardson and their family arrived in the village of Rochester (now Sheboygan Falls) in 1845, they purchased 200 acres with the intention of farming. Settling next to the Mullet River, Joe decided to put up a mill instead. The rest is history. This view of the Richardson Mill and homes is found in the 1875 Sheboygan County Plat Book.

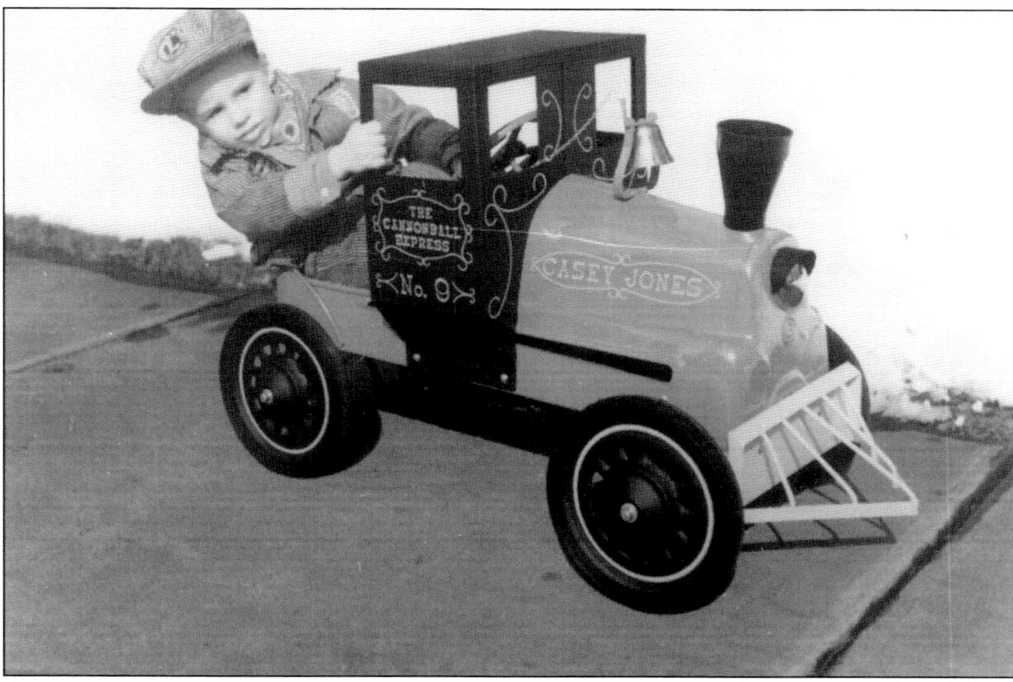

CANNONBALL EXPRESS. Dan Garton is trying out his Cannonball Express toy train made by his family's toy company. The name Garton was for many years synonymous with the name Santa Claus. The hottest pedal car ever produced was Garton's 1950s Kidillac. The company was sold in 1973, and shortly thereafter ceased production. The pedal cars have since become nostalgic collector's items.

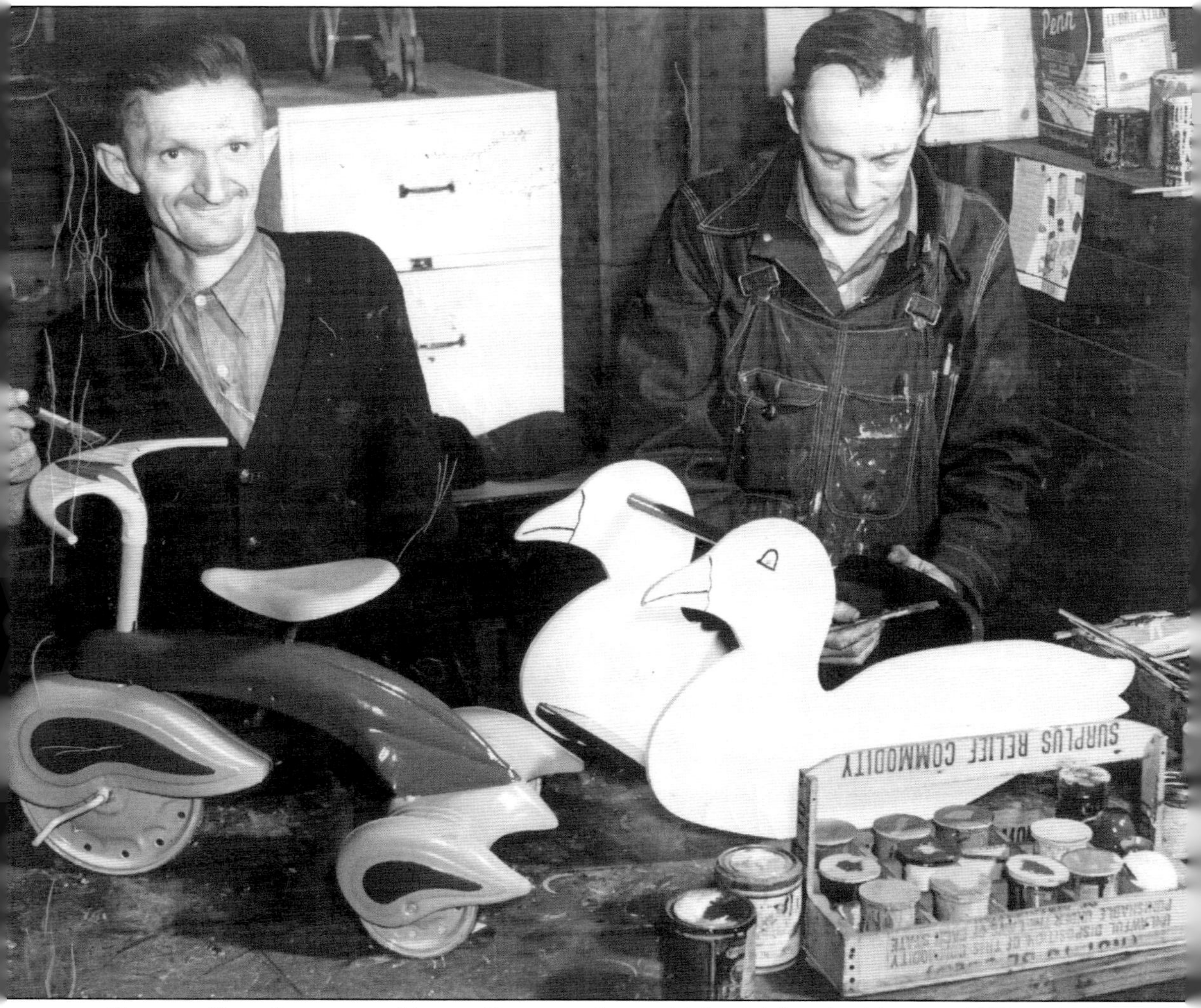

GARTON TOY PAINTERS. Garton Toy started in a 30 by 50 foot building in 1879 with the manufacture of washboards and fish boxes. While working in Sheboygan lumber mills and woodworking plants after his emigration from Canada, Eusebius B. Garton toyed with the idea of developing a motion conveyance having play value for children. He later attached four wooden wheels to a cigar box and proceeded to enter the toy wagon business. Garton Toy expanded to a large riverside plant with branch offices in Seattle, New York, Chicago, Dallas, and San Francisco. The company produced the toys of every child's dreams—coaster wagons, sleds, pedal cars, and tractors. Here we see Garton employees William Mohr and John Hintzleman painting toys in 1941.

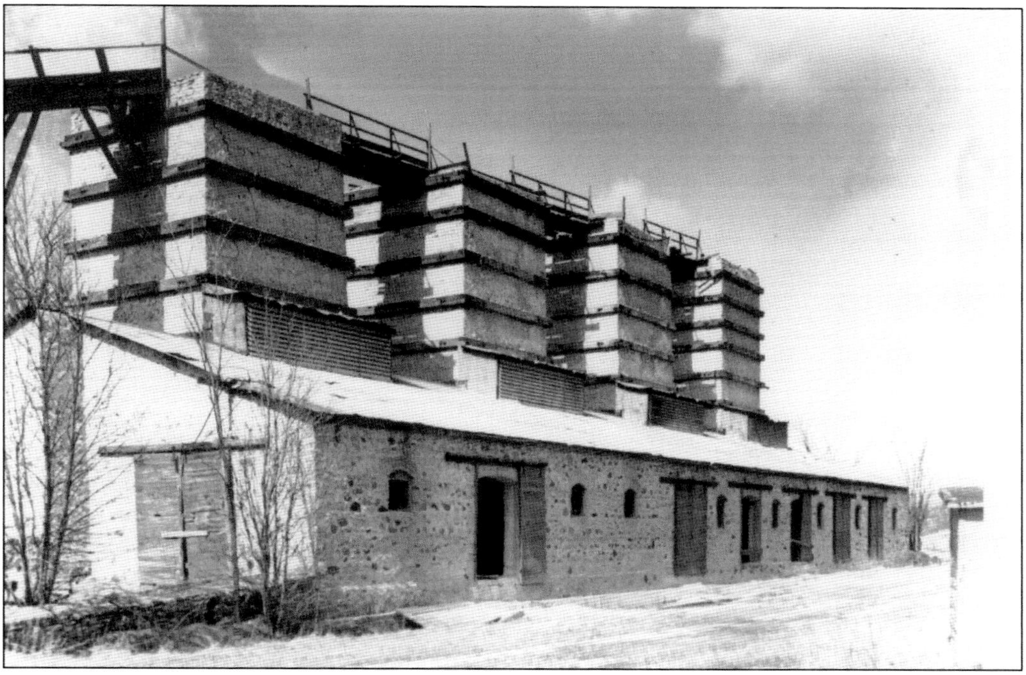

Rhine Mills Lime Kilns. This photo was taken in the late 1930s. The kilns were erected during WWI to manufacture lime. They were kept in operation until 1926. They stand at the east edge of the Sheboygan Marsh.

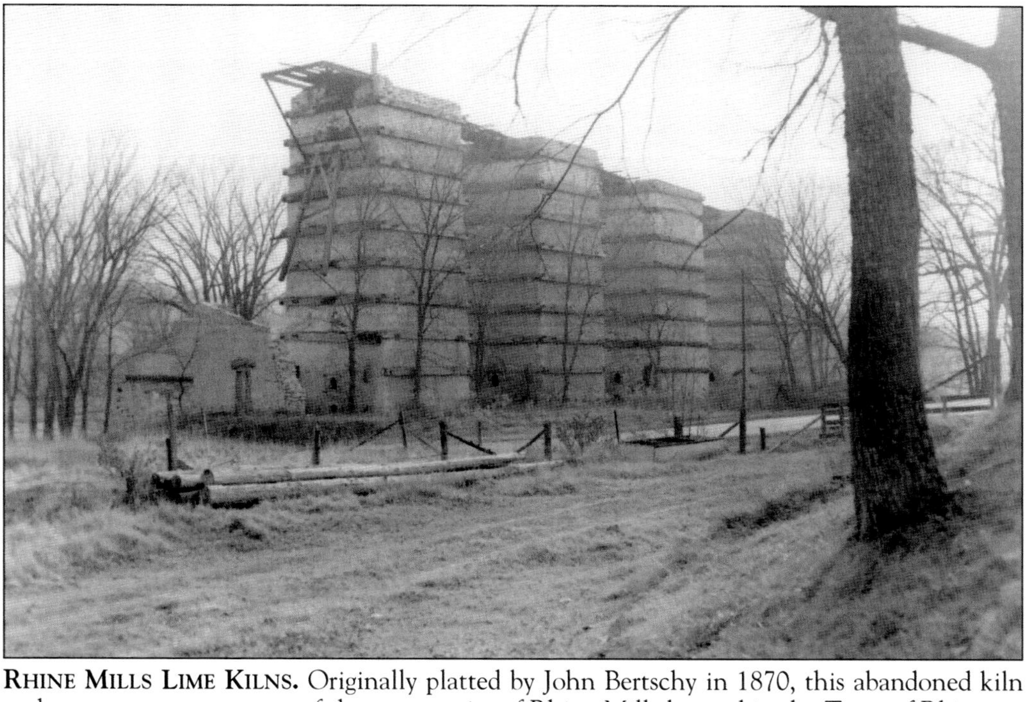

Rhine Mills Lime Kilns. Originally platted by John Bertschy in 1870, this abandoned kiln and quarry was once a part of the community of Rhine Mills located in the Town of Rhine on County Road MM. This photo was taken in November of 1956. Notice the extent to which the wooden structures at the top of the kilns has deteriorated since the previous photo.

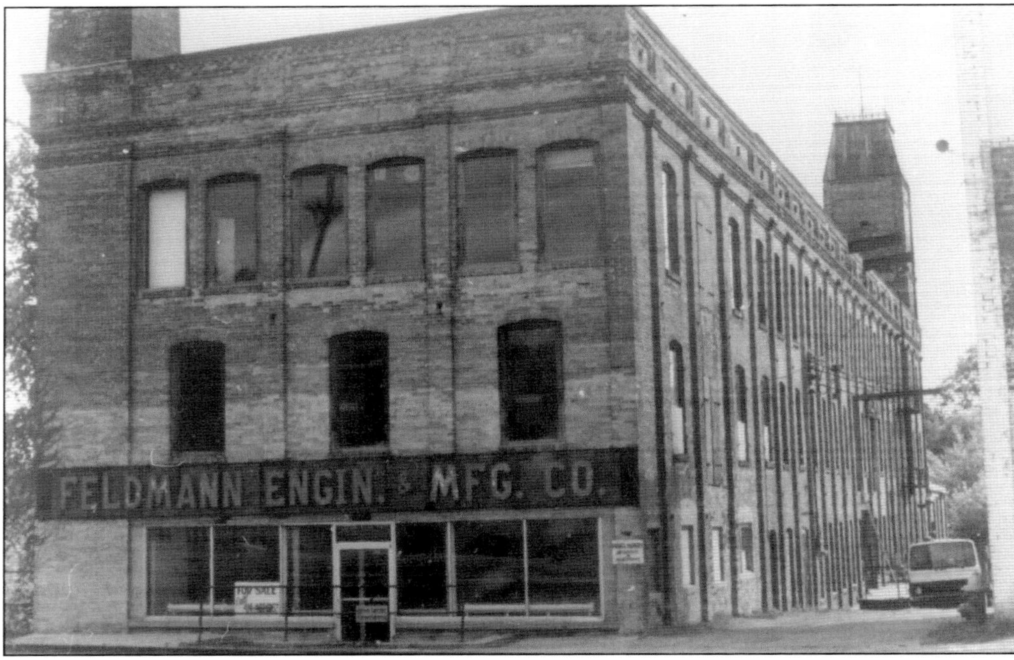

THE FELDMANN PROJECT. Originally the Brickner Woolen Mills, this building was also the home of Feldmann Manufacturing, the maker of the Jiffy Ice Drill, among other things. After Feldmann Manufacturing moved north into the Sheboygan Falls industrial park on Forest Avenue, this facility sat vacant. In 1991, the Feldmanns graciously donated the structure to the city to be rehabbed into affordable housing. The building is now the outstanding Brickner Woolen Mills' Apartments, located adjacent to the Sheboygan River at Monroe Street.

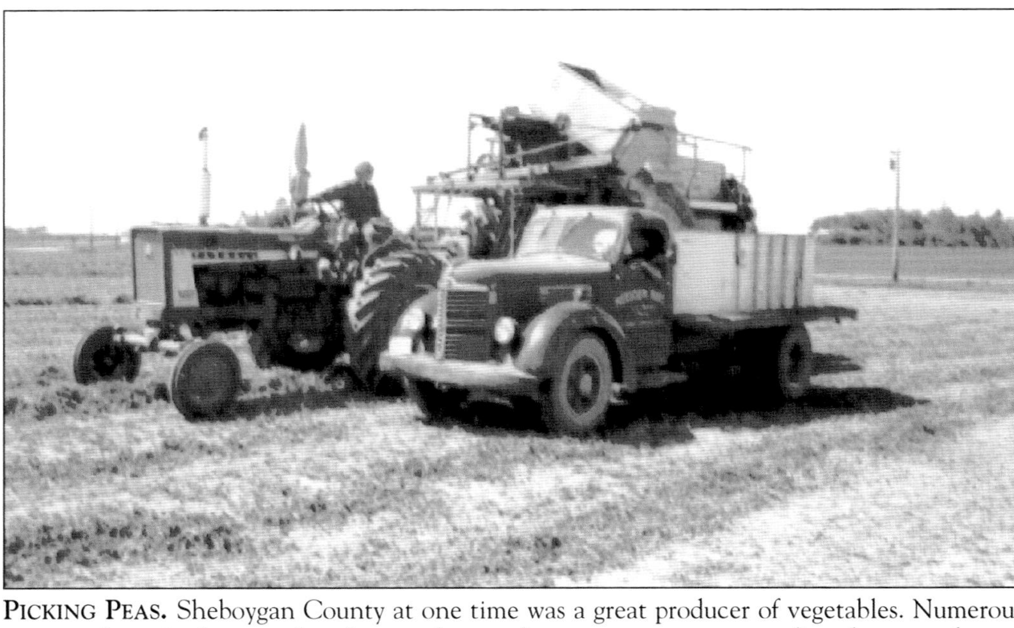

PICKING PEAS. Sheboygan County at one time was a great producer of vegetables. Numerous canning factories harvested and canned green beans, carrots, potatoes, lima beans and peas. This pea viner is harvesting a crop of peas. Krier, Stokely, and Larson were three of the largest canning operations.

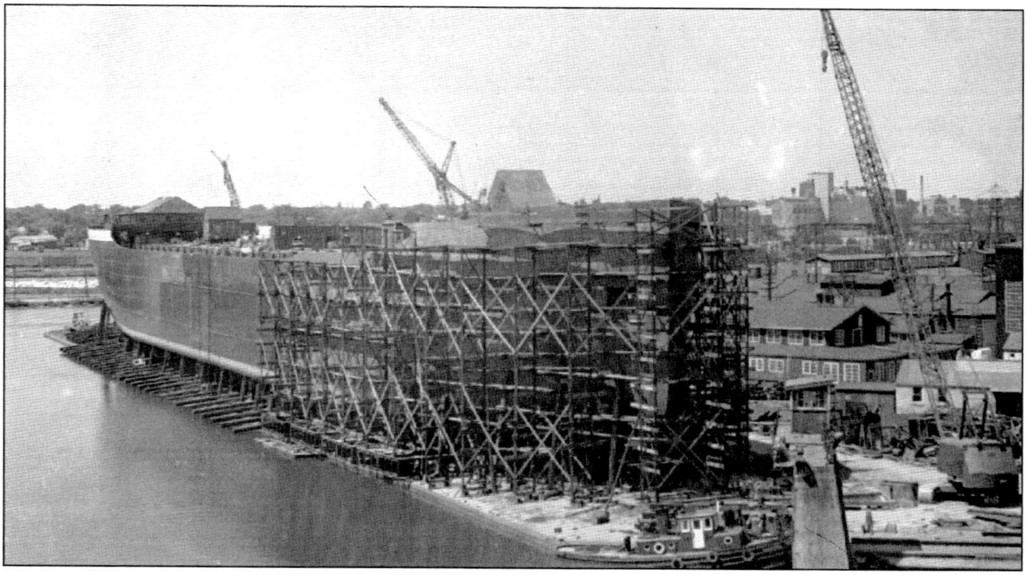

SHIPBUILDING. Shipbuilding started in Sheboygan soon after the settlement of the county. The center of the industry was the Sheboygan River east of Eighth Street into the harbor and west of Eighth Street to Fourteenth Street. It was a steady source of year-round employment between 1845-1896. The largest employer was Riebolt and Wolters, which employed 175 men. The company built steamers, steam barges, tugs, dredges, and dump scows. This company built the largest freighter that emerged from Sheboygan. It was called the "Helena" and was launched in 1887.

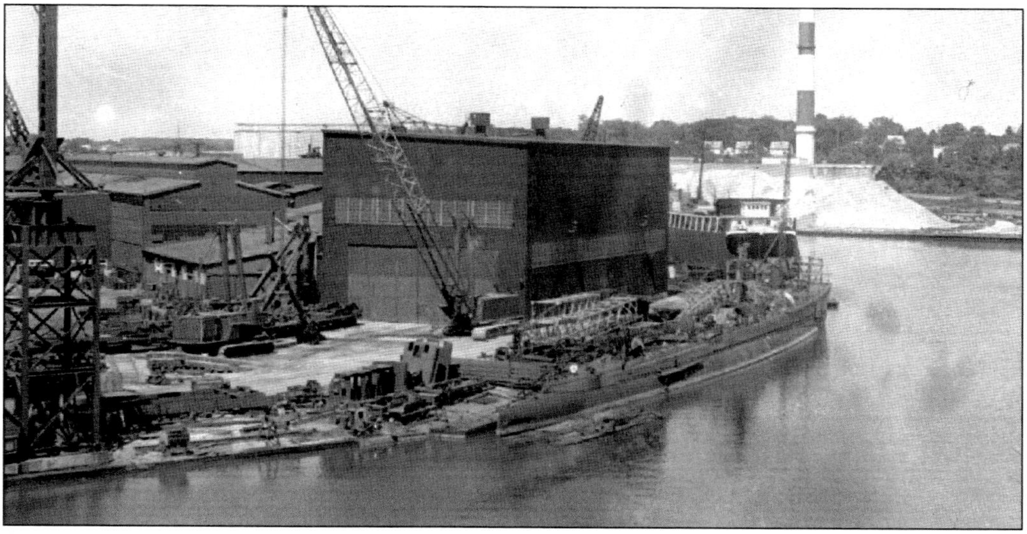

SHIPPING. Many great vessels passed through the harbor either to stay or on their way to Chicago. In 1868, more than one thousand vessels that carried passengers laid over. When they departed, they took along wood products, eggs, butter, cheese, flour, peas, beer, wool, fish, wagon parts, tanned hides, and other goods that were produced in Sheboygan County. In 1867, Sheboygan sent 490,079 bushels of wheat to market. Sheboygan's port was an important port along the routes for the exchange of people and materials. Captain A.E. Goodrich purchased land in 1905 and built a huge warehouse on Kirkland Dock, near the south pier. Goodrich founded the Goodrich Transit Company in 1856 out of Chicago. This stop was discontinued in 1919, but resumed again in 1923. In October of 1933, Goodrich was forced to declare bankruptcy and his docks were sold.

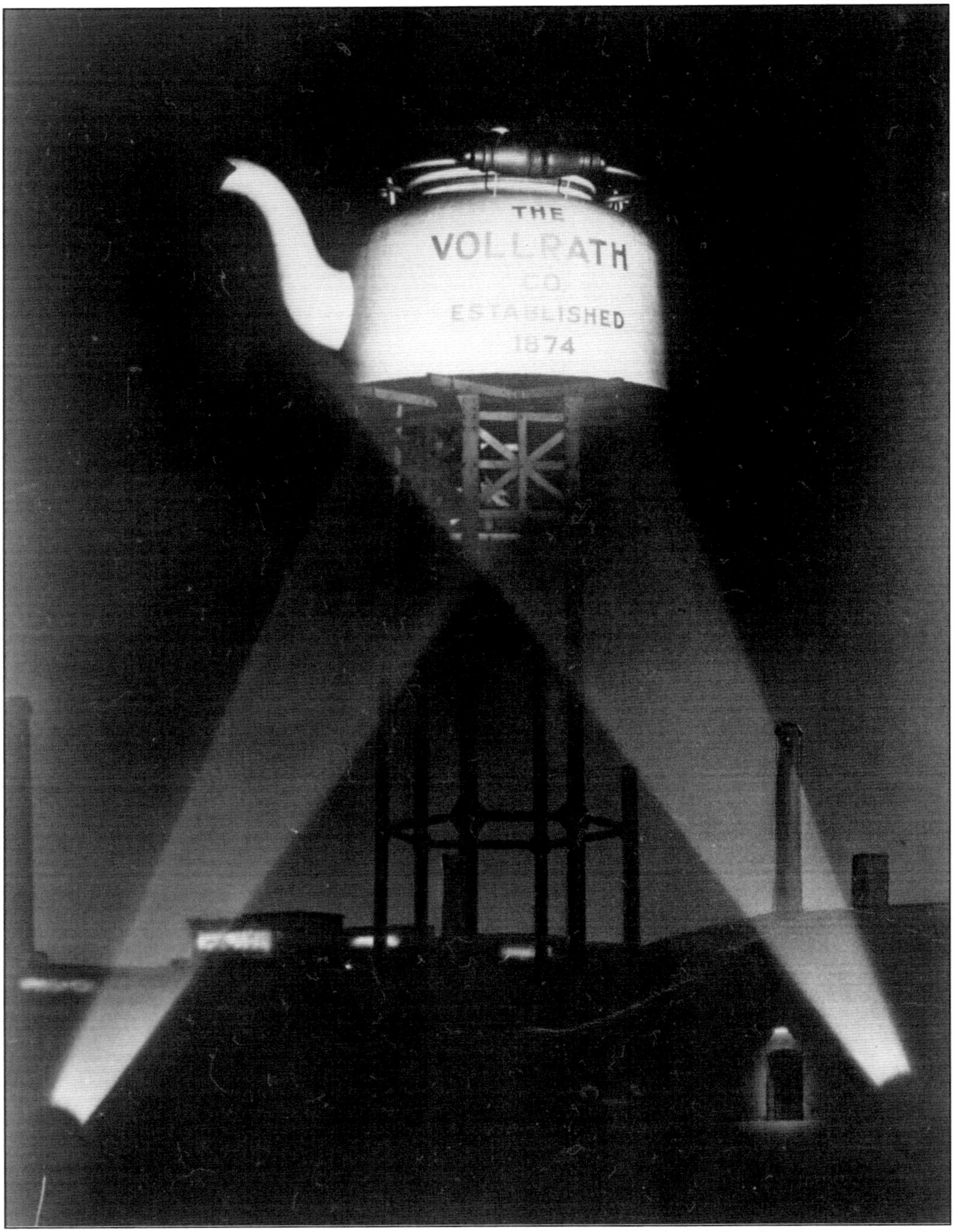

VOLLRATH TEA KETTLE. This large tea kettle was built as part of the Vollrath Company display at the St. Louis World's Fair in 1904. It was later installed at the Vollrath plant at Eighteenth and Erie Avenue in Sheboygan (shown here in 1912). Henry William, a pattern maker for the Falls Machine Company of Sheboygan Falls, constructed the kettle, made of wood, to correct scale of the company's regular tea kettles. It was then coated to resemble the special blue ware for which the Vollrath Company was famous. It held approximately 2,250 gallons of water. For years it was a unique and famous landmark of Sheboygan. The kettle stood until the beginning of WWII, but no one seems to remember its fate.

Five

EARLY TRANSPORTATION

Transportation has changed more than nearly anything else since the formation of Sheboygan County in 1835. Men traveled by foot and canoe, then by ship and locomotive, streetcar, and bicycle. Finally, the automobile and airplanes entered the lives of Sheboygan County citizens, and the world became so much smaller. Following are a number of interesting examples of Sheboygan County's transportation growth.

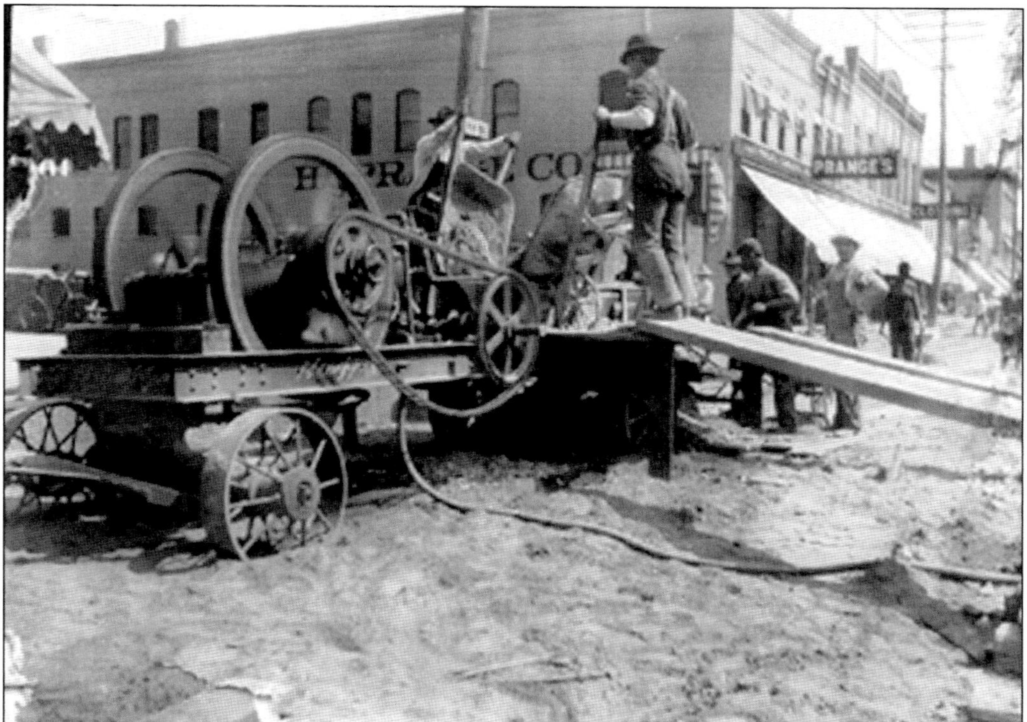

STREET PAVING. This photo shows the initial paving of Eighth Street in Sheboygan. H.C. Prange Company is in the background. Notice the materials are being hauled in wheelbarrows.

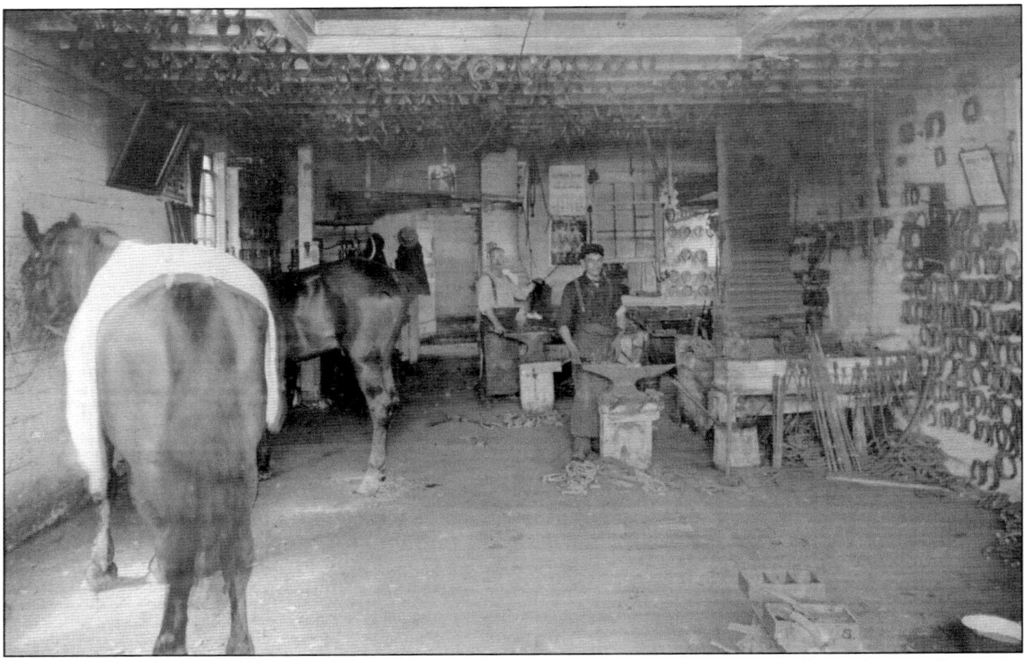

WILLIAM BEHREND BLACKSMITH SHOP. This blacksmith shop was located in Plymouth in the early 1900s at the intersection of Mill and North Streets. Note the abundance of horseshoes. Interior shots of these businesses were seldom taken due to lack of adequate lighting.

Andrew Clicquennoi

Automobile and Carriage Painting

Painting and Repairing Promptly Attended to

Refinishing of Automobiles

First-Class Work—Best Materials used—Valentine's Vanadium Varnish, Murphy's, Beckwith-Chandler's, and other high-grade varnishes.

During the winter months your car could be getting a fine new finish instead of standing idle. Call or telephone and I'll arrange to handle your job. Do it now, so you can be sure of delivery at the right time.

I Also Refinish Wagons, Carriages, etc.

SHOP	RESIDENCE
1520 North Thirteenth Street	1832 North Eighth Street

HARNESSED HORSES. The type of harness worn by these horses caused harnessmakers to spend many hours making and repairing each one. It was an early form of job security. Note the long strands covering the animals' backs. They were designed to keep flies and insects from bothering the horses.

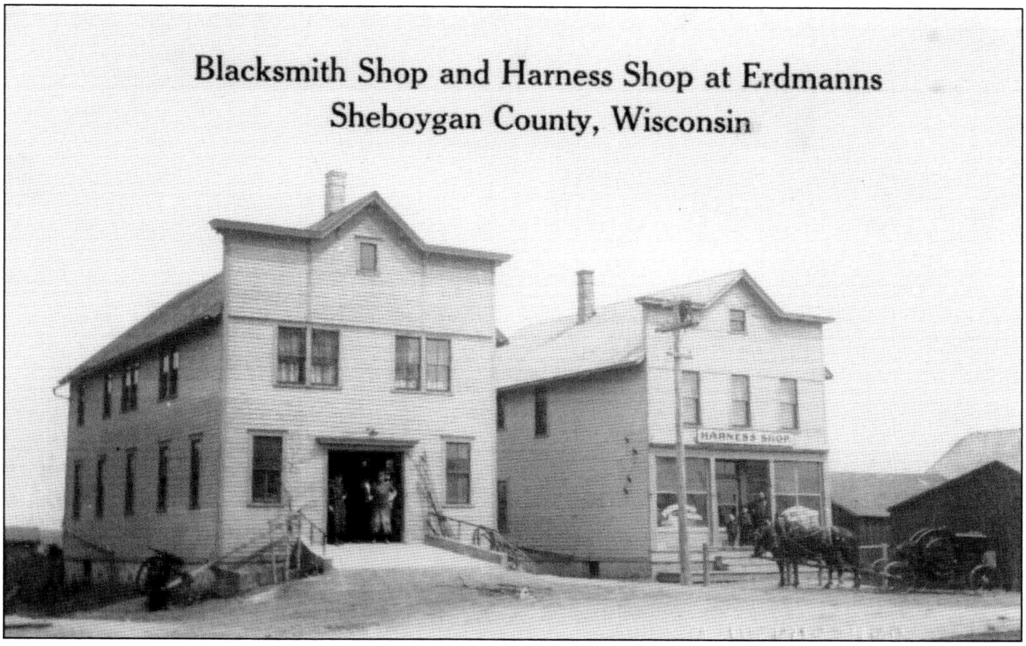

BLACKSMITH AND HARNESS SHOPS AT ERDMANN. Often these two businesses were located in close proximity to each other. They made business easier for customers since a farmer could have his horse shod at the same time he was having his harnesses fixed.

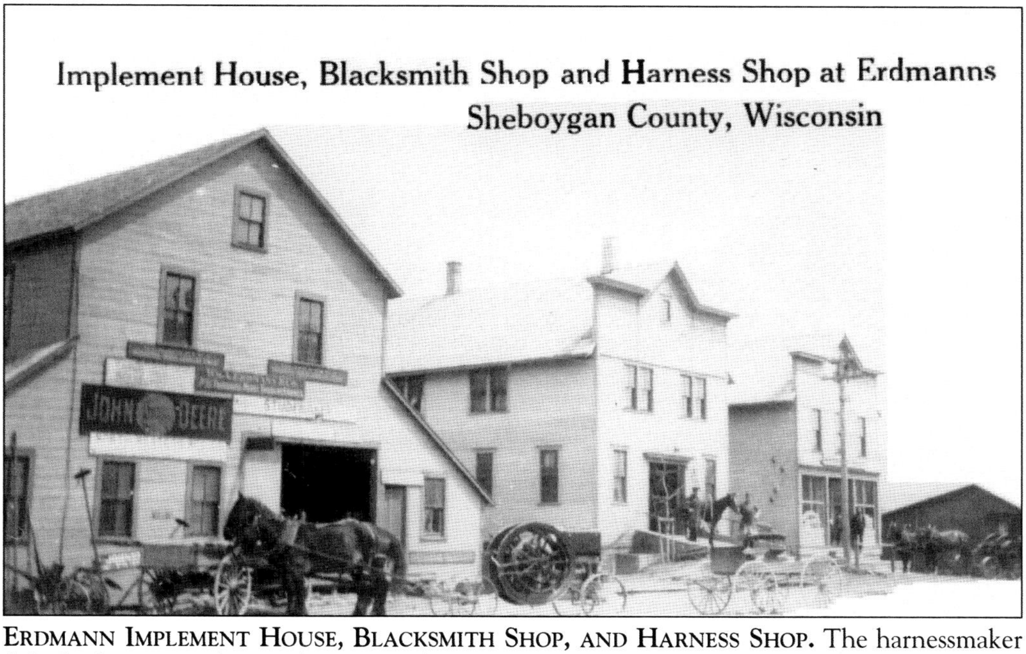

ERDMANN IMPLEMENT HOUSE, BLACKSMITH SHOP, AND HARNESS SHOP. The harnessmaker did a big business as long as farmers used work horses. When tractors began to replace the horses, both they and the harness makers began to disappear. It was the job of the harnessmaker to make the reins, check reins, traces, breeches, bellybands, and other leather parts in a harness.

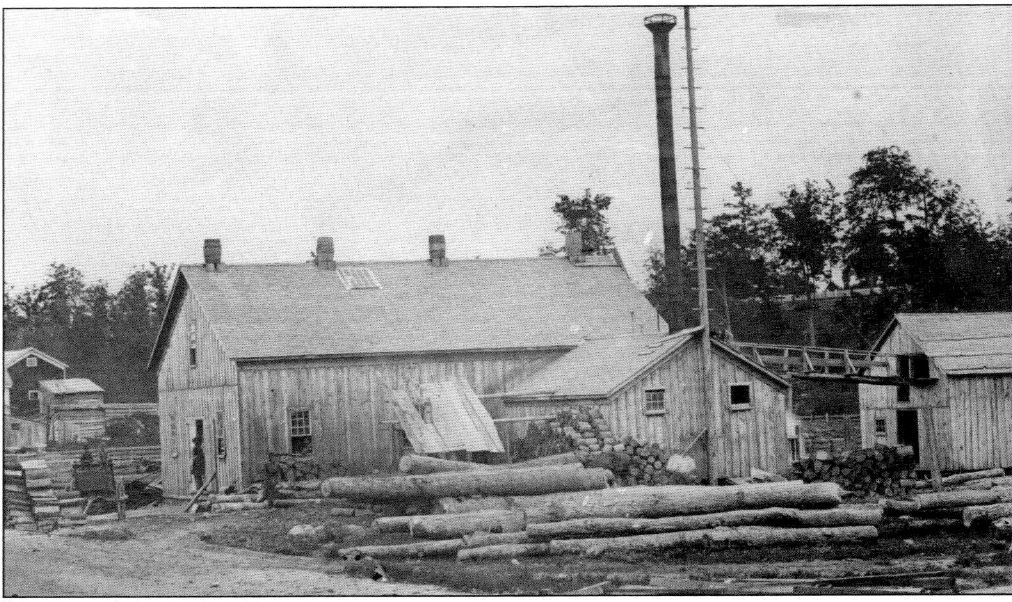

HUB AND SPOKE FACTORY. Built about 1860, this hub and spoke factory located on the corner of Mill and Stafford Streets in Plymouth provided the wheels upon which the transportation of the nation depended. Shown are the wooden logs, which would soon be transformed into wagon and carriage wheels.

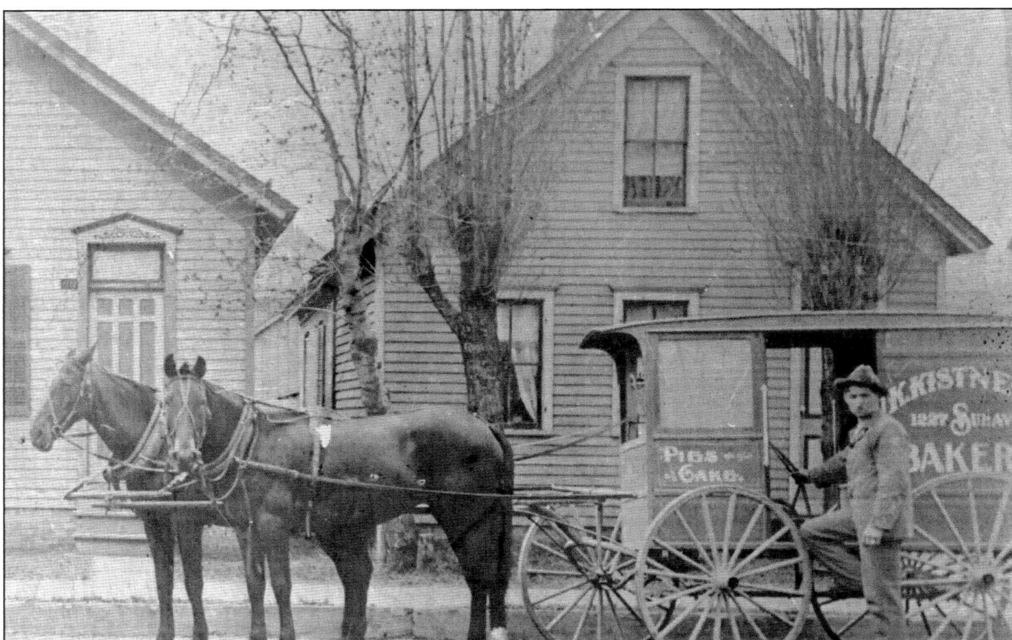

KISTNER BAKERY WAGON. The baker made his rounds early in the morning years ago, usually starting at 4 a.m. He sounded his whistle in the predawn hours to rouse out customers who wanted fresh bakery goods for breakfast. The picture above shows 16-year old Fred Muhs with one of the horse-drawn delivery wagons of the Kosmus Kistner Bakery. Muhs later established his own bakery.

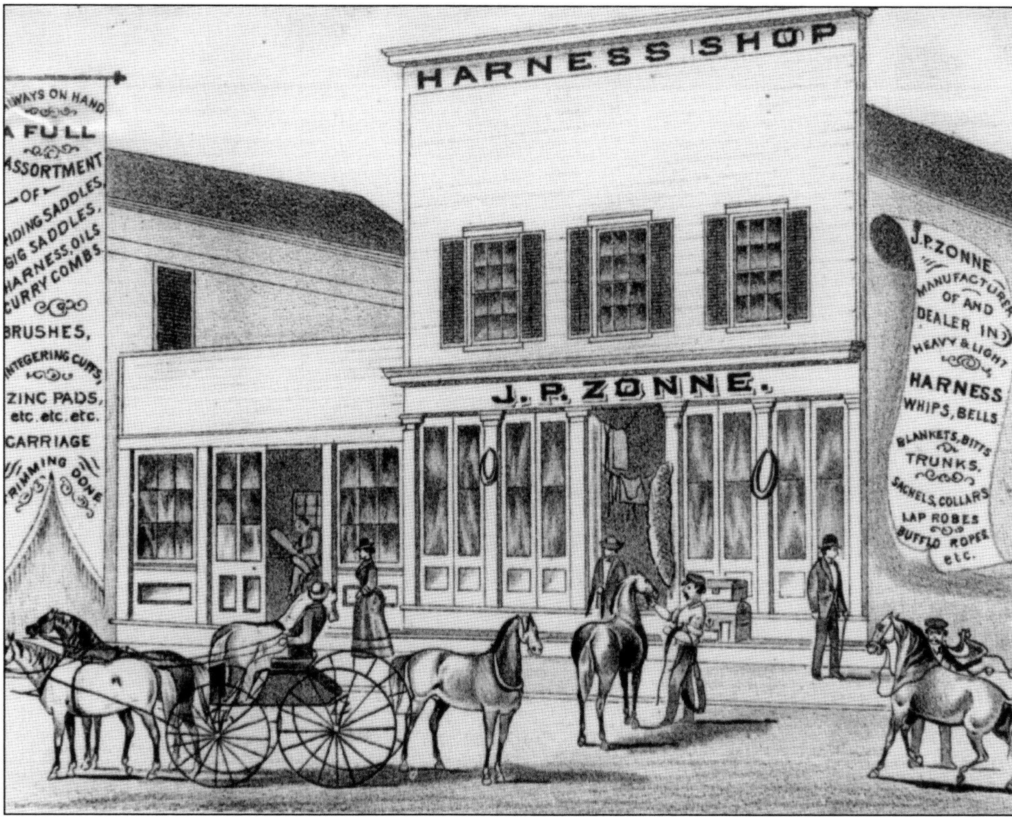

J.B. ZONNE HARNESS SHOP. This ad from the 1875 Sheboygan County Atlas extolled the virtues of J.B. Zonne's Harness Shop in Sheboygan Falls. It is noted that Zonne "sells cheaper than any other shop in the county." Items sold included whips, blankets, harnesses, zinc pads, buffalo robes, and saddles.

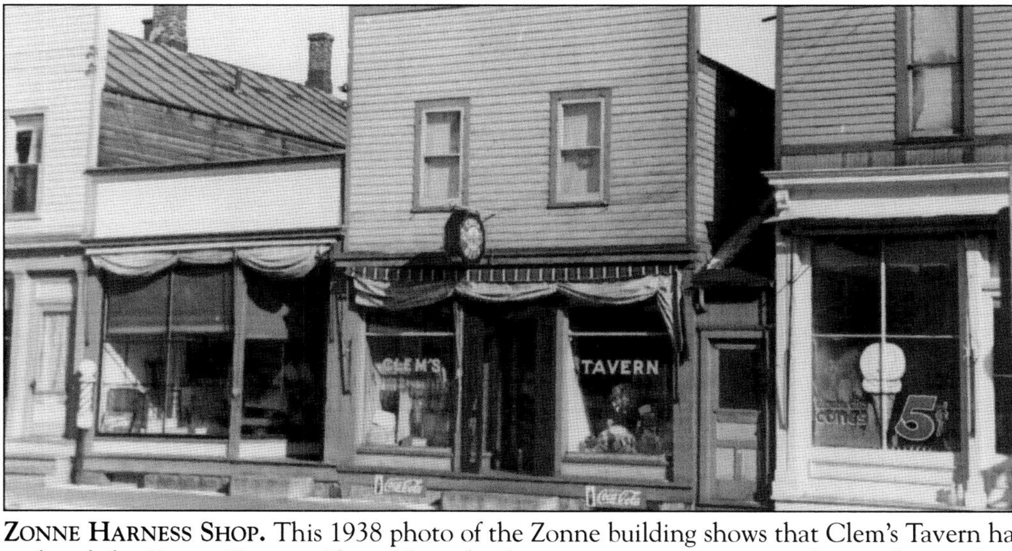

ZONNE HARNESS SHOP. This 1938 photo of the Zonne building shows that Clem's Tavern has replaced the Zonne Harness Shop. Note the five-cent ice cream cones advertised next door. Coca Cola has also made an appearance in advertising.

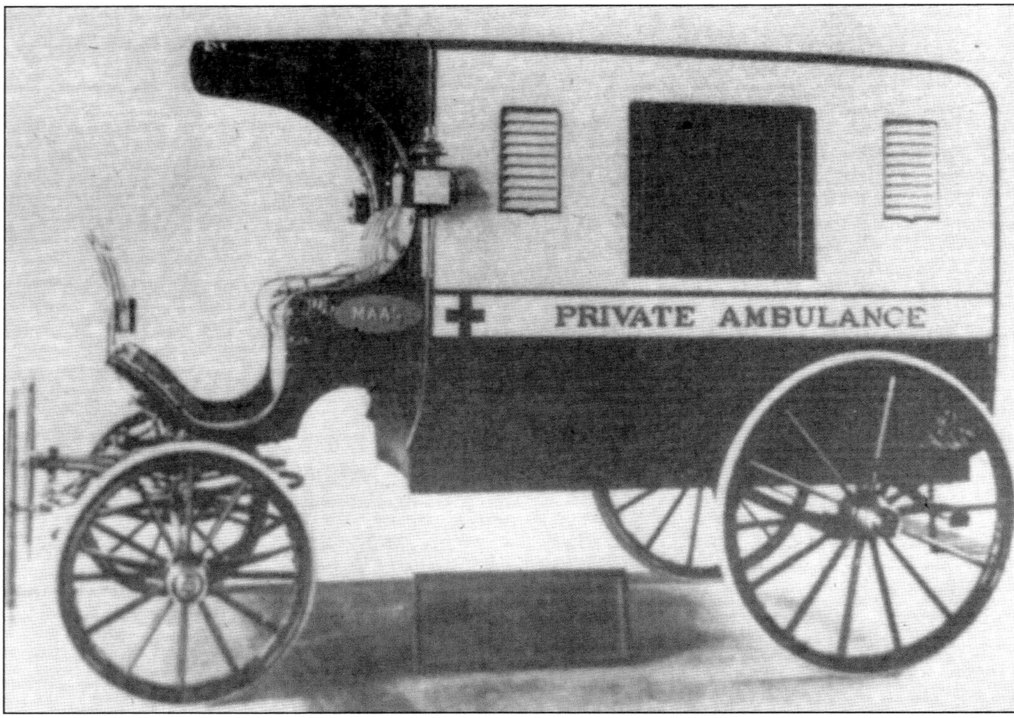

HORSE-DRAWN AMBULANCE. This private ambulance, produced by Maas, would have been the type that carried a Sheboygan County resident to the doctor or hospital.

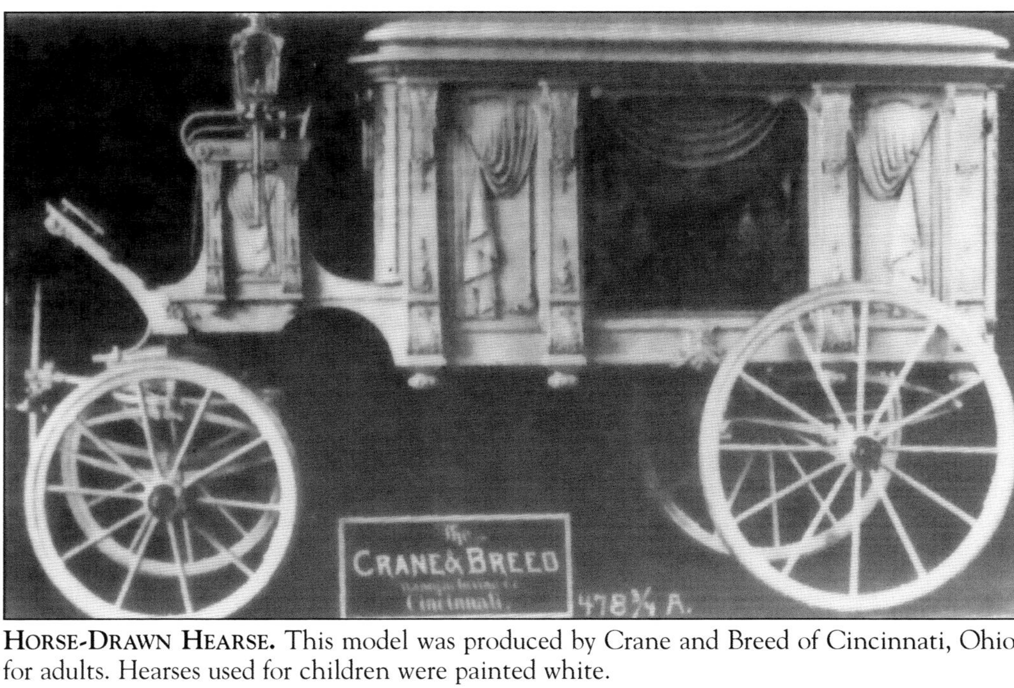

HORSE-DRAWN HEARSE. This model was produced by Crane and Breed of Cincinnati, Ohio, for adults. Hearses used for children were painted white.

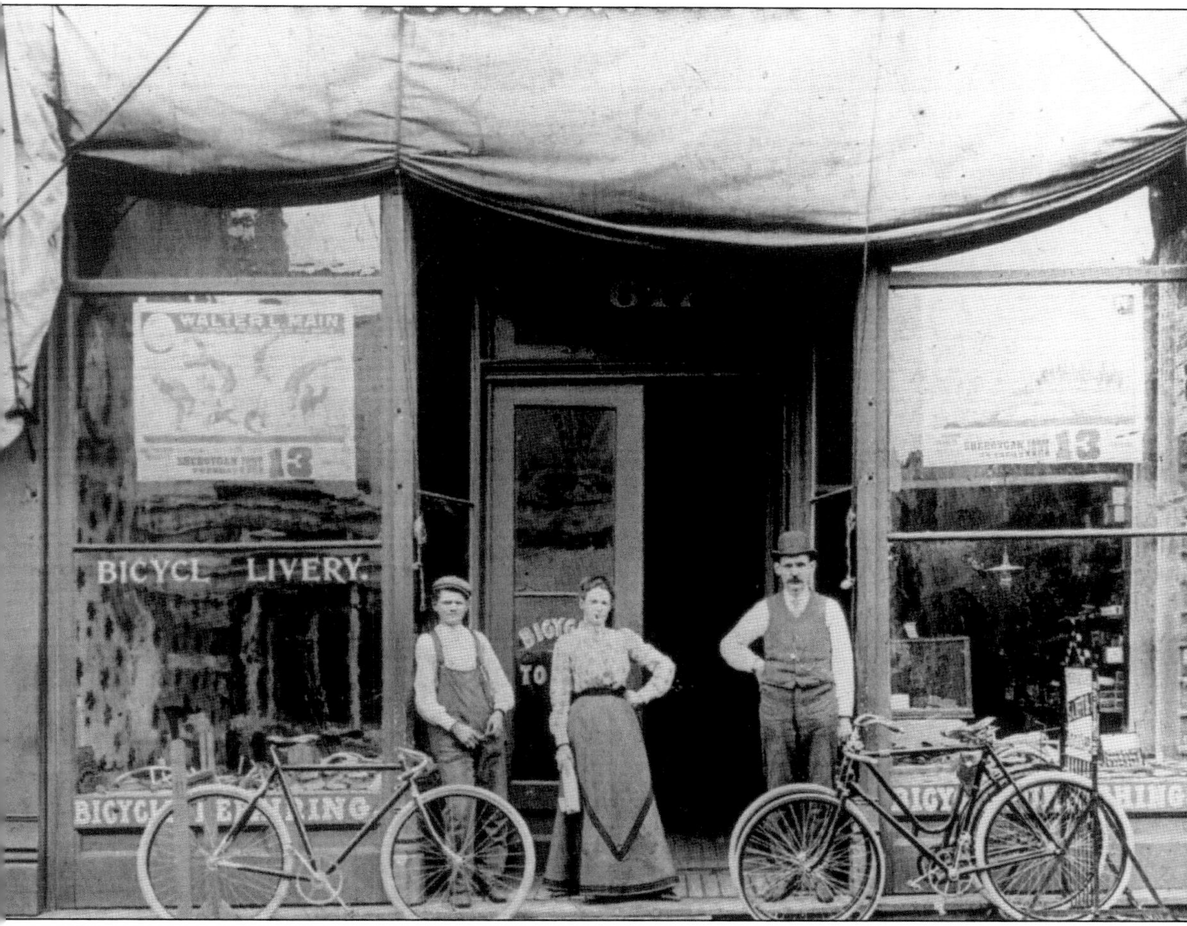

S.A. TIFFT AND COMPANY BICYCLE LIVERY. Located at 617 North Eighth Street, Tifft's is said to have been Sheboygan's first bicycle shop, established in 1898. The bicycle shown is the model named "Yellow Fellow" made by Jenkins Machine Company. Jenkins made bikes at that time. An early bicycle rider was known as a wheelman or cyclist. Occasionally, a wheelman would operate his bicycle or "wheel" at an excessive rate of speed. This would put pedestrians and other cyclists at risk. The offender was referred to as a scorcher. Speed limits of from five to ten miles per hour had to be established, and scorchers who violated them would either be fined or jailed. Bicycling was a leading form of entertainment for both men and women during the latter part of the nineteenth century. The ladies, due to modesty, wore special costumes—long, full skirts, such as the one in this picture, so that their limbs would be concealed from view.

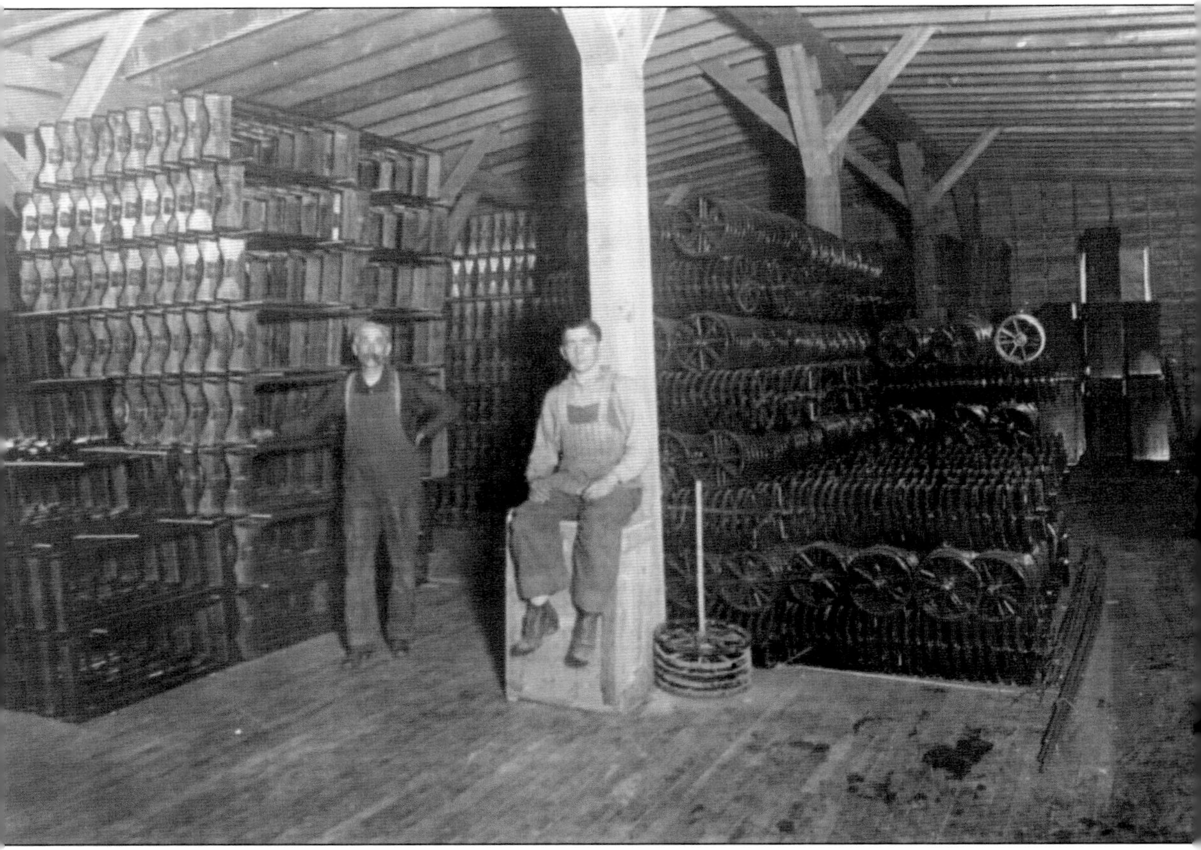

White Wagon Works Interior Shot. The White Wagon Works, organized by Arthur White, was founded on patents granted to him in 1900. White coaster wagon patents were different because previously boys' wagons had solid pulling bars. White made it possible to tilt the handle, thereby allowing a youth to sit or kneel in the wagon and still be able to steer. This company was located in the building on Broadway in Sheboygan Falls that later became Bemis Manufacturing. It was razed in 1999 and is now the site of Settler's Park.

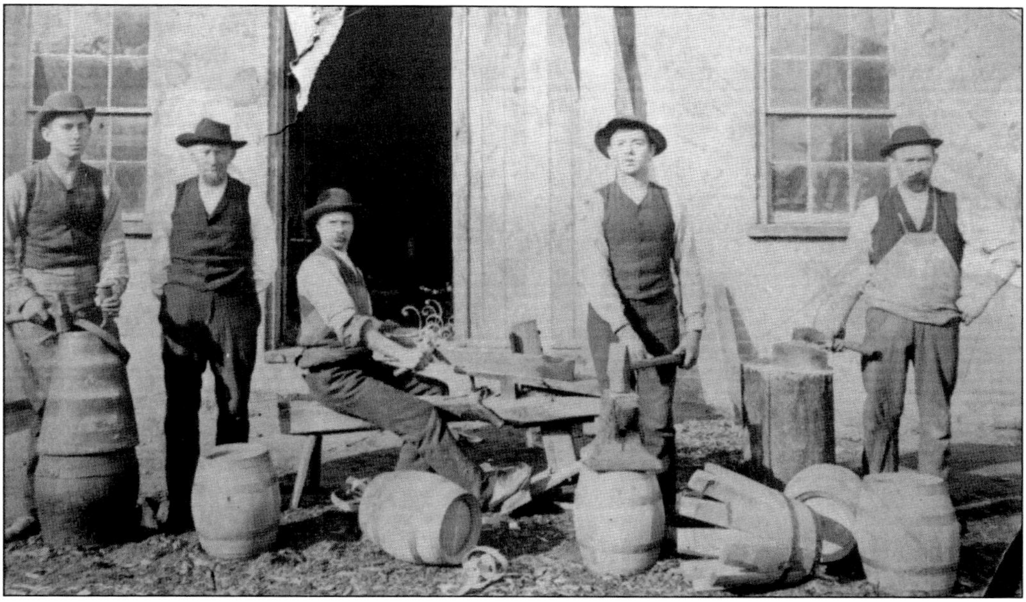

OEHLER COOPER SHOP. The Oehler Brothers operated their cooperage on North Ninth Street between Niagara and Ontario in Sheboygan. Wooden beer kegs were made in large quantity in Sheboygan years ago. The brewing industry utilized them. This photo shows the tools and methods used in making the kegs. The unidentified man in the center is seated on a schnitzelbank and is forming barrel staves with a drawknife. Otto Oehler is standing behind a cone-shaped device presumably used for forming metal hoops for the kegs. The Oehler Cooper shop also made wooden cisterns.

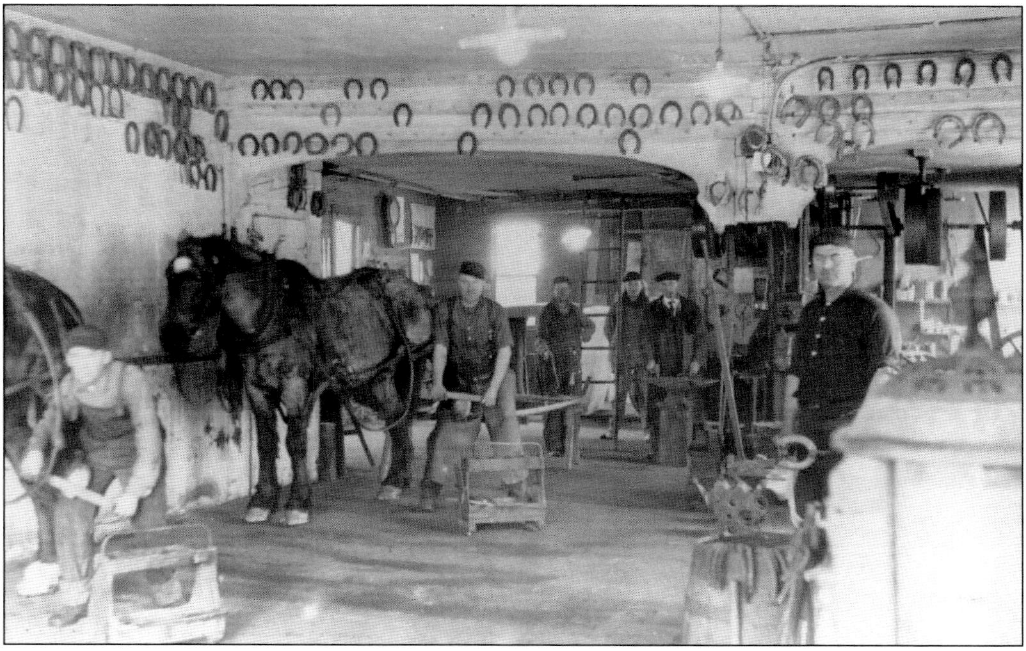

BLACKSMITH SHOP. This is the Robert Rusch Blacksmith Shop, located on South Eleventh at Indiana Avenue. From left to right are Art Bagemehl, John Roelse, Louie Jakum, unidentified, unidentified, and Robert Rusch. This photo is unusual because of the bright interior.

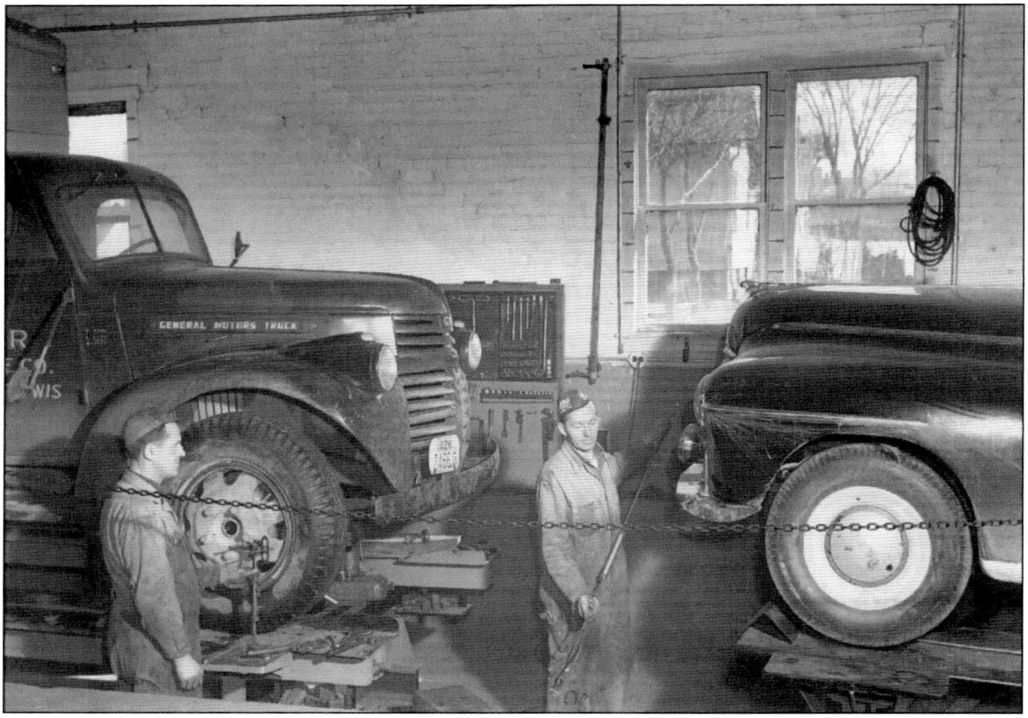

Robert Rusch Auto Rebuilding. Located at 1129 Indiana Avenue, Sheboygan, the same location as the blacksmith shop. The company has made the transition from horse-drawn transportation to the motor vehicle. This photo was taken about 1947. At left is Arthur Bagemehl and to the right is Harvey Oldenburg. They are shown as they stand working in the trenches in the days before the hydraulic lift.

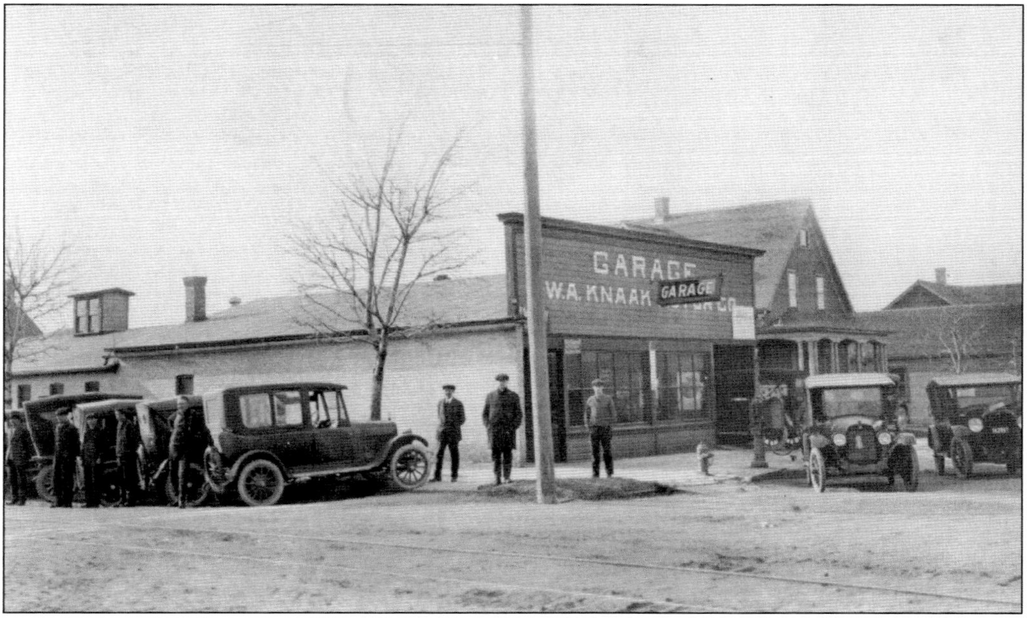

W.A. Knaak Garage. Located at Thirteenth and Georgia Avenue in Sheboygan, this garage was one of the earliest to service motor cars. This photo was taken in the early 1910s.

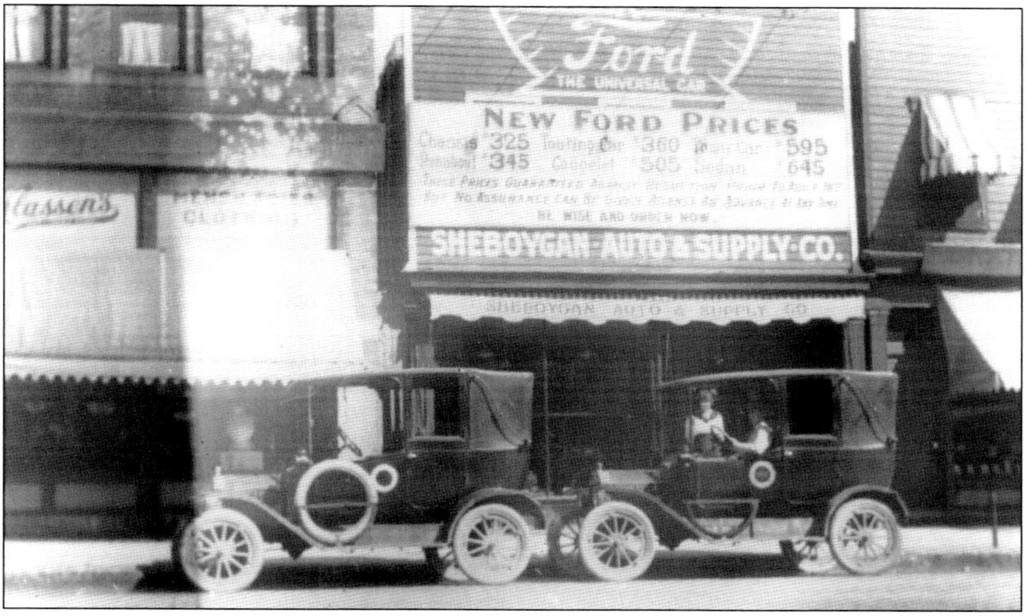

SHEBOYGAN AUTO AND SUPPLY. The billboard at Sheboygan Auto and Supply advertises that new Ford cars were on sale. The pricing was as follows: Touring Car–$360, Coupelet–$505, and Runabout–$345. It advertised, "Be Wise and Buy Now."

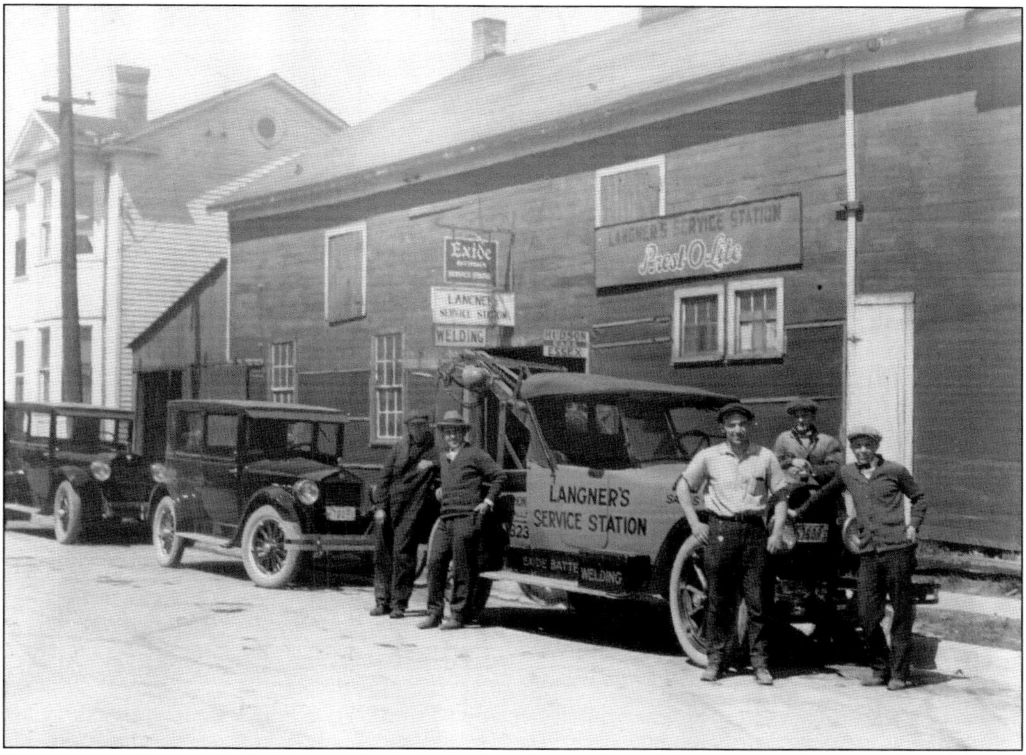

LANGNER'S SERVICE STATION. This station was located in Sheboygan Falls. The photo is from 1925. The men pictured from left to right are Cletus Painter, Elmer Gerber, two unidentified, and Arno Langner.

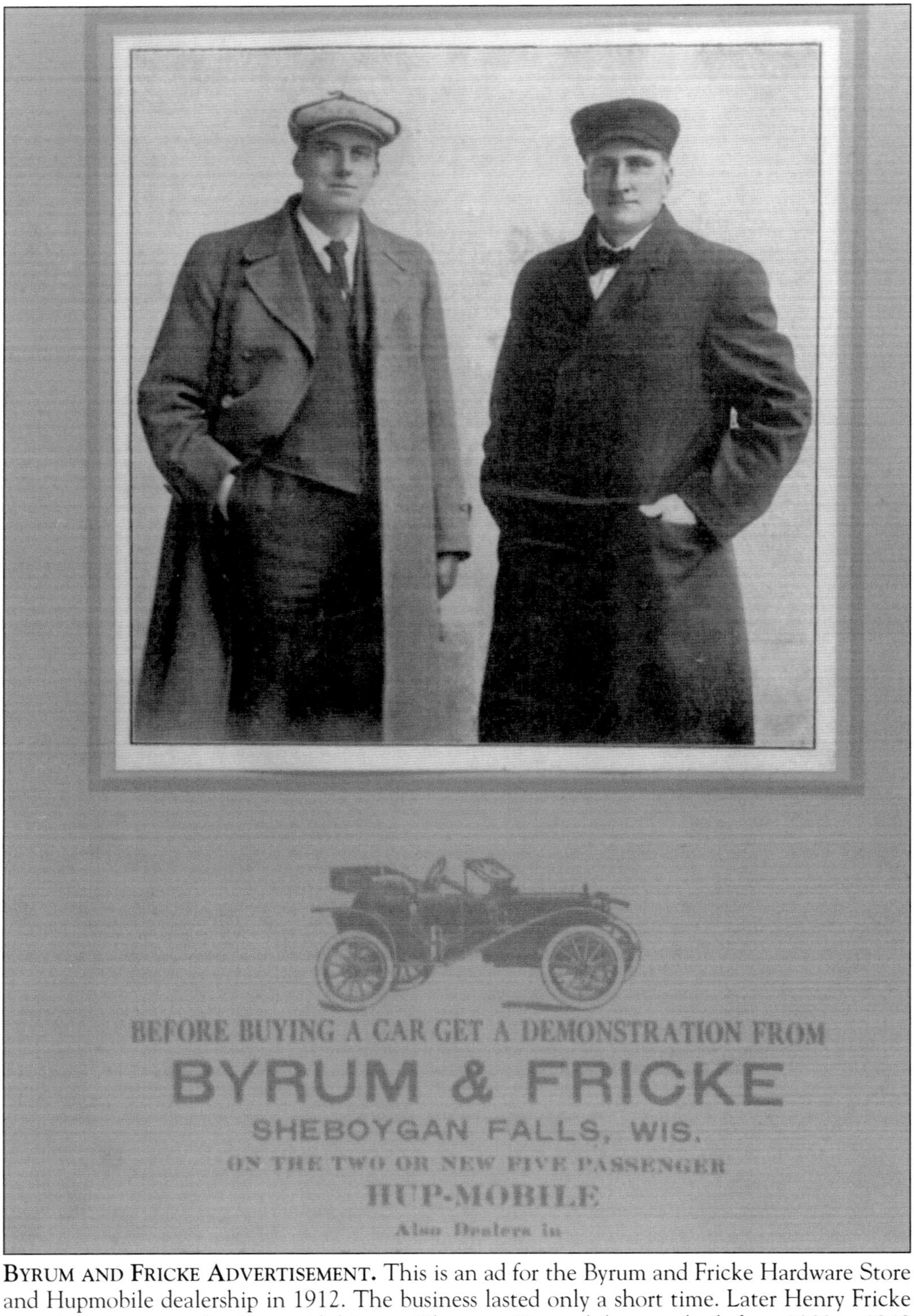

BYRUM AND FRICKE ADVERTISEMENT. This is an ad for the Byrum and Fricke Hardware Store and Hupmobile dealership in 1912. The business lasted only a short time. Later Henry Fricke went into the garage business with his son, Clarence. Hupmobiles were built from 1909 to 1940 by the Hupp Motor Company of Detroit, Michigan. It is the Hupmobile which is pictured on the back of a United States ten dollar bill.

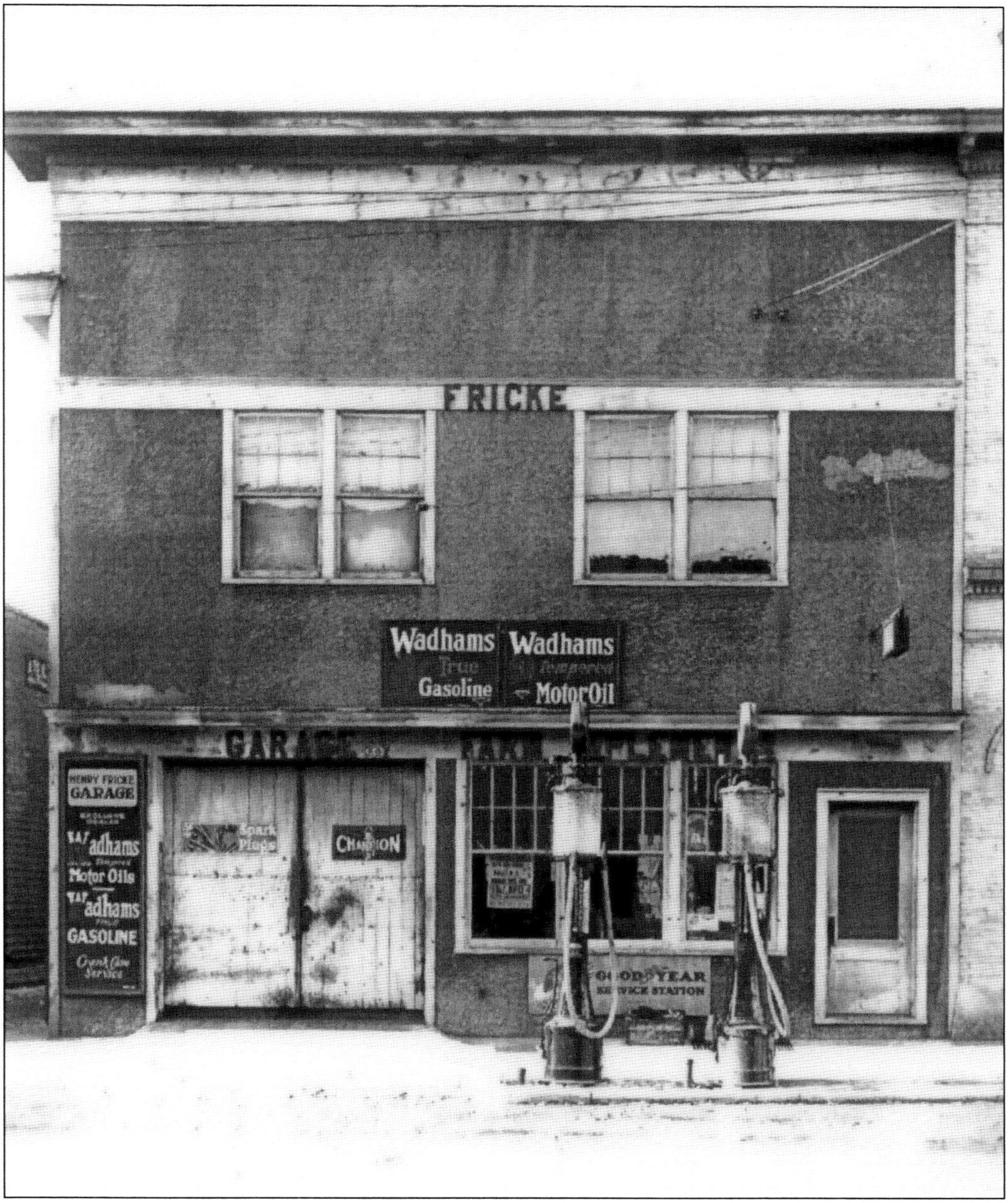

FRICKE GARAGE. This image shows Fricke Garage on Broadway Street in Sheboygan Falls as it looked in the 1920s. It later became Fricke Bicycle Shop, and is currently a part of Fire House Pizza. Note the old suction gas pumps in front of the building. The gas was drawn from underground tanks by a hand pump into the glass globes near the top of the pump. The globes had markings indicating gallon amounts up to a total of five or ten gallons. When the operator pumped the desired amount of gas into the globes, he opened the hose and let gravity pull the gas from the globe to the tanks of customers.

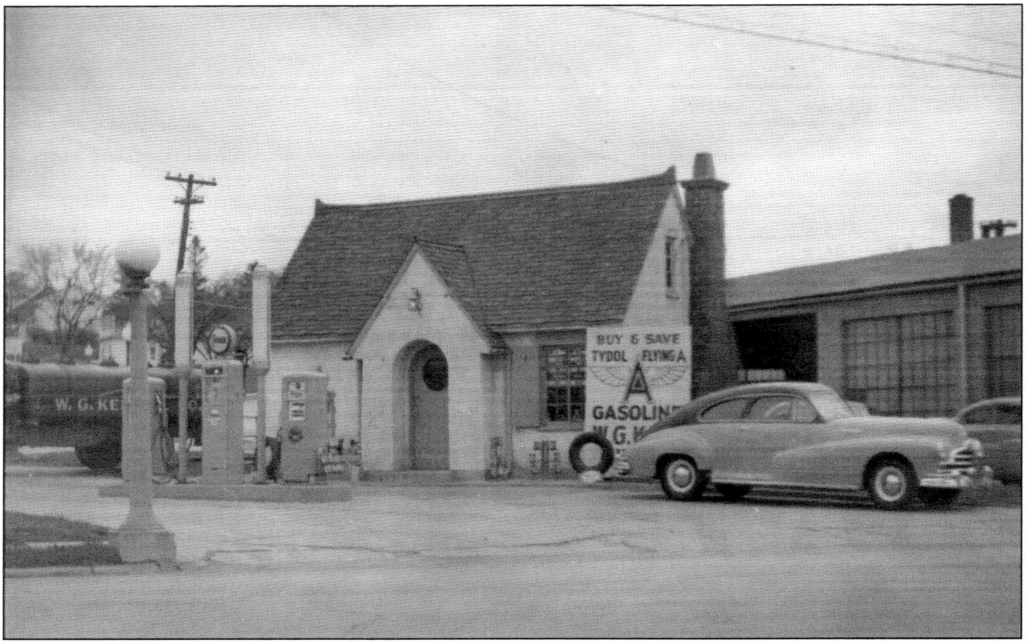

SHEBOYGAN FALLS GAS STATION. This quaint station, located on the northeast corner of Poplar and Monroe Streets, just west of the Ford dealership, urges its customers to "Buy Tydol, Flying A Gasoline and Save." The photo was taken in 1953.

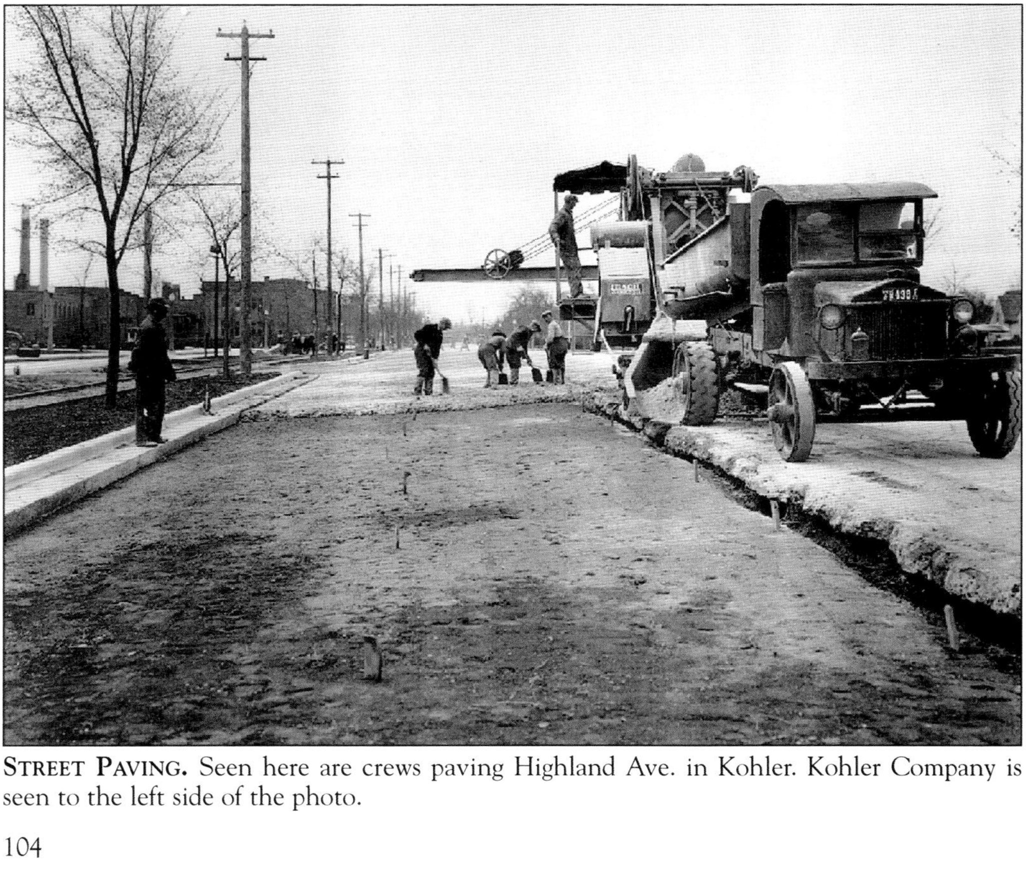

STREET PAVING. Seen here are crews paving Highland Ave. in Kohler. Kohler Company is seen to the left side of the photo.

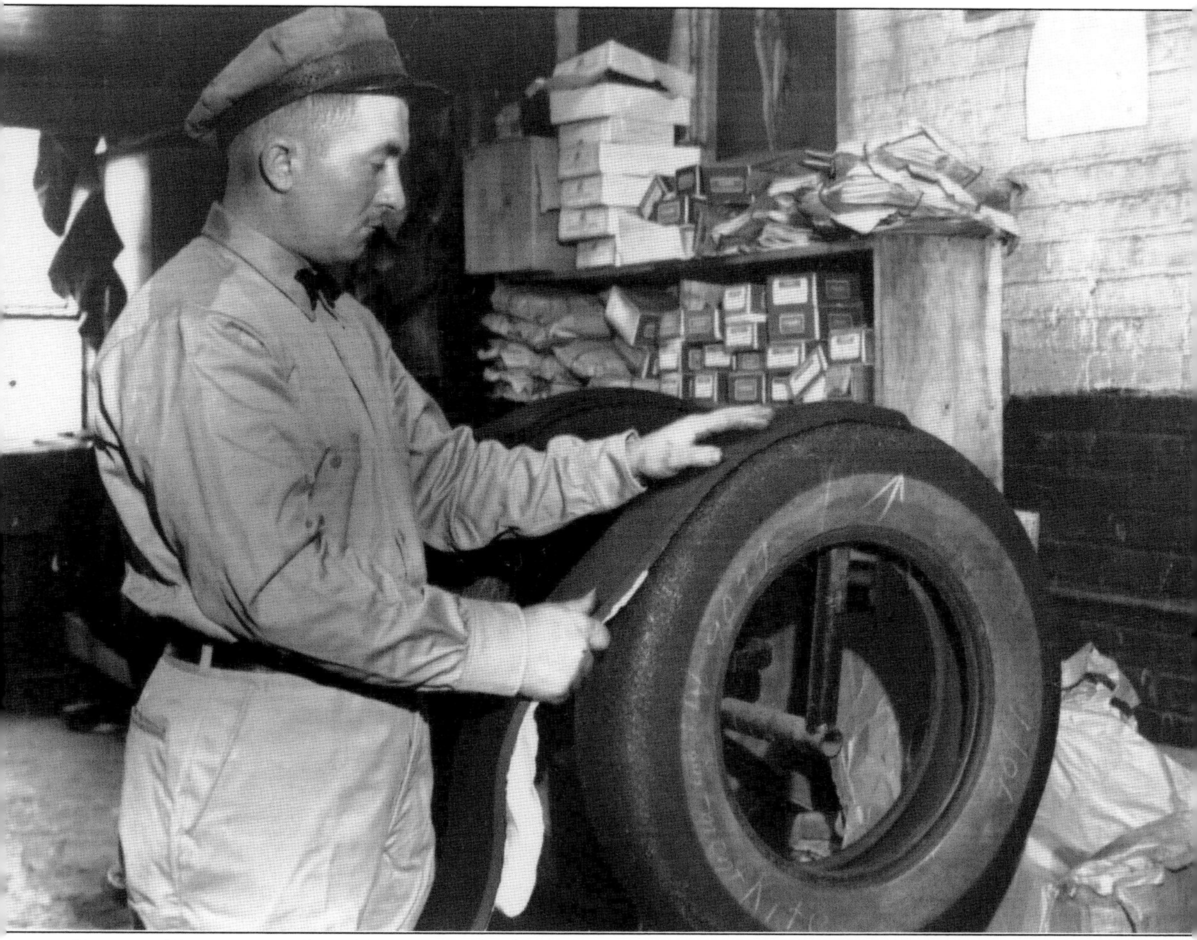

GRASSE BROTHERS OIL COMPANY. Before tires were improved to the point that they are now, tire recapping was a vital job. This was especially true during the years of WWII, when rubber was in short supply. Here, we see Elmer Koppelmann, Sr., a Grasse Bros. Oil Company employee, beginning the process of recapping in 1942. Today, except for truck tires, recapping has all but disappeared.

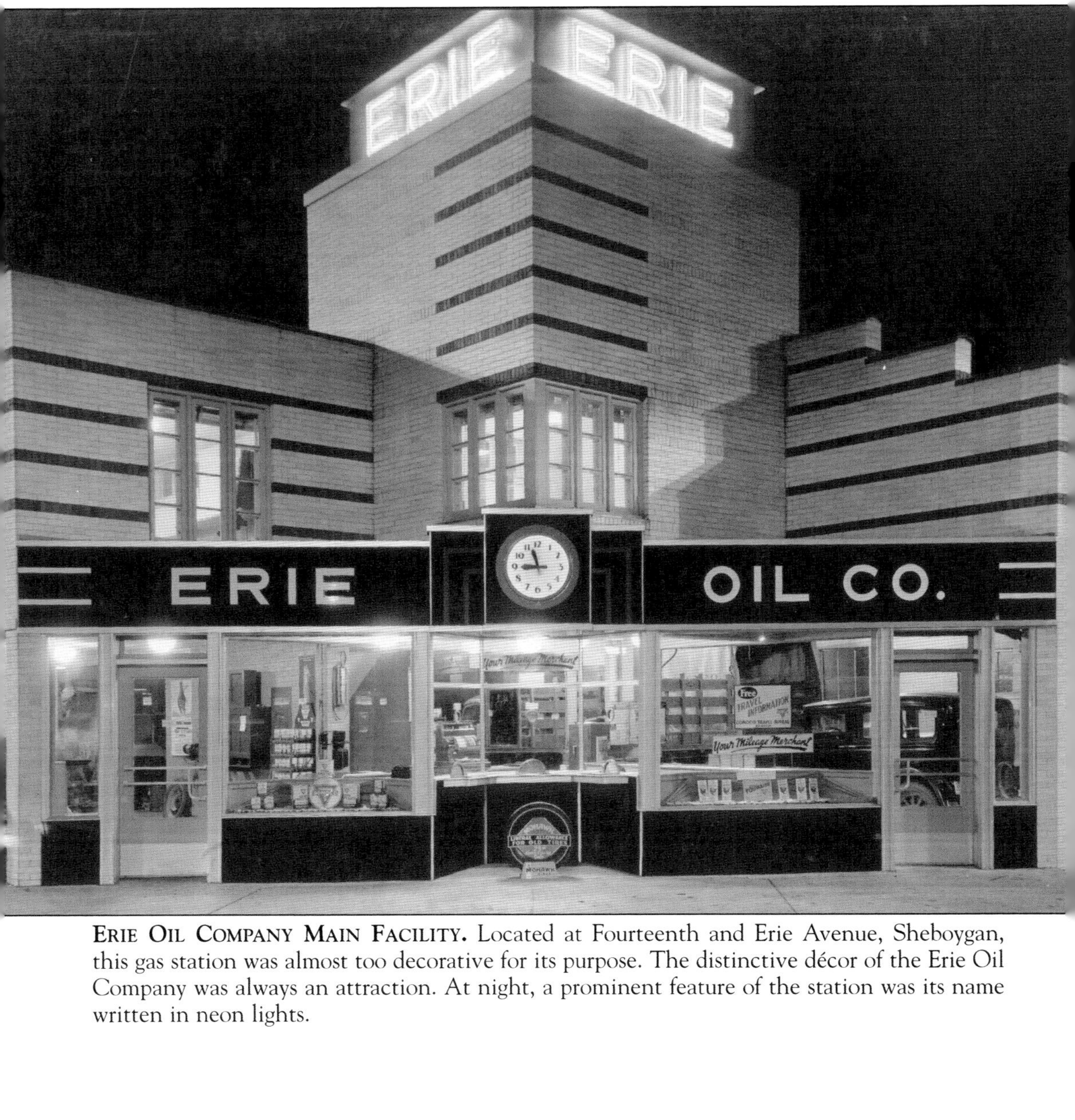

ERIE OIL COMPANY MAIN FACILITY. Located at Fourteenth and Erie Avenue, Sheboygan, this gas station was almost too decorative for its purpose. The distinctive décor of the Erie Oil Company was always an attraction. At night, a prominent feature of the station was its name written in neon lights.

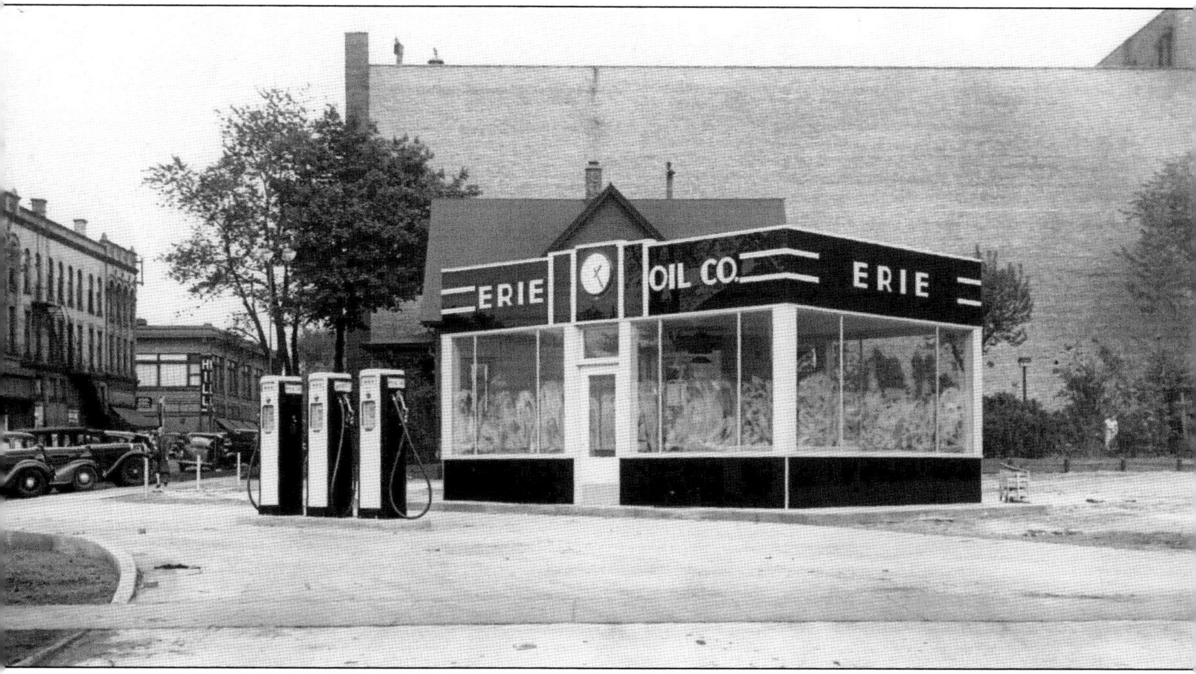

ERIE OIL COMPANY GAS STATION. This photo shows an unused gas station at Ninth and Niagara Streets in Sheboygan on May 27, 1939. This same Art Deco design was used at all of the Erie Oil Company Stations.

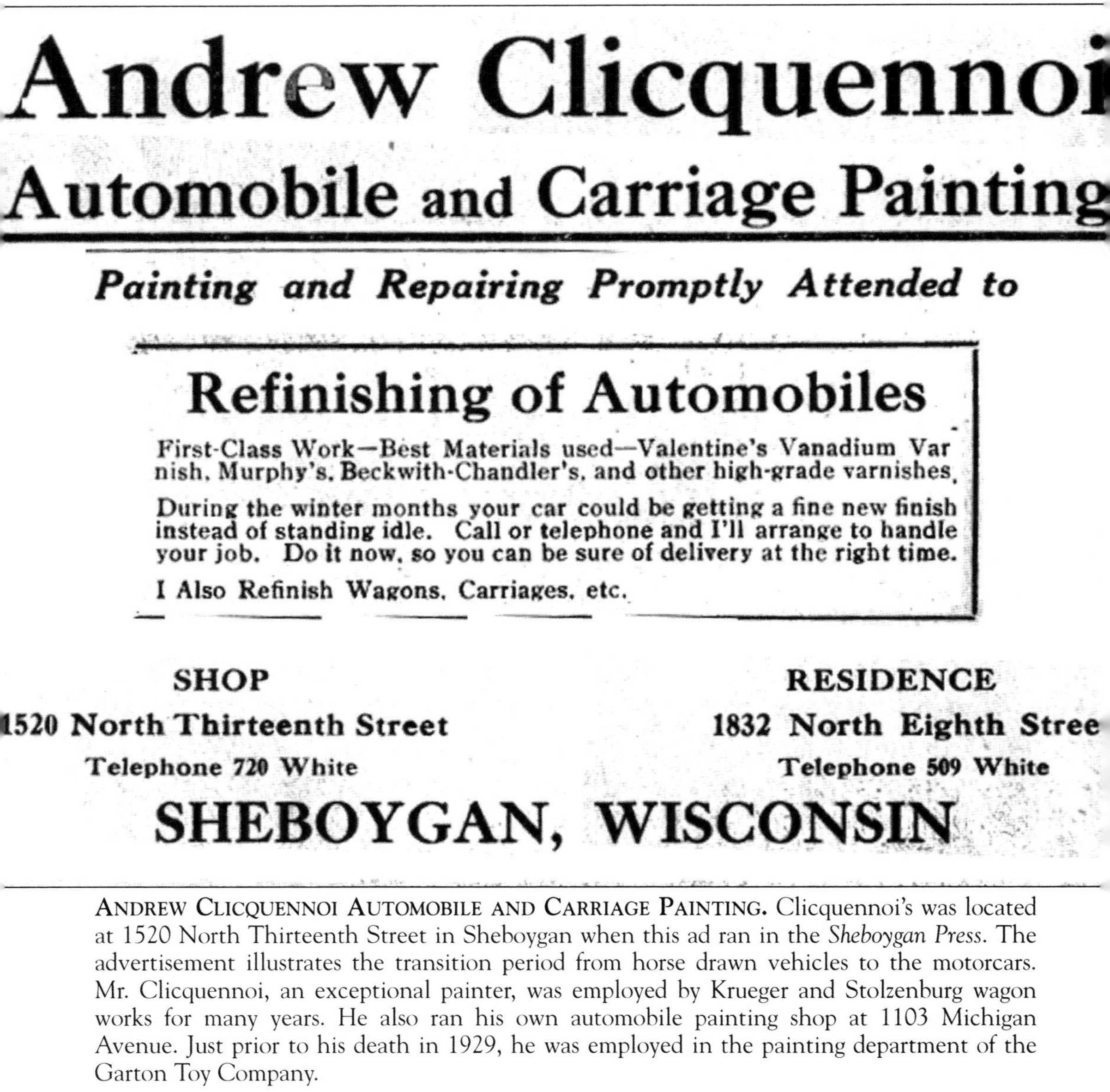

ANDREW CLICQUENNOI AUTOMOBILE AND CARRIAGE PAINTING. Clicquennoi's was located at 1520 North Thirteenth Street in Sheboygan when this ad ran in the *Sheboygan Press*. The advertisement illustrates the transition period from horse drawn vehicles to the motorcars. Mr. Clicquennoi, an exceptional painter, was employed by Krueger and Stolzenburg wagon works for many years. He also ran his own automobile painting shop at 1103 Michigan Avenue. Just prior to his death in 1929, he was employed in the painting department of the Garton Toy Company.

Six

Odds and Ends

There are always items that don't fit into any one broad category—the odds and ends. Sheboygan County's business history is as diverse as any county in the state of Wisconsin. Much of this diversity remains only in story form. The town of Mitchell had cranberry bogs, but no photo exists. The town of Greenbush had a muskrat farm, but we again have no photo. Following are a few of the more interesting odds and ends of which we are fortunate to have photographs.

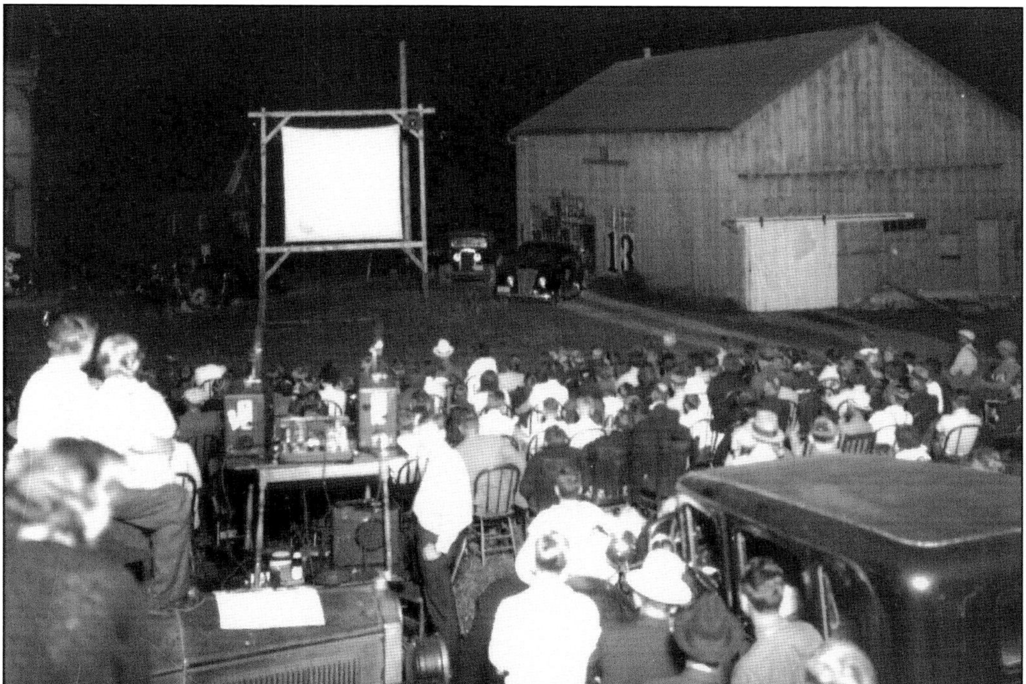

Movie History. Perhaps this is an image of the first outdoor movie or drive-in in Sheboygan County. Seen here in a farmyard, a makeshift screen has been set up for a movie. The projector is in the foreground. This photo was taken in the 1930s.

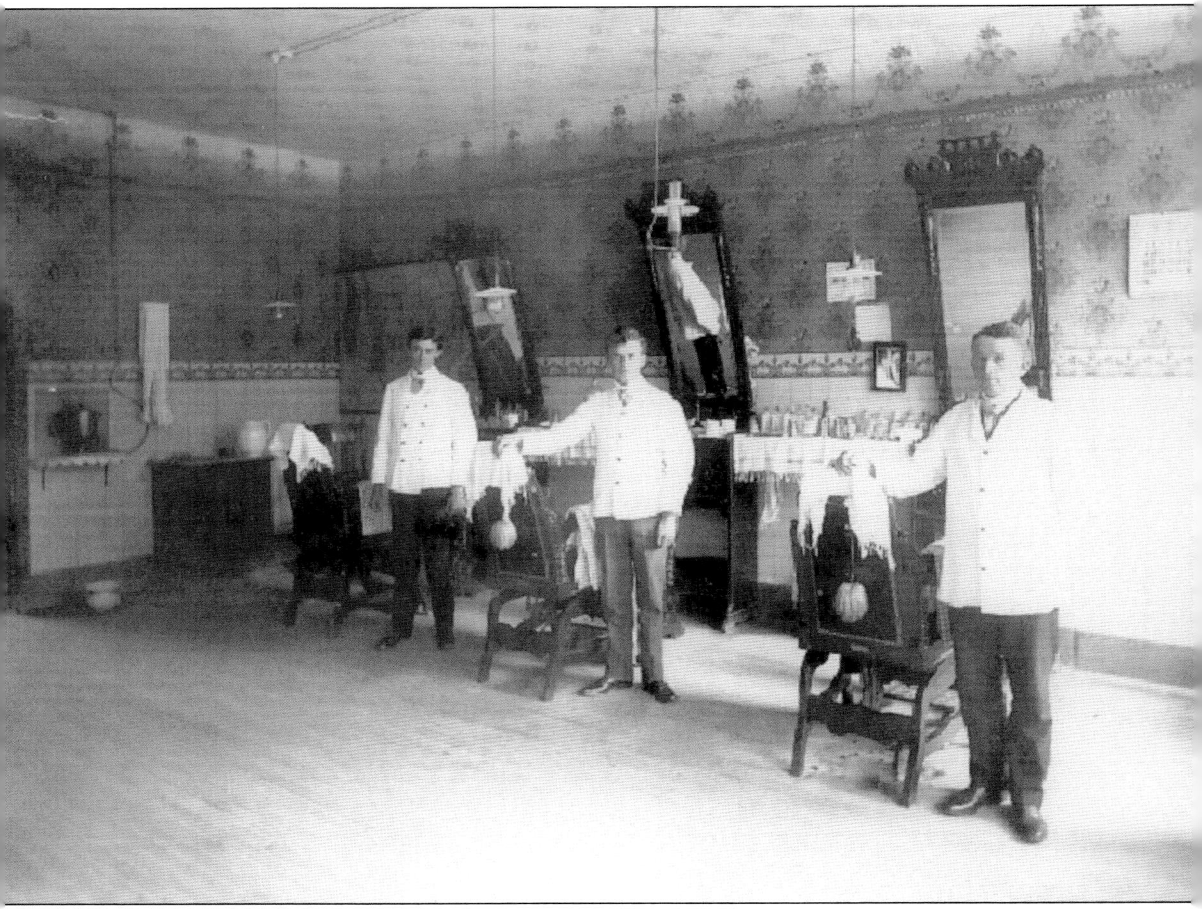

WILLIAM FLAIG BARBER SHOP. William Flaig's barbershop stood on the site of the first Sheboygan Clinic at 1118 N. Eighth Street in Sheboygan. Flaig was a barber for 54 years, until his death in 1946. This picture was taken about 1910. Notice the rigid barber chairs and ornate mirrors.

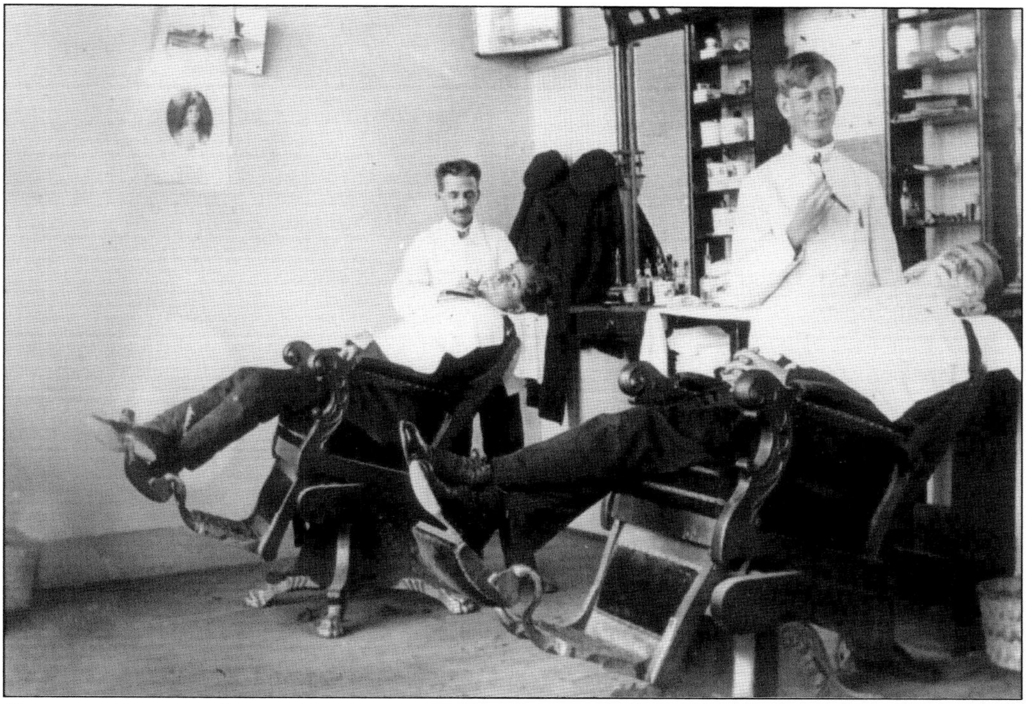

GUYETTE BARBER SHOP. Also known as the Dayton Barber Shop, this business was located on Monroe Street in Sheboygan Falls, between Broadway and Buffalo in the Guyette building. The barbers shown here are Charles Dayton (rear) and George Hartenberger (foreground). The customers are Charles Prinsen (rear) and Andrew Pfeiffer (foreground).

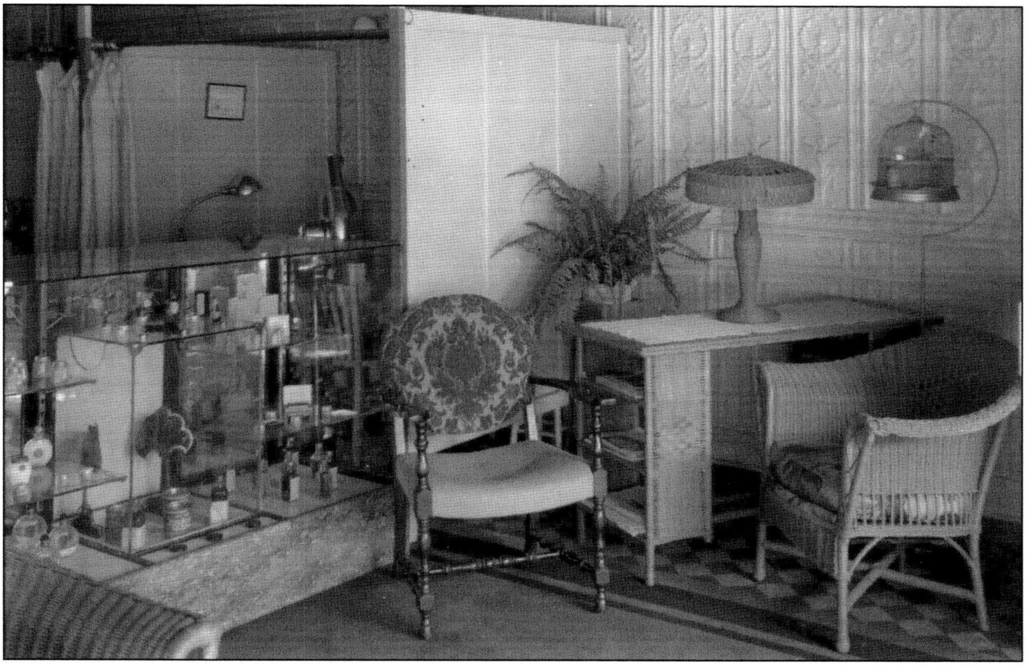

POWDER PUFF BEAUTY SALON. The reception area at the Powder Puff contained the very latest products for hair and beauty care.

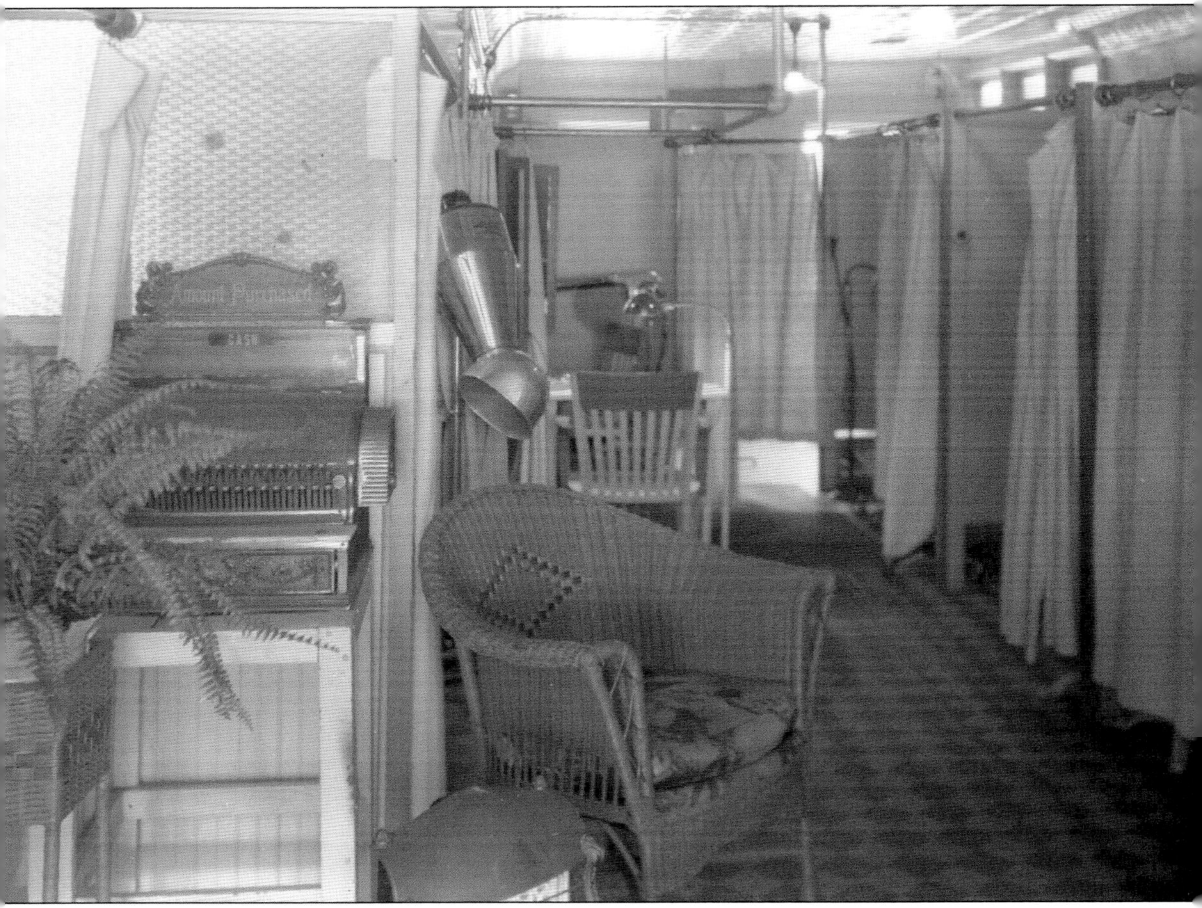

Powder Puff Beauty Salon. This beauty parlor was located at 710 Center Avenue in Sheboygan in 1930. Note that each station could be self-contained for privacy. This shop also had the latest equipment such as the hair blower next to the cash register.

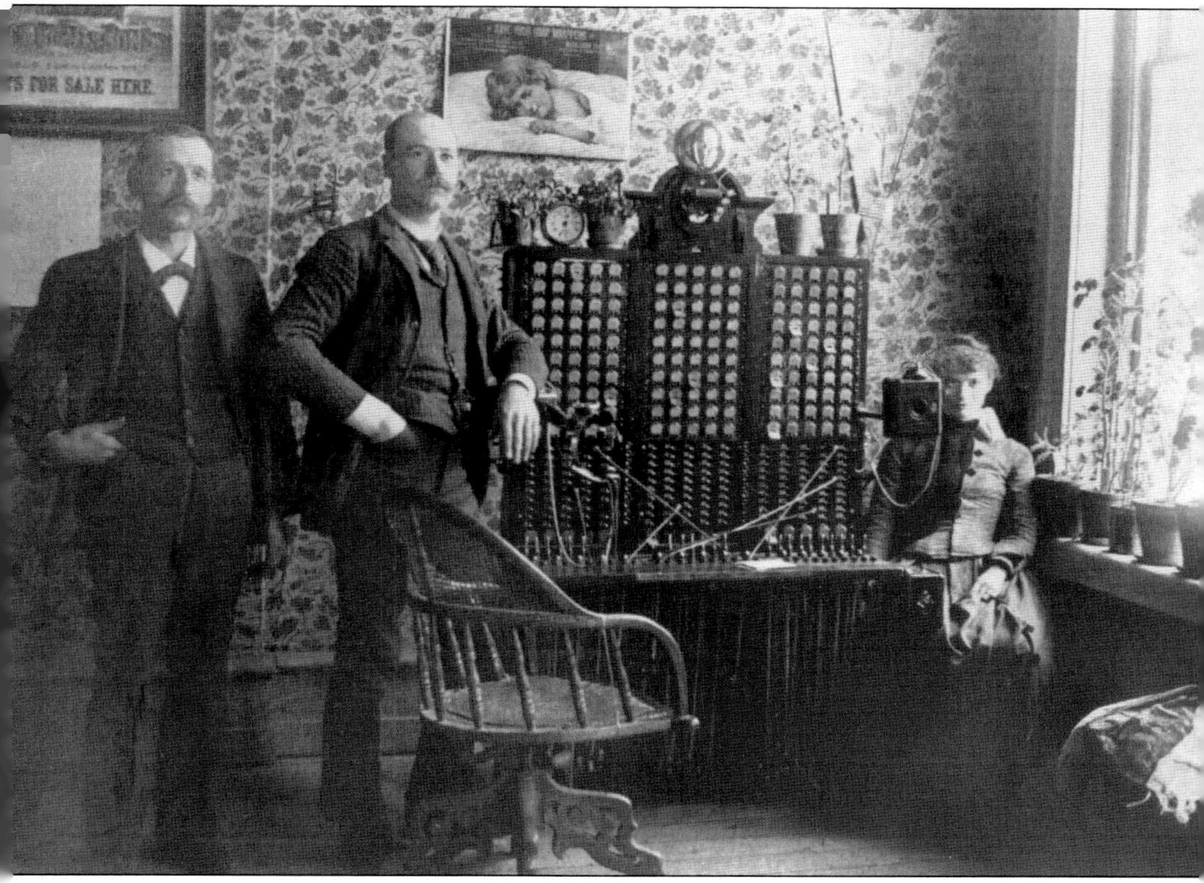

BELL TELEPHONE SWITCHBOARD. Sheboygan's first telephone service started in 1890 in this office at Eighth and Pennsylvania Avenue. George Best, the lineman and night operator, is on the left. Manager Ed Farrell is on the right.

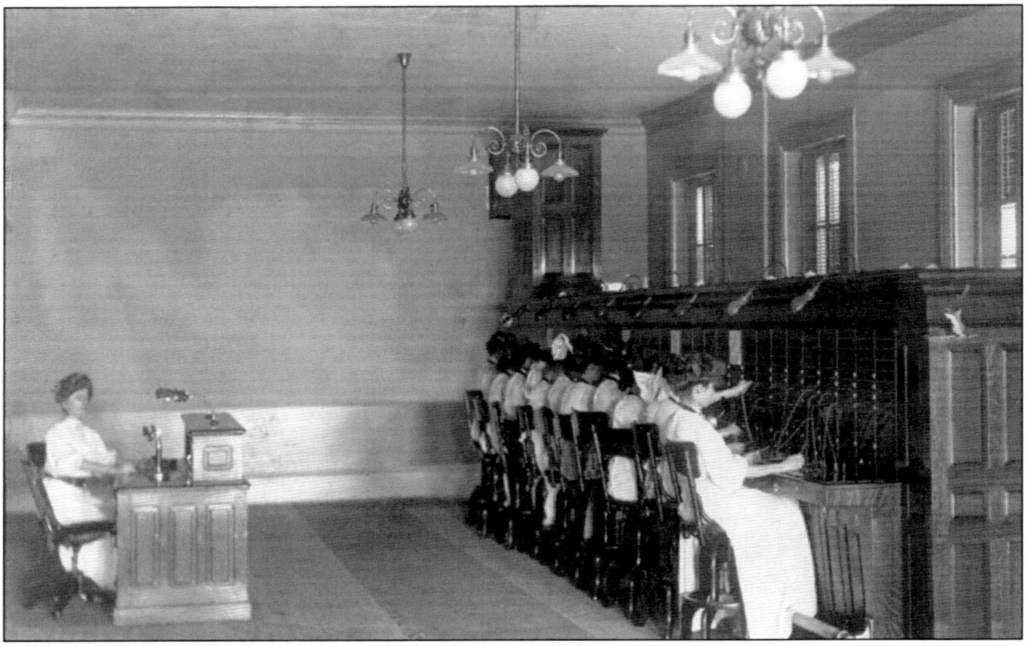

TELEPHONE OPERATORS. This is a later view of a telephone operator's workplace after the telephone had become more widely available, and more operators were needed.

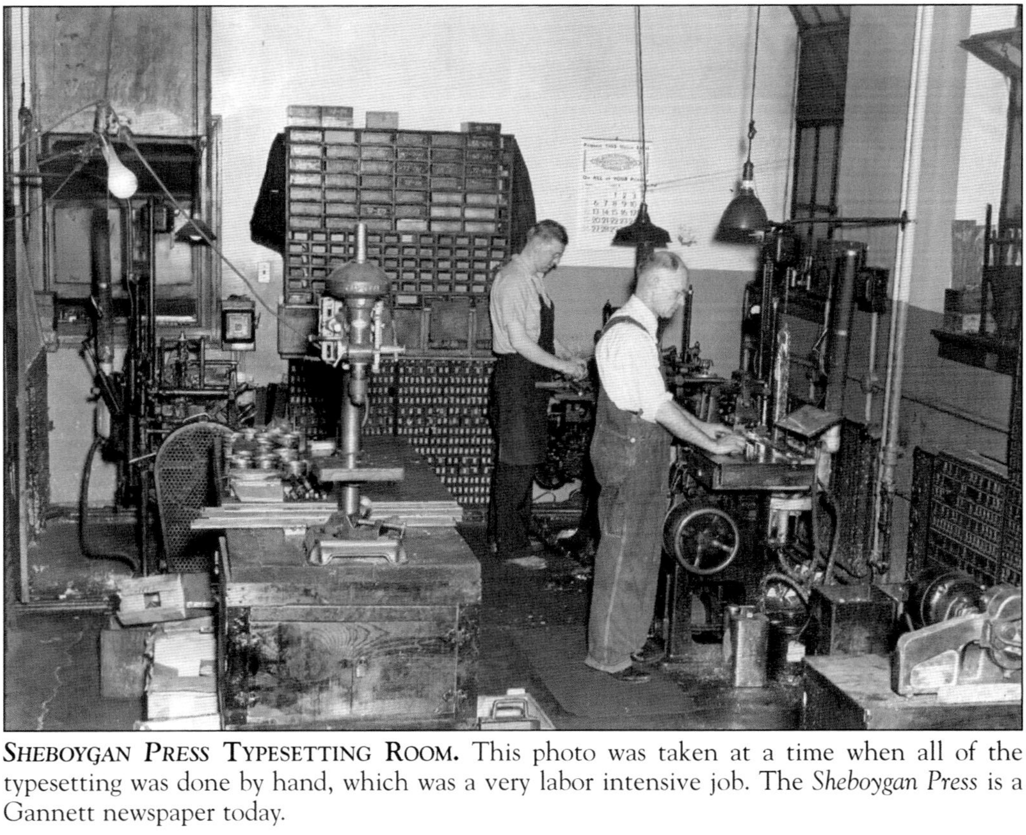

***SHEBOYGAN PRESS* TYPESETTING ROOM.** This photo was taken at a time when all of the typesetting was done by hand, which was a very labor intensive job. The *Sheboygan Press* is a Gannett newspaper today.

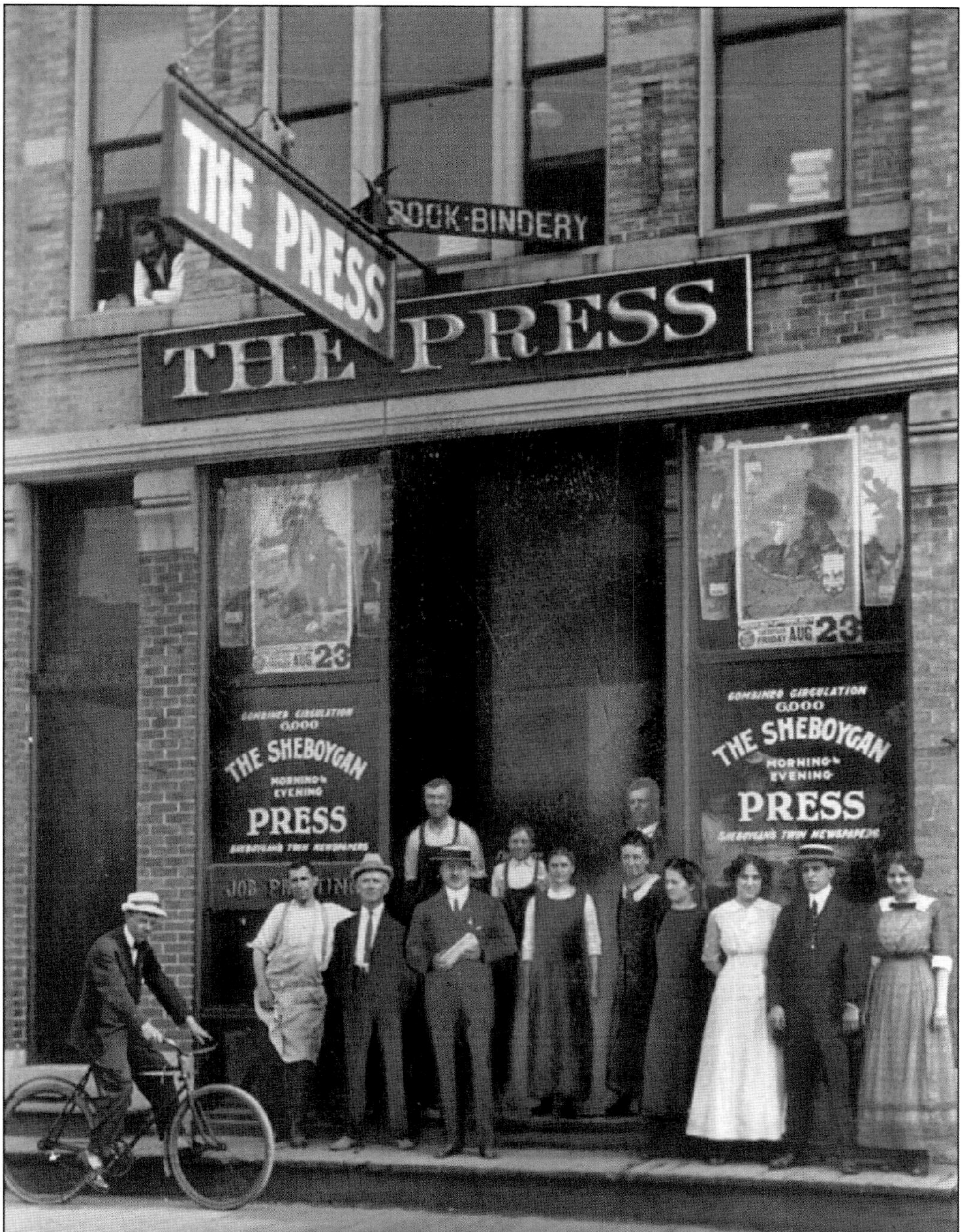

OLD SHEBOYGAN PRESS BUILDING. The *Sheboygan Press* published both morning and evening editions back in the days when this picture was taken in 1912. It was described as "Sheboygan's Twin Newspapers," and had a circulation of 6000. It was published in a plant between Eighth and Ninth Streets on Pennsylvania Avenue. The *Press* was one of eight newspapers published in Sheboygan at that time, and is the only one still published today. The others were *The National Demokrat*, *Amerika*, *Daily Journal*, *Herald*, *Telegram*, *Zeitung* and *Saturday Star*.

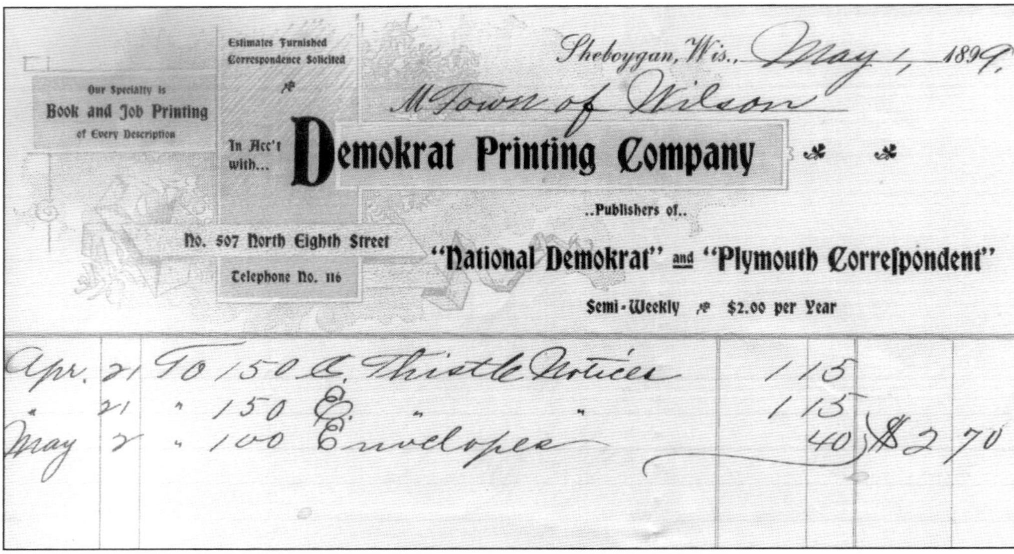

Estimates Furnished
Correspondence Solicited

Our Specialty is
Book and Job Printing
of Every Description

Sheboygan, Wis., May 1, 1899

M Town of Wilson

In Acc't with... Demokrat Printing Company

..Publishers of..

No. 507 North Eighth Street

"National Demokrat" and "Plymouth Correspondent"

Telephone No. 116

Semi-Weekly $2.00 per Year

Apr.	21	To 150 C. Thistle Notices	1 15	
"	21	" 150 E. "	1 15	
May	2	" 100 Envelopes	40	$2 70

DEMOKRAT PRINTING COMPANY. Located at 507 North Eighth Street in Sheboygan, the Demokrat Printing Company, along with publishing a semi-weekly newspaper, operated a print shop. Note the telephone number of 116 and the subscription rate of $2.00 per year.

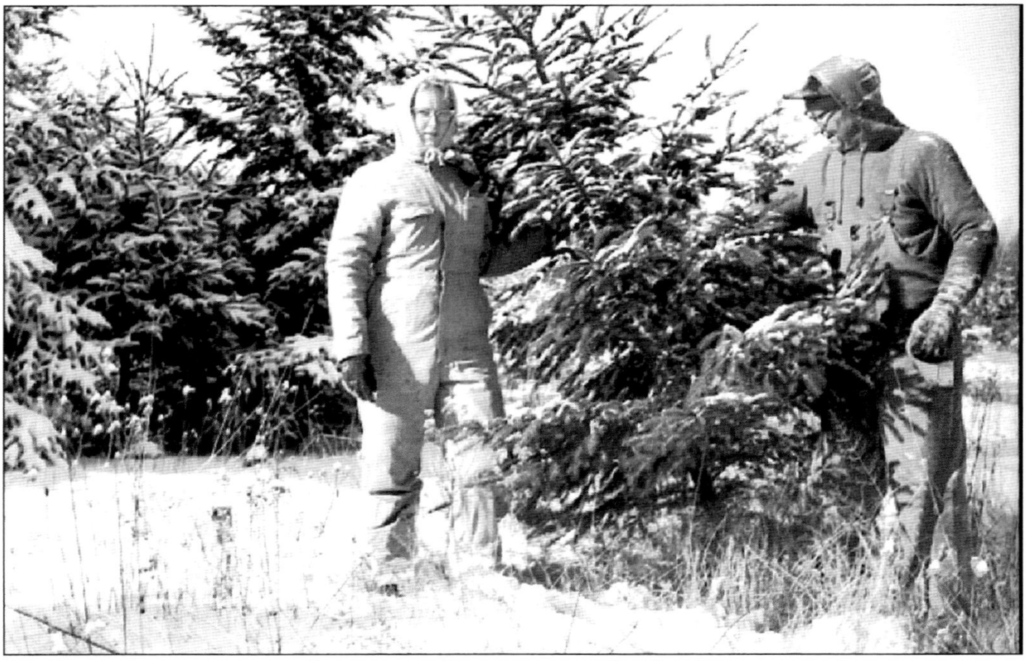

CHRISTMAS TREE FARM. Each year 35 million American families bring a real Christmas tree into their homes to become a warm and glowing part of their holiday celebration. In 1842, Charles Minnegerode introduced the custom in Williamsburg, Virginia. His tree was described as splendidly decorated with strings of popcorn, gilded nuts, and lighted candles. The fourteenth president of the United States, Franklin Pierce, was the first president to set up a Christmas tree in the White House. The enduring tree symbol remains a firmly established part of our holiday customs, engaging not only our senses of sight, touch, and smell, but also our sense of family, spirit, and tradition. This photo is from one of the many tree farms in Sheboygan County.

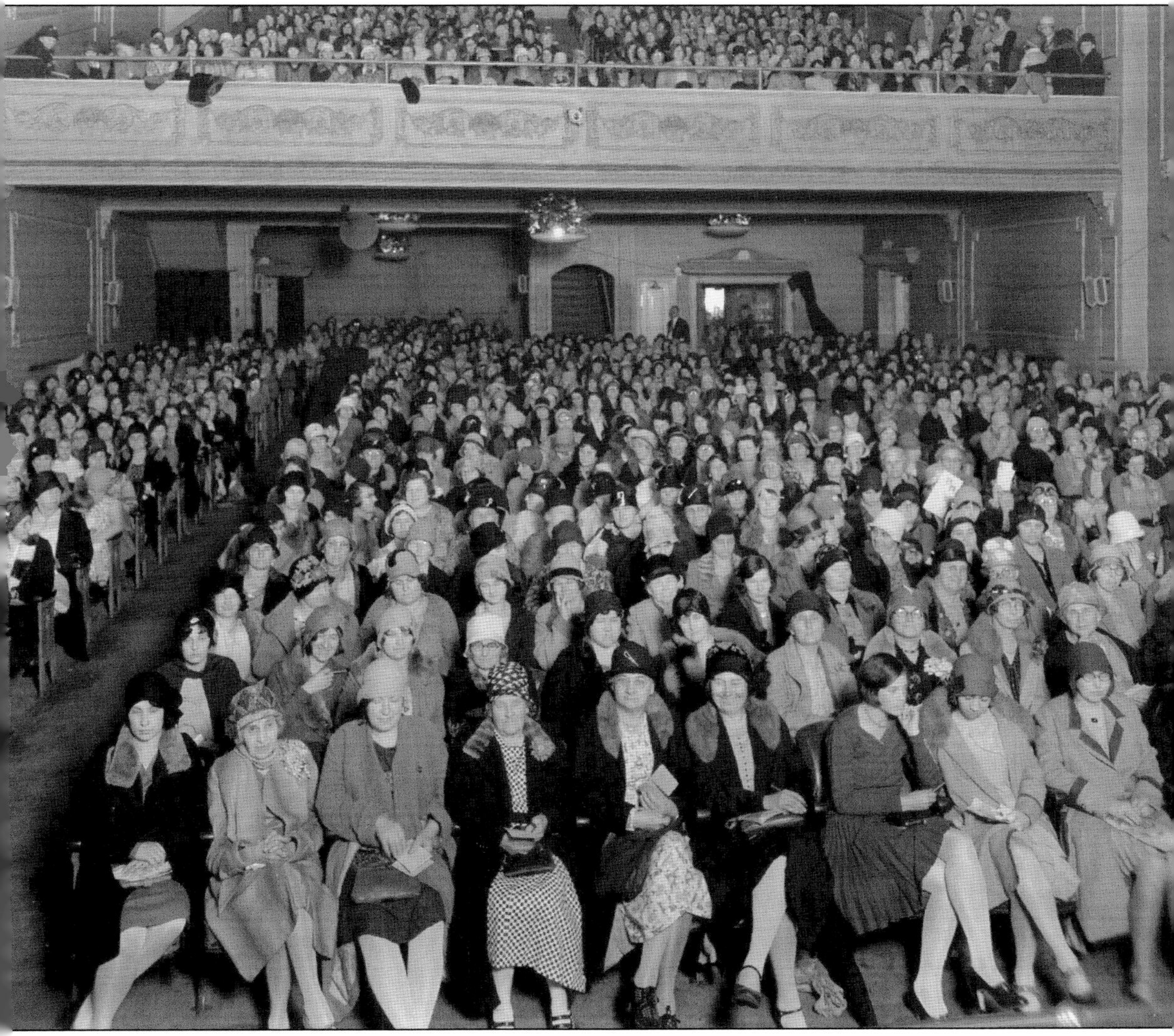

SHEBOYGAN PRESS COOKING SCHOOL. The *Sheboygan Press* periodically sponsored forums on a wide variety of topics. Shown here is a cooking school held at the Rex Theater in Sheboygan. As the photo shows, it was very popular with the ladies of the county. The photo was taken in September of 1927.

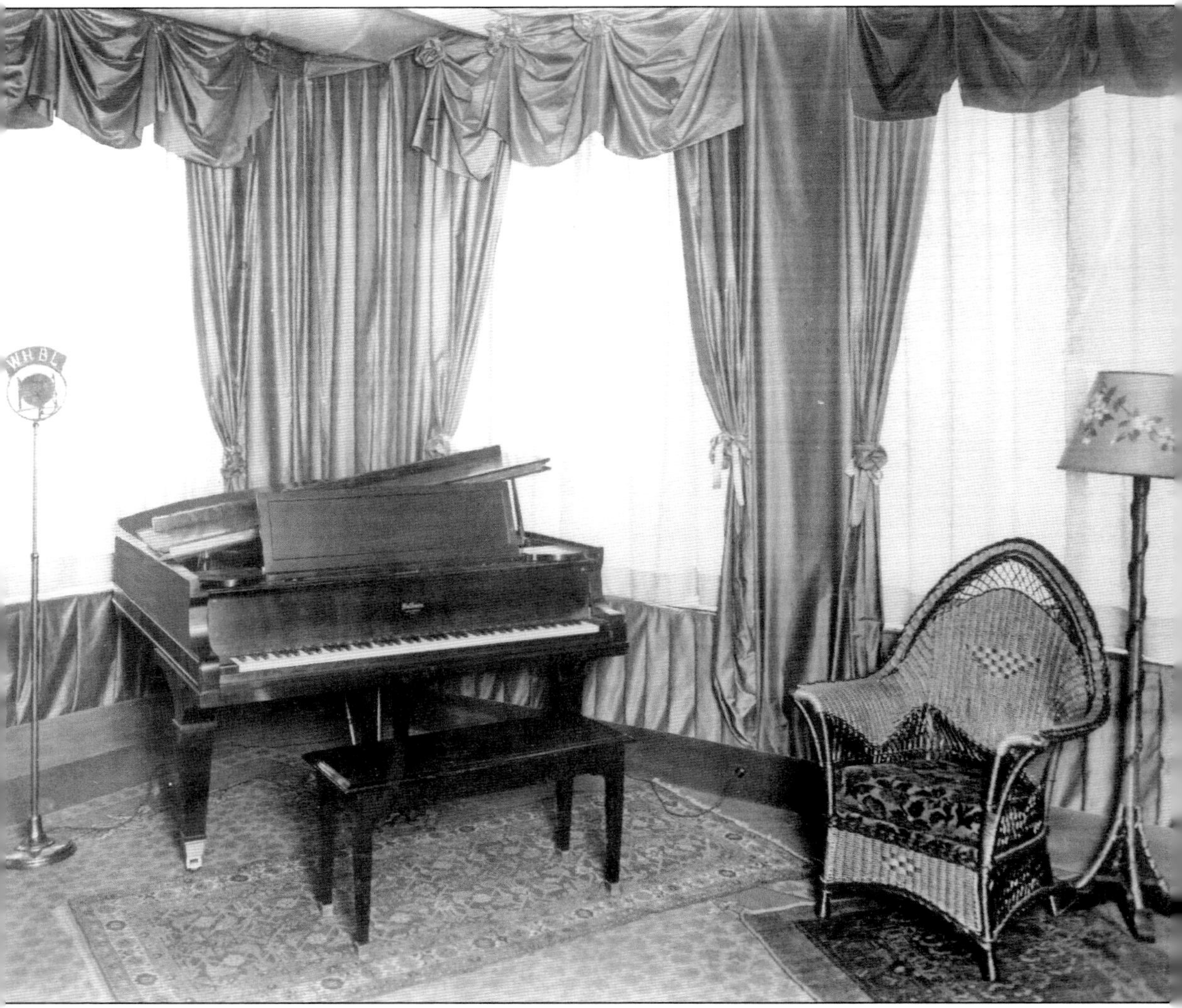

WHBL STUDIO. Taken in April of 1928, this shot of the WHBL Radio Studio in Sheboygan looks far different from today's utilitarian, technology-filled studios. Our earliest radio station went "on the air" November 7, 1927. At first, known as WHBM, the name was changed to WHBL in 1928. WHBL was owned by the Werner Family, who also owned the *Sheboygan Press*. Later, Charles Broughton purchased the radio station. In 1947, it was incorporated as WHBL, Inc. General Manager Paul Skinner was hired by Broughton to run the station. He was a band singer with the Bill Carlsen Orchestra in Sheboygan. As time went by, four other stations, WKTS, WPLY, WSHS and WWJR joined WHBL in bringing the Sheboygan area a variety of music, news, and entertainment.

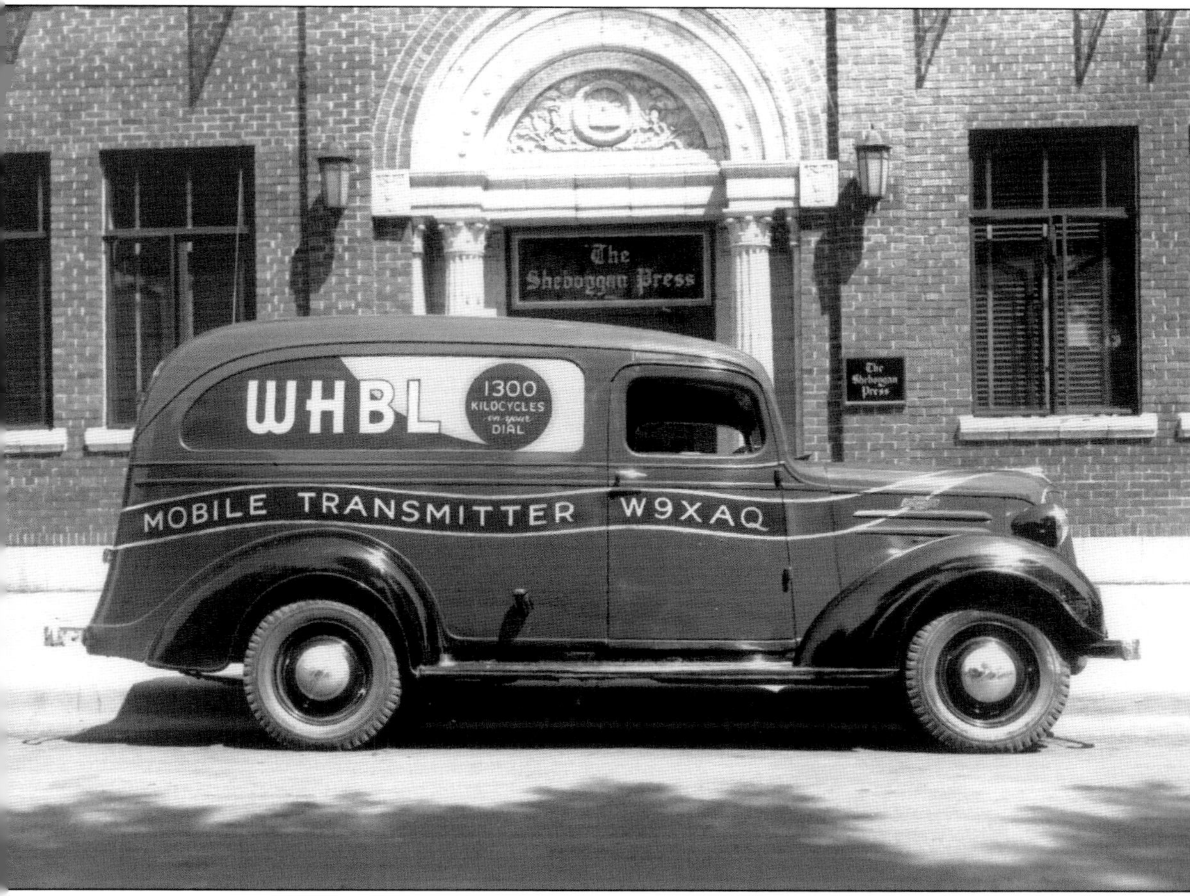

WHBL MOBILE TRANSMITTER. Standing in front of the Sheboygan Press Office on Center Avenue in Sheboygan, this mobile unit was able to travel to find news and do interviews. At first, WHBL had an off and on schedule during the day, broadcasting for an hour or two, then going off the air, then returning to the air. It continued as a part-time station until November of 1935 when the FCC assigned it a new frequency of 1300 kilocycles and permitted full-time operation. Ground was broken on April 1, 1936 for an AM transmitter building and tower one and one-half miles south of the city.

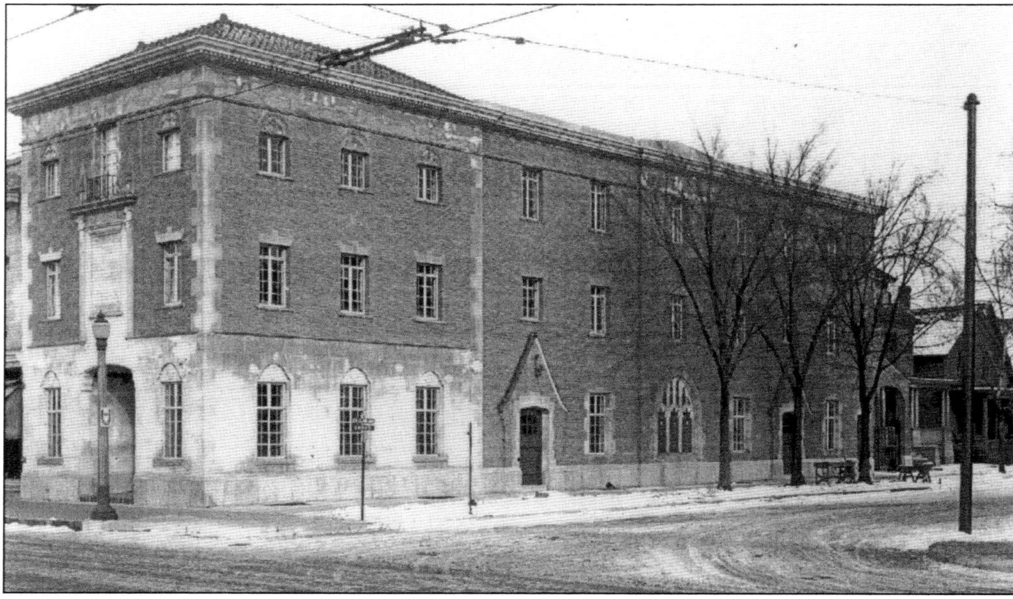

Ballhorn Funeral Temple. Built in 1928, a three-story structure designed to furnish the best in funeral service to the public. German immigrant John Ballhorn was a cabinet-maker living in Glenbeulah when he decided to move his family to Sheboygan. The Ballhorns had the first crematory (1947) located in a funeral establishment in Wisconsin.

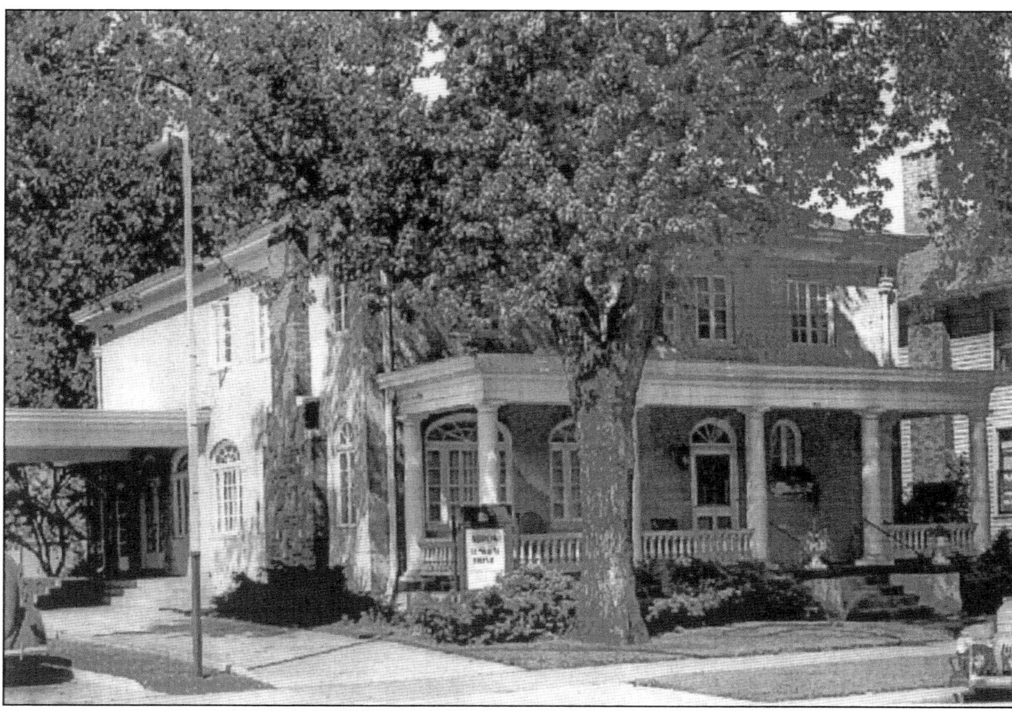

Kroos Funeral Home. Max Kroos established his business in 1901. Shown here is the first building in Sheboygan to be erected specifically as a funeral home (1924). It was also the first to have a motorized hearse and the first to offer organ music as a part of its service. Today it is the Rettke funeral home at 1119 Michigan Avenue.

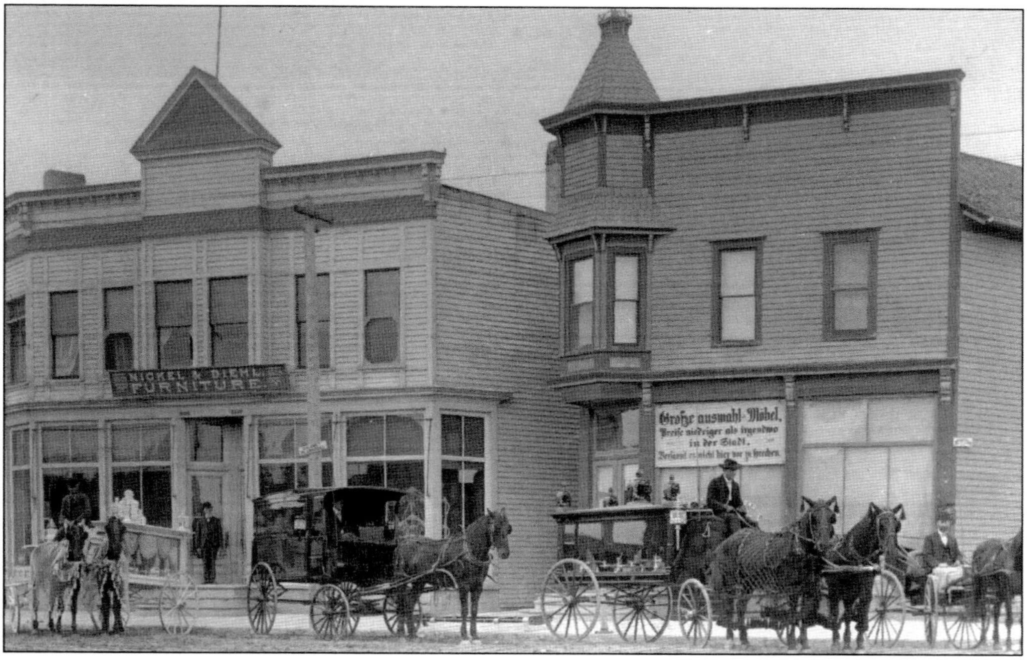

Nickel and Diehl Funeral Home. Founded by Jacob Nickel and Joseph Diehl in 1892, it was located in the 1500 block of Calumet Drive in Sheboygan. After 1908 and the death of Joseph Diehl, the business was operated solely by the Nickel family. Mrs. Meta Nickel was one of the first women to be licensed as a funeral director and embalmer in the state of Wisconsin, and the very first in Sheboygan. In 1975 the business became the Nickel-Lippert Funeral Home when it was purchased by Mr. and Mrs. Roland Lippert.

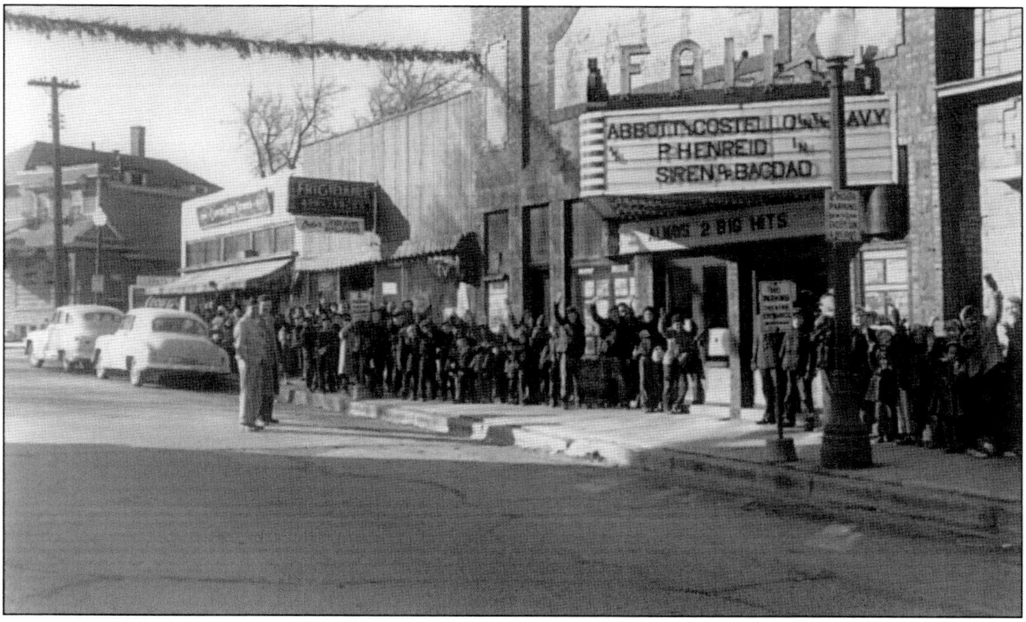

Sheboygan Falls Theater. A good movie always packs them in. This is the Sheboygan Falls Theater showing Abbott and Costello in *In the Navy* and Paul Henried in *Siren of Baghdad*. In the 1940s and 1950s seeing two features for the price of one was very common.

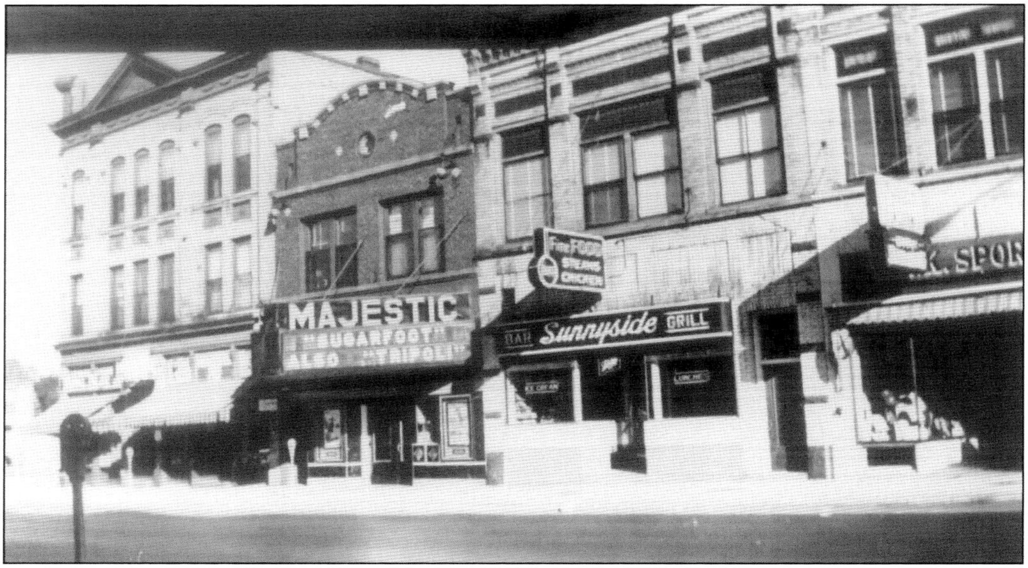

MAJESTIC THEATER. The Majestic Theater was located at 408 East Mill Street in Plymouth. This theater was located on the north side of the street, just to the east of Division Street. Taken on September 7, 1954, the photo shows that the movies showing at the time were *Sugarfoot* and *Tripoli.*

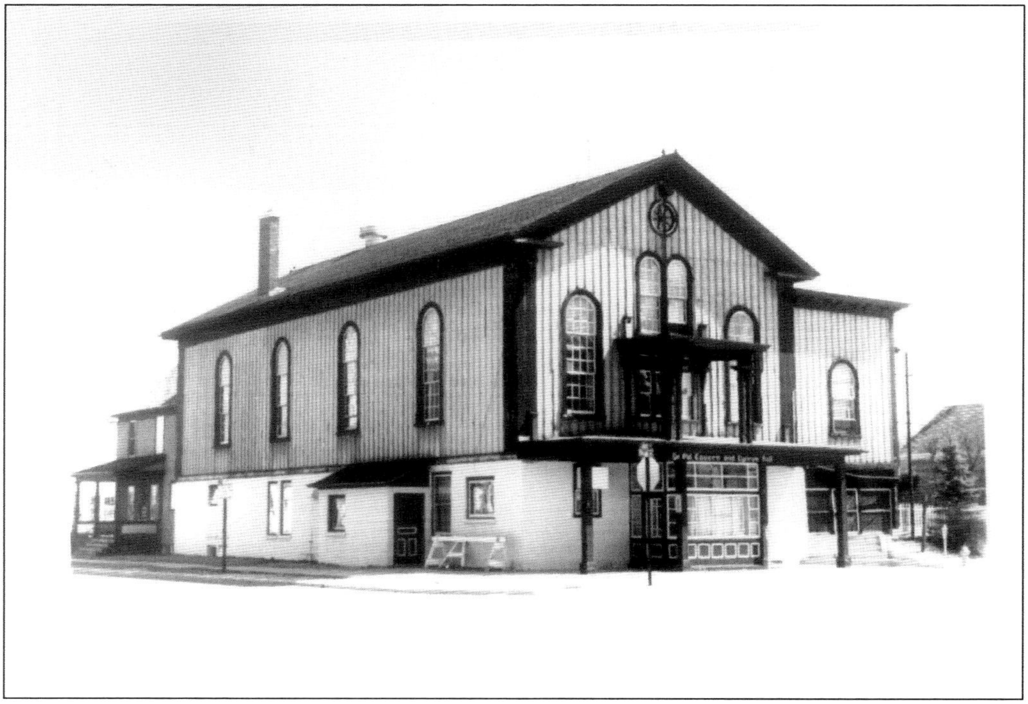

LYCEUM HALL, PLYMOUTH. Lyceum Hall has been a fixture in Plymouth since the German immigrants built it in 1869. It is located on the southeast corner of Smith and Main Streets in Plymouth. It was built as a public meeting house and place for dramatic and musical entertainment. It became the civic center of Plymouth after the Cold Spring Tavern burned. Lyceum Hall still stands today and houses a tavern and hair salon.

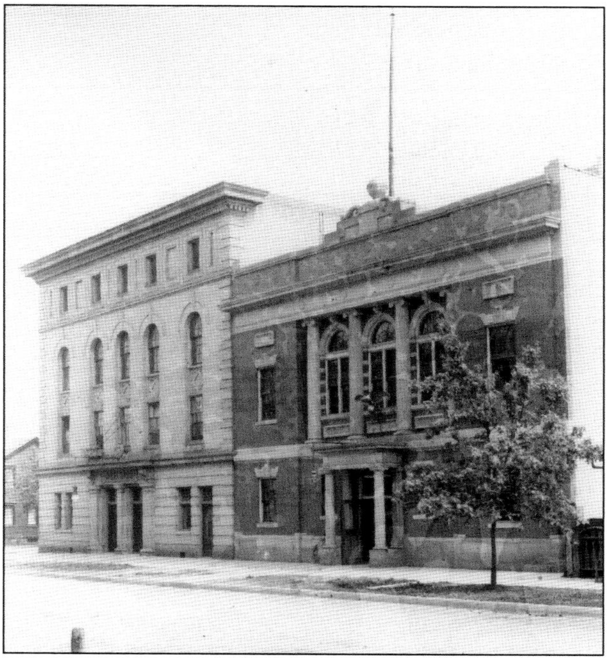

EAGLES' CLUB AND NEW OPERA HOUSE. Located on the corner southwest corner of Seventh Street and New York Avenue in Sheboygan, this beautiful set of buildings met a sad ending. The Eagles' Club, also known as the Playdium, burned. The Opera House was razed to make room for six parking spaces.

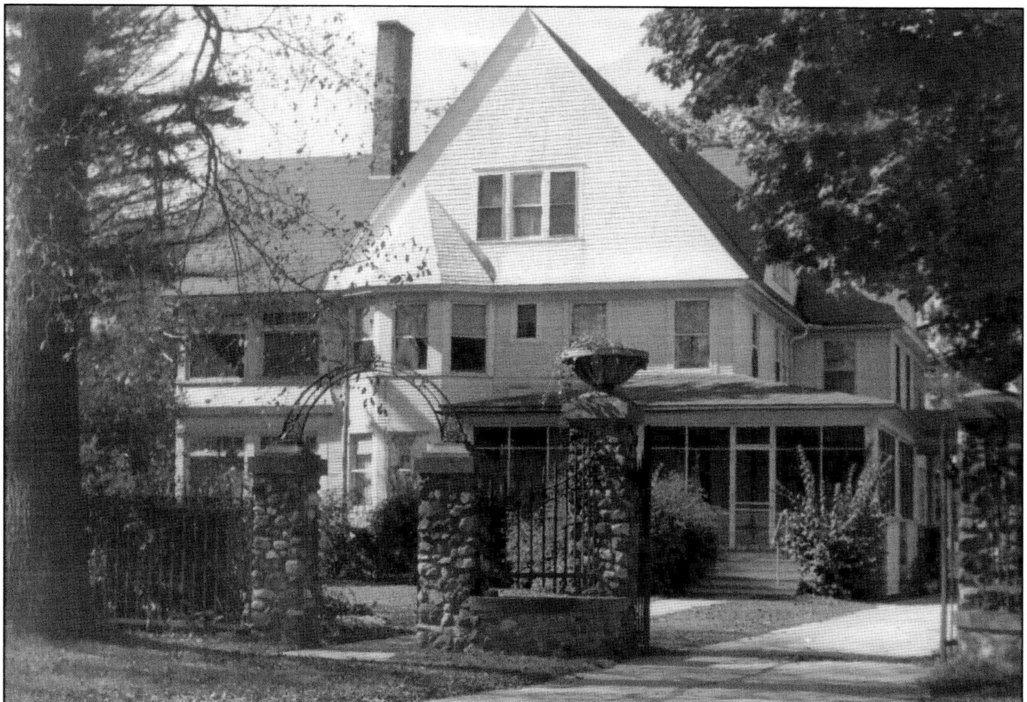

PINE HAVEN RETIREMENT HOME. Pine Haven Christian Home was developed through cooperation between eighteen Reformed and Presbyterian Churches in Sheboygan County. This agreement began in 1950. The Reiss Summer Home on the outskirts of Sheboygan Falls was purchased as the first facility. Along with this home, another 37.5 acres was purchased from Pinehurst farms. The facility has expanded greatly over the years. This photo, taken in 1955, shows the original retirement home.

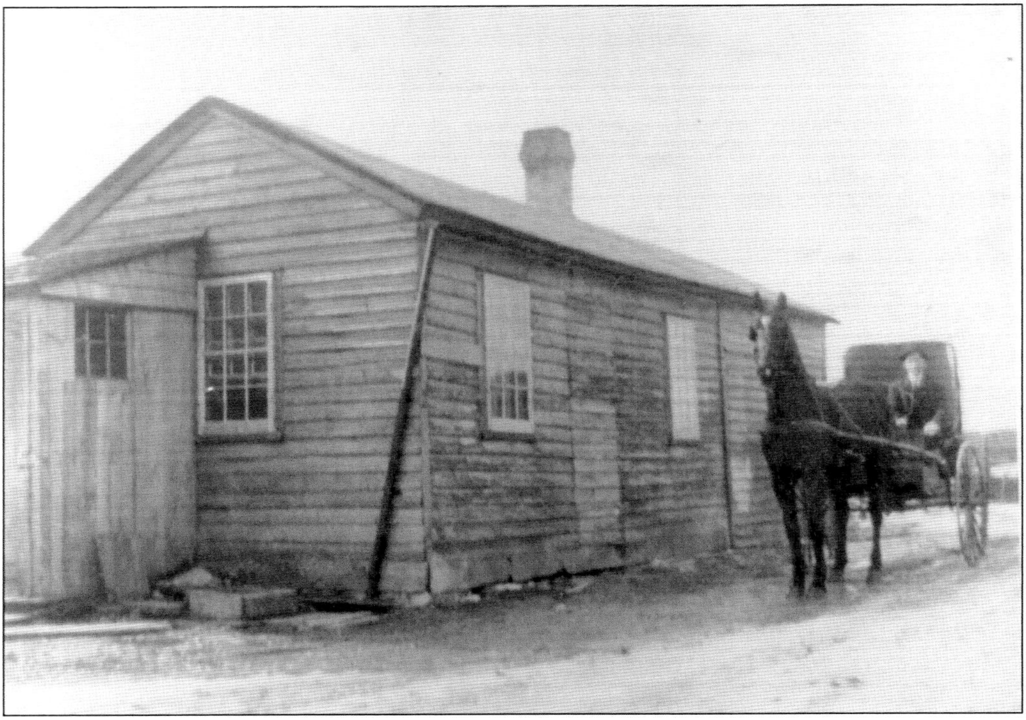

TOLLGATE #3. Located one mile northwest of Howards Grove, this toll gate on the Sheboygan and Calumet Road was operated by Mr. Burhop during the 1870s. It was discontinued in 1901. The compensation for collecting toll was the free use of the little house and $110 annually in cash.

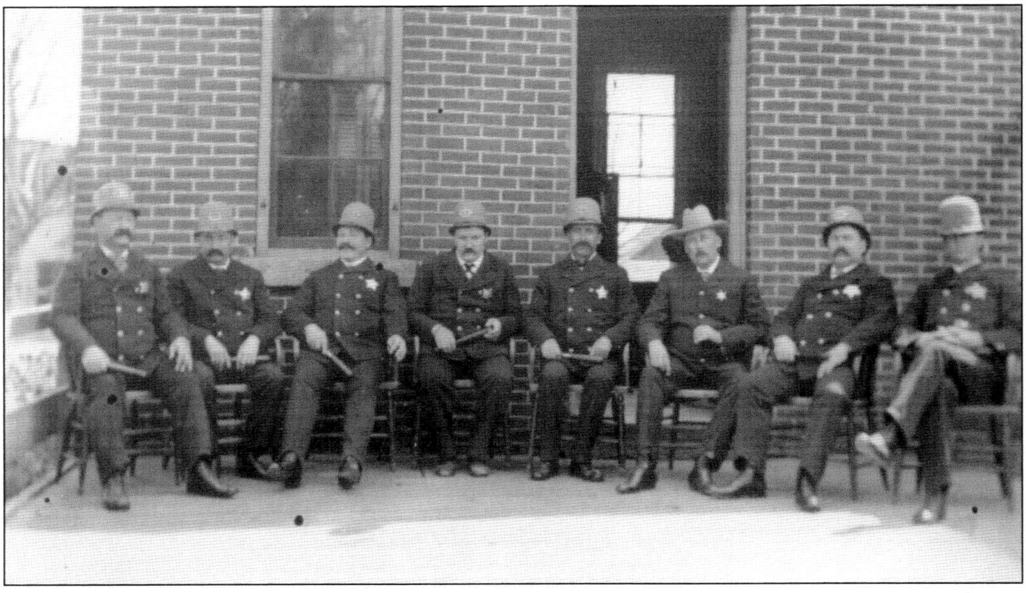

THE BEAT COP. The beat cop, who walked his territory each day or night, exists almost exclusively as a memory of the past. In large cities, a policeman on foot can still be seen in downtown areas, but in the residential sections, they patrol in a squad car. The speed of traffic has brought about other changes as well. The horse-drawn patrol wagon, sometimes called a Black Maria, and its foot gong, has made room for the patrol car with its siren.

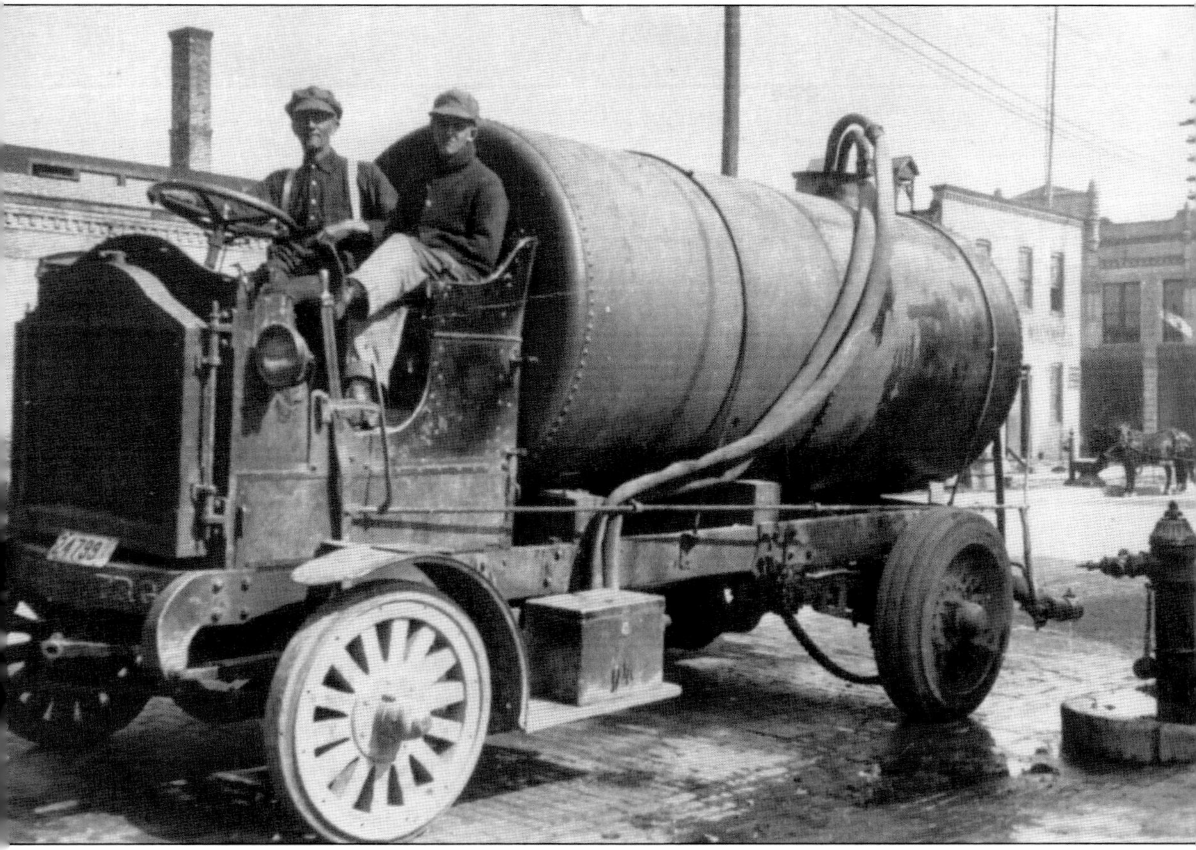

CLEAN STREETS. The street cleaner's job began as a means to deal with horse droppings. The man in the white uniform, with a brush, scoop, and waste can has vanished. His job was vital to the community. He also cleaned up trash and debris. Once streets were paved, a more mechanical type of cleaner was used. Seen here is the city street flusher used in Sheboygan. It was the precursor of today's street sweeper. Notice the street is paved with brick, not concrete.

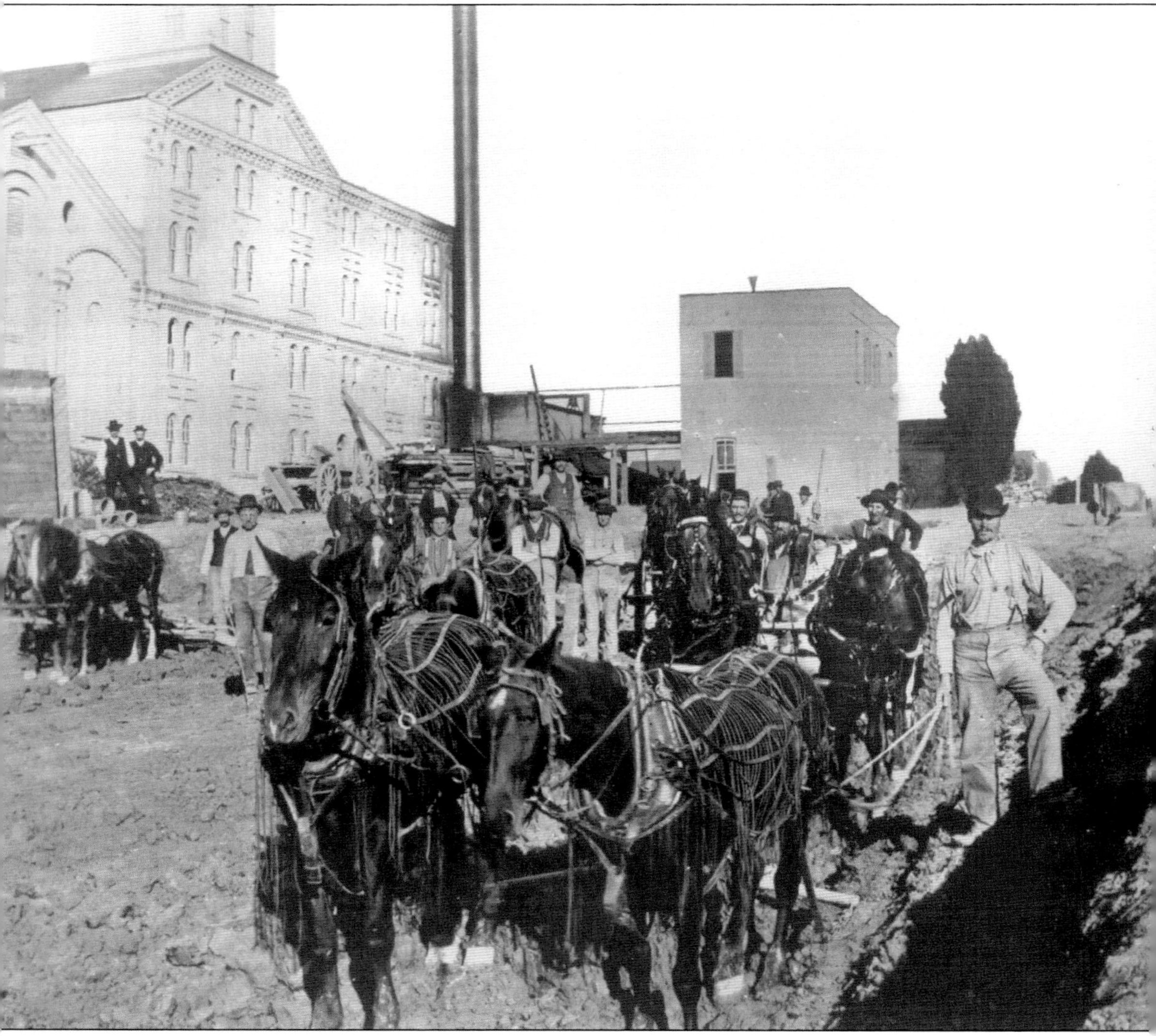

EARLY ROAD GRADING. This photo, taken May 15, 1893, shows men and horses grading New Jersey Avenue at south Fifteenth Street in Sheboygan. The building in the background is a part of the Schreier Malting complex.

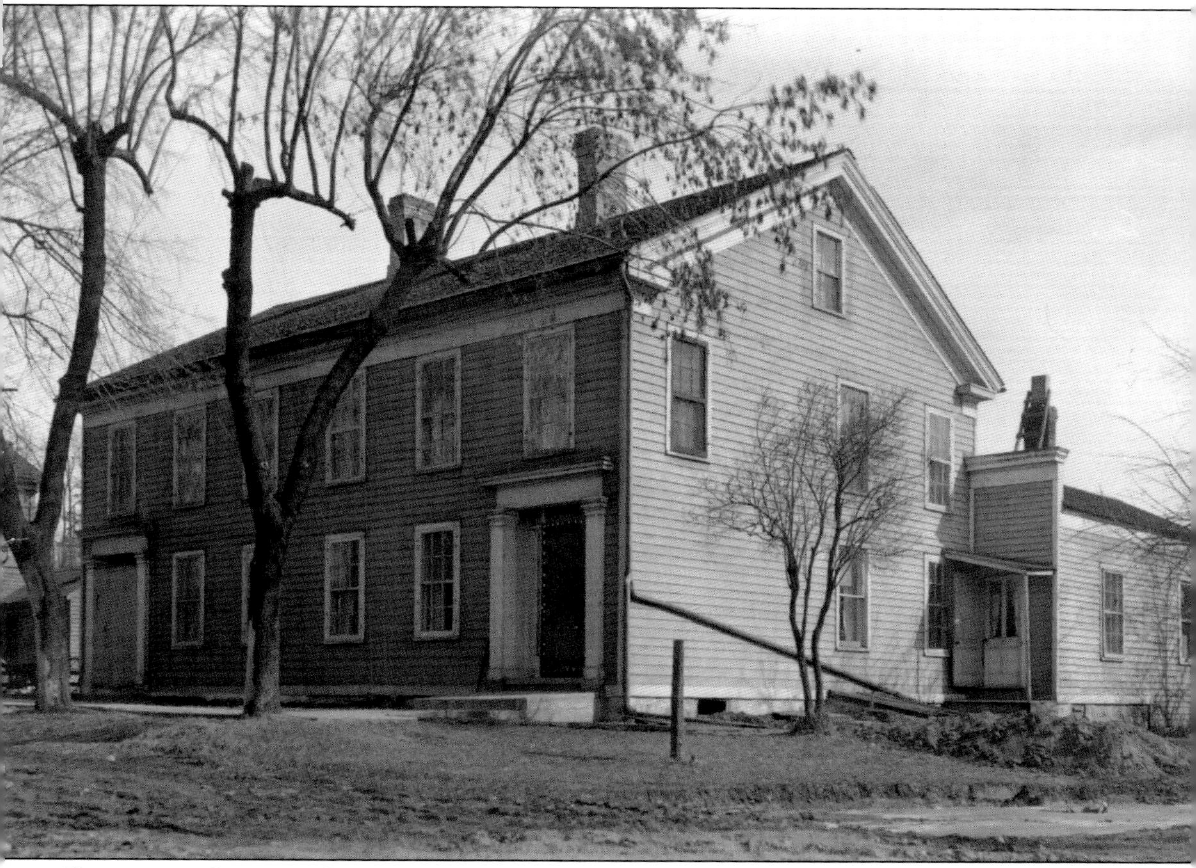

ROCHESTER LUMBER COMPANY MILL HOUSE. Built in 1837 by the Rochester Lumber Company for boarding its workers, it also served as the first home for early settlers in the county, accommodating their families until they could build their own homes. At the time of the 1850 United States Census, more than thirty people lived in the Mill House. Charles Cole purchased the structure in 1860 for two of his sons. The Mill House became a two-story, wood frame Greek Revival building with a side-gabled roof and returned eaves. The house rests on a limestone foundation. A wall was built through the middle of the house, dividing it exactly in half. Called the double or "mirror" house by local residents, the house remained a two-family home until the late 1960s, when it was remodeled into a four-family apartment house.

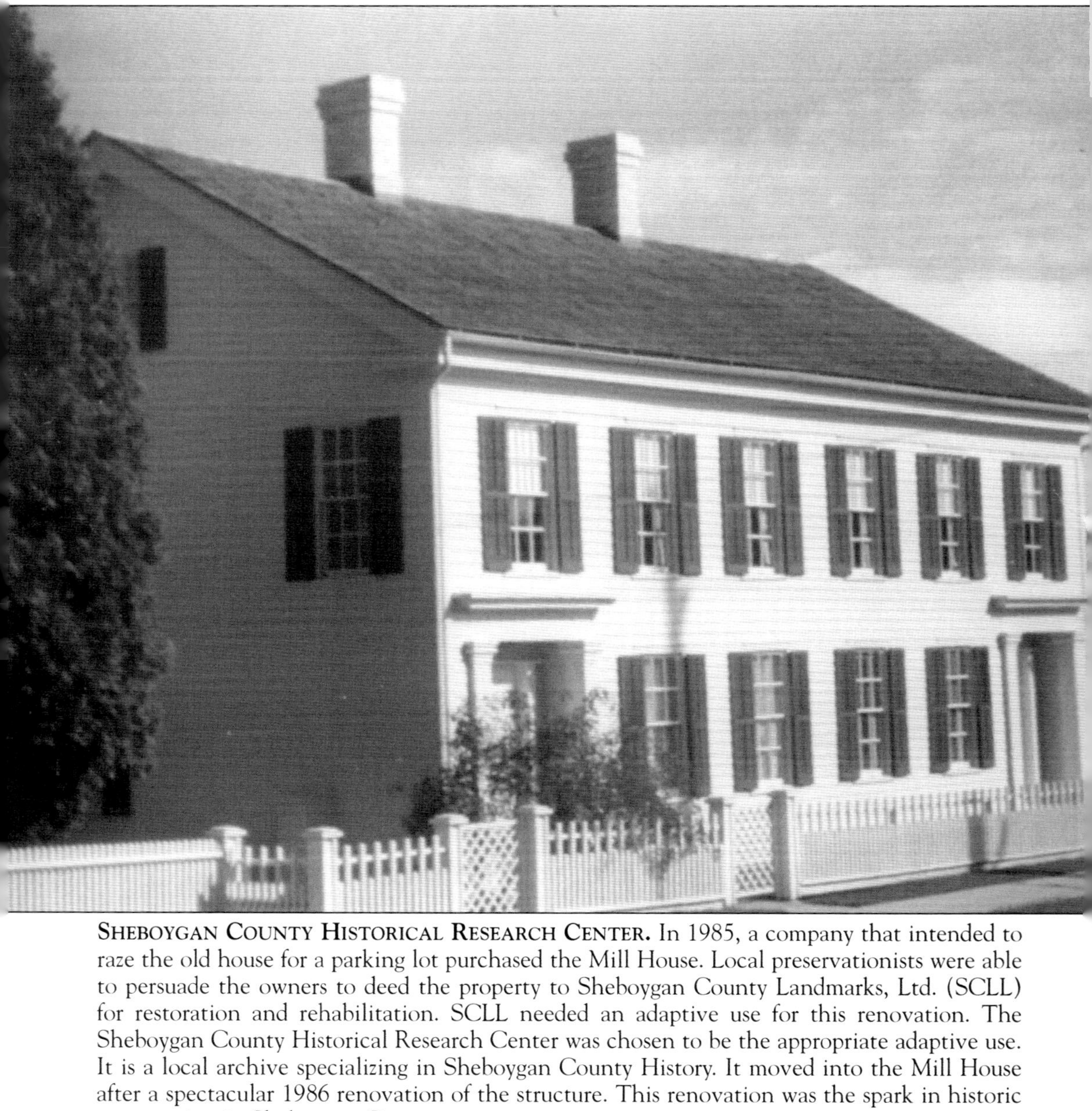

SHEBOYGAN COUNTY HISTORICAL RESEARCH CENTER. In 1985, a company that intended to raze the old house for a parking lot purchased the Mill House. Local preservationists were able to persuade the owners to deed the property to Sheboygan County Landmarks, Ltd. (SCLL) for restoration and rehabilitation. SCLL needed an adaptive use for this renovation. The Sheboygan County Historical Research Center was chosen to be the appropriate adaptive use. It is a local archive specializing in Sheboygan County History. It moved into the Mill House after a spectacular 1986 renovation of the structure. This renovation was the spark in historic preservation in Sheboygan County.

The Mill House is one of five buildings in the Cole Historic District. The entire district is listed on the National Register of Historic Places. The Cole District is the largest group of Greek Revival buildings in their original locations west of the East Coast.